16/-

FOUR SACRED PLAYS

FOUR SACRED PLAYS

by

DOROTHY L. SAYERS

LONDON
VICTOR GOLLANCZ LTD
1959

First published March 1948
Second impression March 1957
Third impression June 1959

Printed in Great Britain by
The Camelot Press Ltd., London and Southampton

CONTENTS

THE ZEAL OF THY HOUSE

PREFACE

A schoolboy, asked to state what he knew of Mary Tudor, replied: "She was known as Bloody Mary but she was not half as bloody as you'd think."

We might reasonably expect Miss Sayers, since the previous plays written or performed at the invitation of the Friends of Canterbury Cathedral have concerned prelates and kings who have come to violent and untimely ends, to write with relish of archbishops and assassination, for she has already proved herself to be thoroughly at home with peers and homicide. But, like Mary Tudor, she has not fulfilled our sanguine expectations. Many will be relieved to find that her hero is an architect, that such violence as there may be is accidental, and that, though a rope is the instrument of his downfall, it is accessory to a windlass and not to a gallows.

At a time when all works of fiction are prefaced by a passionate declaration that the author's characters are entirely imaginary, it is a pleasant change to have to vouch for the authenticity of the main protagonists in this play. It is true that, while most people are familiar with the names of those who damaged or were murdered in Canterbury Cathedral, William of Sens, who designed and built the greater part of it, is not as well known as he ought to be. When the choir was burnt down in 1174, he was chosen by a nervous Chapter to undertake the work of reconstruction. Then as now, that a foreigner in competition with native contractors should be selected for such a task must have caused furious comment. Nevertheless, in the face of official timidity and practical obstacles, he succeeded in raising from the ashes of Lanfranc's work the leaping choir which we cherish to-day. This creation, magnificent as it is, might hardly seem to be suitable material for a dramatic work. But Miss Sayers chooses William of Sens to be the vehicle for her theme of the artist who in the supreme moment of mastery over his craft may be thrown down and destroyed

9

by a consuming and wasting infirmity, the germ of which is in us all and which too often, fostered by our unawareness, destroys virtue and vitality with its insidious infection. Though few may have fallen physically as far and as hard as William, many have fallen away artistically and have perished without the revelation which was granted to him.

The only scenes which may be suspect historically are those between William and the Lady Ursula. It might be considered a little unfair to credit William with an imaginary intrigue; but, in fact, Miss Sayers has ingenious and moderately sound reasons for doing so.

Our authority for these events is the contemporary chronicle of Gervase the Monk. After recording with horror and enthusiasm the fire and the rebuilding, he refers to William's accident in a strange and pregnant sentence; he attributes the calamity to "either the Vengeance of God or the Envy of the Devil." Can we not detect in this the verdict of one who, while full of admiration for the Master's work, has watched with disapproval, and not a little envy, the pride and licence which the artist has been at little pains to conceal, and now records a well-merited if lamented punishment with righteous satisfaction? Herein may be the clue to some such fall from grace as that which Miss Sayers suggests in the scenes between the arch tect and his admirer.

For the rest the play deal with well-established facts. Avoiding sham archaism and the fusty language which is too often expected and provided in plays of period, it presents the Middle Ages as being very little removed in essentials from our own. Petrol and patent medicines have taken the place of the windlass and the faith-healing of the pilgrims, but human fallibility and the inspiration of the artist remain constant. The Archangels who from time to time descend into the arena and direct the destinies of the groundlings need not bewilder the reader or the spectator. They represent the Will of God, Fate, Providence, Accident or what you will and, in the final scenes, that bright flash of intuition which occasionally illuminates even the most clouded conscience.

LAURENCE IRVING.

The Zeal of Thy House was written for presentation by the Friends of Canterbury Cathedral, and was first acted in the Chapter House at the Canterbury Festival, 12th–18th June, 1937, with Mr. Harcourt Williams as William of Sens and a mixed cast of professional and amateur performers.

It was first presented in London by Mr. Anmer Hall at the Westminster Theatre, on 29th March, 1938, with Mr. Harcourt Williams, Mr. Frank Napier and Mr. Michael Gough in their original parts, and with the original music and costumes.

Mr. Williams and Mr. Napier were the producers on both occasions. The special music was composed by Mr. Gerald H. Knight, the Cathedral Organist at Canterbury.

The present text is that of the play as first written. At Canterbury, it was presented without interval, and in a slightly shortened form. In London, an interval was found necessary between Parts II and III, and the following chorus was accordingly inserted at the beginning of Part III:

The Lord God of Heaven hath given me all the kingdoms of the earth; and He hath charged me to build Him an house at Jerusalem.

That every man should eat and drink and enjoy the good of all his labour, it is the gift of God.

Not unto us, O Lord, not unto us, but unto Thy name give the praise;

For we look for a city which hath foundations, whose builder and maker is God.

The only other modification of any importance was in St. Michael's final speech, the last sentences of which were altered as follows:

Behold, then, and honour, all beautiful work of the craftsman, imagined by men's minds, built by the labour of men's hands, working with power upon the souls of men, image of the everlasting Trinity, God's witness in world and time. And whatsoever ye do, do all to the Glory of God.

With the help of these modifications, the play in its original form should prove sufficiently elastic to adapt itself for production in any theatre or place of public or private performance.

DOROTHY L. SAYERS.

DRAMATIS PERSONÆ

Angelic Persons:

MICHAEL ⎤
RAPHAEL ⎬ Archangels
GABRIEL ⎦

CASSIEL, the Recording Angel

A YOUNG CHERUB, Thurifer to Raphael

Religious:

THE PRIOR OF CHRISTCHURCH ⎤
STEPHEN, the Treasurer
THEODATUS, the Sacristan
MARTIN, the Guest-Brother and Infirmarian ⎬ Choir Brothers and members of the Cathedral Chapter
AMBROSE, the Choirmaster
WULFRAM, the Director of the Farm
ERNULPHUS, the Director of the Kitchen and Distillery
PAUL, the Gardener
HILARY, the Almoner
SILVESTER, the Painter
GERVASE, the Historian and Clerk ⎦

HUBERT, an Oblate, Superintendent of the Rough Masons

Laymen:

WILLIAM OF SENS, Architect to the Cathedral

JOHN OF KENT ⎤ Rival Architects
HENRY OF YORK ⎦

SIMON ⎤
WALTER ⎬ Workmen
HUGH
GEOFFREY ⎦

A YOUNG BOY

THE LADY URSULA DE WARBOIS

Monks; Lay-Brothers; Workmen; Pilgrims of both sexes

Two Cantors and a Choir of Mixed Voices

The action takes place during the years 1175–1179.

NOTE.—The names Michaël, Raphaël, are to be pronounced as trisyllables throughout.

I

At the opening of the play, the scene is set as for a meeting of the Chapter, with seats about a long table. The CHOIR *having entered and taken their places, they sing the hymn following:*

CHOIR

Disposer supreme, and judge of the earth,
Thou choosest for Thine the weak and the poor;
To frail earthen vessels and things of no worth
Entrusting Thy riches which aye shall endure.

Those vessels soon fail, though full of Thy light,
And at Thy decree are broken and gone;
Then brightly appeareth the arm of Thy might,
As through the clouds breaking the lightnings have shone.

[*During the singing of the second half of this verse, there enter* MICHAEL, RAPHAEL *with his* THURIFER, GABRIEL *and* CASSIEL *the Recorder. They pass slowly to the steps while the next verse is sung.*

Like clouds are they borne to do Thy great will,
And swift as the wind about the world go;
All full of Thy Godhead while earth lieth still,
They thunder, they lighten, the waters o'erflow.

℣. He maketh His angels spirits.
℟. And His ministers a flaming fire.

MICHAEL

I am God's servant Michael the Archangel;
I walk in the world of men invisible,
Bearing the sword that Christ bequeathed His Church
To sunder and to save.

RAPHAEL

I am God's servant
Raphael the Archangel; and I walk
In the world of men invisible; I receive
Prayer spoken or unspoken, word or deed
Or thought or whatsoever moves the heart,
Offering it up before the Throne.

GABRIEL

I am
God's servant the Archangel Gabriel,
The heavenly runner between God and man,
Moving invisible.

CASSIEL

God's Recorder, I,
That keep the Book and cast up all accounts,
Cassiel, chief scrivener to the Courts of Heaven.

℣. Their sound is gone out into all lands.
℟. And their words into the ends of the world.

[*During the singing of the following verse, the* ANGELIC
PERSONS *depart severally,* MICHAEL *standing above* RAPHAEL
on the right side of the steps, and the THURIFER *kneeling below
them;* CASSIEL *with his book on the left side of the steps with*
GABRIEL *above.*

CHOIR

Oh, loud be Thy trump and stirring the sound,
To rouse us, O Lord, from sin's deadly sleep;
May lights which Thou kindlest in darkness around
The dull soul awaken her vigils to keep.

[*The Recorder,* CASSIEL, *sits at his desk;*

RAPHAEL *hands his censer to the* THURIFER, *and sits.*

MICHAEL

What is our business here to-day in Canterbury?
16

CASSIEL (*slapping the Book rather sharply open and running his finger down the page*)

A meeting of the Cathedral Chapter to choose an architect for the rebuilding of the Choir after the great fire of 1174.

RAPHAEL (*reminiscently*)

Ah, yes—the choir. I was sorry to see the old one go. It was very beautiful, and a favourite haunt of mine. Prayer had soaked into the stones and sanctified them.

CASSIEL (*austerely*)

Mankind are exceedingly careless of their possessions. I have an entry against one Tom Hogg, neathered, who neglected to clean his chimney and so had his thatch set on fire. The sparks were blown across the road and lodged under the lead roof of the church. In a short time all was ablaze.

GABRIEL

A heavy consequence for a light offence. Was that your doing, Michael?

MICHAEL

It was. I bore the flame betwixt my hands and set it among the rafters. We fanned it with our wings, my angels and I, riding upon the wind from the south.

CASSIEL (*muttering to himself over the Book*)

. . . and seven, twenty-six . . . and three, twenty-nine . . . and nine, thirty-eight. . . .

RAPHAEL

Was it done to avenge the murder of the Archbishop?

CASSIEL

. . . and six. Put down four and carry eight.

MICHAEL

I do not know. I am a soldier. I take my orders.

CASSIEL (*casting up a column and ruling a line beneath it*)

We all do that, Michael. Your interference in the matter does not affect the debit against Tom Hogg. He stands charged with Sloth to a considerable amount. What use was made of his sin is neither here nor there. It is a question of economics.

MICHAEL

Quite so. I could have done the work perfectly well myself, with a thunderbolt. Hogg's sin was not in the least necessary.

GABRIEL (*in humorous resignation*)

Nothing that men do is ever necessary. At least, that is my experience. I find them very amusing.

[*The sound of the "Veni Creator" is heard from the lower end of the Chapter-House as the* CHOIR-MONKS *enter in procession.*

RAPHAEL

I find them very pathetic.

GABRIEL

You see them at their best, Raphael; as Michael sees them at their worst.

MICHAEL

I find them very perverse. If God were not infinite, they would surely exhaust His patience.

CASSIEL

They make a great deal of work in the counting house. Happily, being an angel, and not a man, I like work. The hatred of work must be one of the most depressing consequences of the Fall.

GABRIEL

Some men work like angels—and whistle over their work. They are much the most cheerful kind.

[*In the meantime,* RAPHAEL *has met the* MONKS *at the foot of the steps and now precedes them to the Chapter, swinging his censer before them. The last verse of the hymn is sung by the* MONKS *standing about the table. Then all sit.* RAPHAEL *comes down to sit beside* MICHAEL. CASSIEL *opens the Book at a fresh page and prepares to take minutes of the meeting.*

PRIOR

Brethren, the business before us is, as you know, the appointment of an architect for the new choir. Our earlier discussions have brought the number of suitable candidates down to three. To-day we have to make our final choice.

THEODATUS

Under God's guidance.

PRIOR

Under God's guidance, of course, Father Theodatus. The three men in question are John of Kent, William of Sens, and Henry of York.

STEPHEN

Have we got the estimates, Father Prior?

PRIOR (*handing papers to* STEPHEN)

I have two of them here. Henry of York's is lower than John of Kent's. He thinks he can restore the existing fabric without pulling it all down and rebuilding.

WULFRAM

Will that be safe? Some of the masonry looks to me very insecure. John of Kent is a local man—he has had more opportunity to judge. Besides, it would look well to give the work to a local man.

ERNULPHUS

John is very young—young men are always full of extravagant ideas. No experience.

HILARY

One must encourage young men. The future is with the young.

19

STEPHEN

John's estimate is certainly rather high. I don't think we can countenance extravagance.

PRIOR

We must consider expense, of course, Father Treasurer. Perhaps we had better have the architects in and hear what they have to say. Father Gervase—if you will be so good——

[GERVASE *goes out by door, right.*

AMBROSE

Speaking as Choirmaster, may I urge here and now that we should get a man who understands something about acoustics. The old choir——

PAUL

What we want is the old choir restored to what it was before. I dislike this trivial modern stuff they are putting up all over the place, with its pointed arcading and flourishy capitals. Give me something solid, like Ely.

HILARY

One must move with the times, Father Paul. Now William of Sens is a progressive man.

WULFRAM

He is a foreigner. Why should we have a foreigner? Isn't an Englishman good enough? Money should be kept in the country.

STEPHEN

We do not seem to have had an estimate from William of Sens.

[*Re-enter* GERVASE *right with* JOHN OF KENT, WILLIAM OF SENS, *and* HENRY OF YORK.

Not yet. He writes to me here—— Ah, good morning, sirs. Pray come to the table. We have received your letters and considered your qualifications. We are now minded to hear your further opinions, after inspection of the site. You, Master Henry, have submitted a very conservative estimate of the cost of reconstruction.

HENRY

My Lord Prior, I have kept the expense down to the lowest possible figure; and after examination of the standing masonry I have prepared a plan and elevation.

[*Producing it.*

PRIOR

Let us have that.

[HENRY *puts the plan before the* PRIOR *and moves across to left of table.*

HENRY

You will see that I have allowed for keeping the greater part of the standing fabric. (THEODATUS *and* ERNULPHUS *on* PRIOR'S *left examine the plan.*) With the exception of the more grievously damaged portions which I have marked, I see no reason why the present structure may not be restored——

[*He passes plan down to the* MONKS, *on left.*

JOHN

My Lord Prior——

HENRY

—and put into good order along the original lines. The existing outer walls may be retained——

WULFRAM

You think they are not too much weakened by the action of the fire?

JOHN

Weakened? They are calcined in places almost to powder.

21

HENRY

They can be patched and grouted, Master John; and by the addition of supporting buttresses and by altering the pitch of the roof so as to lessen the thrust——

SILVESTER (*who has been studying the plan with* MARTIN)

Will not the effect of the buttresses be somewhat clumsy?

MARTIN

There is something a little mean in the proportions of this roof.

AMBROSE (*who is a man of one idea*)

I should think it would be bad for sound. After all, the chief use of a choir is to hold services in.

MARTIN

The sooner we get *a* choir the better. The singing has been very bad lately. I am ashamed to hear sacred words so howled.

[*Hands back plan to* HENRY, *who takes it across, right, to* WULFRAM.

AMBROSE (*defensively*)

The nave is very awkward to sing in. What with the west end boarded up——

HILARY

Well, we can't be expected to hold our services in full view, not to say smell, of the common people.

AMBROSE

And the east end boarded up——

[ERNULPHUS *quietly falls asleep.*

WULFRAM (*taking plan*)

The draughts are appalling. I caught a shocking cold last Tuesday.

22

AMBROSE

We are singing in a wooden box. You can't sing properly in a box.

PRIOR

Time is certainly of some importance.

STEPHEN

The cost is still more important.

HENRY (*moving up again left of table*)

To repair, according to my plan, will be very much cheaper and quicker than to pull down and rebuild. I could engage to be ready within two years——

JOHN

And in two years more you will have to rebuild again. My Lord Prior——

PRIOR

You, Master John, recommend a complete reconstruction?

JOHN

Recommend? It must be done. Do not be deceived. This botching is useless and dangerous. It is unworthy——

HENRY

Master John, I am older than you and more experienced——

JOHN

You never in your life built anything bigger than a parish church.

PRIOR

Master John, Master John!

JOHN

This is the Cathedral Church of Christ at Canterbury. It must be the wonder of the realm—nay, of the world! Will you insult God with patchwork? Give me the commission, Lord Prior, and I will build you a church worth looking at!

[*Producing plan and elevation, which he passes to* STEPHEN.

HENRY

To the greater glory of Master John of Kent!

JOHN

To the glory of God and of the blessed Saints Dunstan and Elphege.

STEPHEN (*aside to the* PRIOR)

And the entire depletion of the Treasury. Will somebody please tell me where the money is to come from?

THEODATUS

The devotion of the common people is most touching. A poor widow yesterday brought us five farthings, all her little savings.

STEPHEN

Our Lord will reward her. But that will not go very far.

MARTIN

I think we ought to take the long view. Canterbury is the most important church in the Kingdom, and attracts a great many people to the town. What with the visitors and the great increase in the number of pilgrims since the lamented death of the late Archbishop——

ALL

Blessed St. Thomas, pray for us.

[*They cross themselves.*

MARTIN

A little money spent now on building will repay itself handsomely in donations and bequests.

[STEPHEN *passes the plan to* HILARY.

THEODATUS (*rather loudly*)

If the fire was a Divine judgment for the Archbishop's murder——

ERNULPHUS (*waking with a start*)

Eh? the Archbishop? Blessed St. Thomas, pray for us.

[*He crosses himself and falls asleep instantly.*

THEODATUS

I say, if the fire was a judgment, then the new building is a reparation to God, and should be an offering worthy of its high destination and a sufficient sacrifice for the sins of this country.

SILVESTER

No artist can do his best work when he has to consider every halfpenny. Thou shalt not muzzle the ox——

THEODATUS

All this talk about money is sheer lack of faith. God will provide.

STEPHEN

No doubt. But, humanly speaking, the accounts will have to go through the Treasury, and I feel responsible.

HILARY (*passing design to* PAUL)

There is a good deal of elaborate and expensive ornament here, Master John.

PAUL

Modern nonsense, modern nonsense. Let us have the old choir back. Here is a groined roof and a clerestory and a lot of fiddle-faddle. How long is all this going to take?

JOHN (*uncompromisingly*)

Seven years—perhaps more.

MARTIN

Seven years! Have we to put up with half a cathedral for seven years? Why, God made the world in six days!

25

God, Father Martin, was not subject to limitations of funds or material.

JOHN (*angrily aside to* WILLIAM)

Nor to the cheese-paring parsimony of a monastic chapter.

WILLIAM (*who has listened to all this with a quiet smile; with a touch of humour*)

Possibly God is an abler architect than any of us.

PRIOR

We have not yet heard your opinion, Master William. Do you think it possible to restore the remaining fabric?

WILLIAM

Oh, I should think very likely. I should certainly hope to save some of it.

JOHN (*angrily to* WILLIAM)

That is *not* what you said to us outside.

WILLIAM

But I really cannot say—I do not see how anybody can say—without prolonged and careful examination.

AMBROSE

That's very true. Very reasonable.

WILLIAM

That is why I have as yet prepared no estimate or plan. But I have brought some drawings of the work entrusted to me at Sens and elsewhere which will give you some idea of the kind of thing I should like to do here.

[*Hands papers to* PRIOR.

PRIOR

Now, I like that. Extremely fine and dignified. And very modern in feeling.

STEPHEN

And not too ornate.

[WILLIAM *hands them on down right.*

GERVASE

It is wonderful. It is like a poem in stone. I should dearly love to see it. How light—and yet how majestic!

[*He looks admiringly at* WILLIAM.

WILLIAM

Time and cost would depend on the extent of the work. I suggest making a thorough survey before getting out a preliminary plan and estimate. Naturally, I should commit you to nothing without the advice and approval of yourself, Lord Prior and the Father Treasurer.

STEPHEN

Just so. We should object to nothing in reason.

WILLIAM (*he has now got the ear of the house*)

I should be obliged (*firmly*) to stipulate for the best materials.

THEODATUS

God's service demands the best materials.

WILLIAM

But we can effect an economy by making good use of local talent, of which I am sure we must possess a great deal——

WULFRAM

I am all in favour of local talent.

And we may reduce the cost of shipping and carriage by the use of certain mechanical devices of my own invention, which I need not say I shall be happy to place at the disposal of the authorities without extra fee.

PRIOR

Thank you—that is very proper, very generous. . . . H'm. Well, Brethren, I think we have now the facts before us. If these gentlemen would kindly retire for a few moments. . . .

[General movement; GERVASE goes up, right, to door.

ERNULPHUS (*waking with a start*)
Eh, what? what? Have we finished?

SILVESTER

No, Father Ernulphus. The architects are retiring while we deliberate.

ERNULPHUS

Oh, I see. Very good.

[He falls asleep again.

HENRY

Two or three years only, Lord Prior—say four at most—and a strict regard for economy.

[Exit HENRY.

JOHN

Consider, Lord Prior—a structure worthy of its dedication—and safety to life and limb, if you think that matters.

[Exit JOHN.

WILLIAM

Sir, if I am chosen, I will do my best.

[Exit WILLIAM. GERVASE follows them off. The rest examine the plans and documents.

GABRIEL

The motives of mankind are lamentably mixed.

RAPHAEL

They mean well, I assure you.

MICHAEL

Then it is a pity they do not say what they mean.

CASSIEL

It is most confusing. I have worn out my pen trying to keep up with them.

GABRIEL.

That is easily remedied. Allow me.

[*He plucks a feather from his own wing and hands it to* CASSIEL *as* GERVASE *re-enters and shuts the door.*

CASSIEL (*trimming the feather into a pen*)

Thank you.

PRIOR

Well, Brethren?

SILVESTER

I must say, Master Henry's plan seems rather makeshift.

WULFRAM

He is a Yorkshire man. I would as soon have a foreigner as a Yorkshire man.

STEPHEN

He is too anxious to please. First he says two years—then three or four. I should not rely on his estimate.

PRIOR

Are we agreed, then, not to appoint Henry of York? (*The* MONKS *signify agreement.*) Then that leaves us the choice between John of Kent and William of Sens.

MICHAEL

What will they make of that?

CASSIEL

They will choose the man whom God has appointed.

GABRIEL

I shall see to it that they do.

WULFRAM

Let us have John. He is a local man.

[*As the* MONKS *give their votes,* GERVASE *notes them down.*

MARTIN

Yes; his church will attract attention and bring people into the town.

PAUL

Too new-fangled and showy. I am for William. I distrust these go-ahead young men.

HILARY

I have said William all along.

GERVASE

Clearly William is a great craftsman—let us choose him.

THEODATUS

We know nothing about him personally. John is a young man of devout life.

STEPHEN

What has that to do with it? Besides, his manners are abominable. I give my voice for William.

SILVESTER

I like John's plan—we haven't seen William's.

AMBROSE

John's plan looks good from the musician's point of view.

PRIOR

I must not influence you—but I admit I am greatly impressed by William of Sens. . . . Father Gervase, how does the voting stand?

GERVASE

Five have spoken for John and five for William.

GABRIEL

This is where I interfere.

[*He goes up into the Chapter-House.*

PRIOR

Somebody has not voted. Who is it?

[*Everybody stares round at* ERNULPHUS.

MARTIN

It is Father Ernulphus.

THEODATUS

He has been asleep all the time.

[GABRIEL *stands behind* ERNULPHUS.

PAUL

He is getting very shaky, poor old soul.

THEODATUS (*loudly in* ERNULPHUS' *ear*)

Father Ernulphus!

ERNULPHUS (*starting into consciousness*)

Eh? eh? what?

THEODATUS (*shouting in his ear*)

Do you vote for John of Kent or William of Sens?

GABRIEL (*in his other ear*)

William of Sens.

ERNULPHUS (*to* THEODATUS)

Eh? Yes, of course. William of Sens. Certainly.

[*He closes his eyes again.*

THEODATUS (*vexed*)

He hasn't heard a word. (*Loudly*) Father Ernulphus!

ERNULPHUS (*suddenly alert*)

You needn't shout. I'm not deaf. I have followed everything very carefully. I said William of Sens and I mean William of Sens.

[*He shuts his eyes tight with an air of finality.*

THEODATUS

Really, Father Prior!

STEPHEN

You will never move him now.

[*A pause.*

PRIOR

The vote of the Chapter, then, is for William of Sens. If there is no further business, the Chapter is dissolved.

ALL (*rising*)

Glory be to the Father, and to the Son, and to the Holy Ghost. As it was in the beginning, is now and ever shall be, world without end. Amen.

[GABRIEL *goes up and stands above.*

PRIOR (*as the* MONKS *begin to file down, left and right*)

Father Gervase, pray inform the architects of this decision. Thank those that are not chosen for their pains; they shall receive their journey-money from the Father Treasurer. Ask Master William to come and see me. No time must be lost in putting the work in hand, for the night cometh wherein no man can work.

[*Exit* GERVASE, *right, as the* PRIOR *follows the* MONKS *out.*

℣. Be strong, all ye people of the land, saith the Lord, and work; for I am with you, saith the Lord God of Hosts.
℟. No man, having put his hand to the plough, and looking back, is fit for the Kingdom of God.
℣. There is nothing better than that a man should rejoice in his own works, for that is his portion.
℟. Ascribe ye greatness unto our God; He is the Rock, His work is perfect.

[*Re-enter* GERVASE, *right, with* JOHN, HENRY *and* WILLIAM.

JOHN (*indignantly to* WILLIAM)

Trickery, Master William, sheer trickery and cheating. You know well enough that you *cannot* restore a single stone of it.

HENRY (*with equal indignation*)

You will tell any lie in order to get the job. You promise economy, and you will spend their money like water. It is treacherous—it is dishonest——

WILLIAM

You would not only promise, you would *do* them a dishonest piece of work. *That* is treachery, if you like, Master Henry.

[HENRY *bounces down the steps with an angry exclamation.*

JOHN

But why must you flatter and fawn on them? Why pander to all their ridiculous foibles? Cannot you tell them the truth as I do and let the best man win?

BSP

33

The trouble with you, my lad, is want of tact. You can handle stone, but you can't handle men. You must learn to humour fools if you want to get anything done.

JOHN

You stinking fox!

[JOHN *joins* HENRY, *and they go off muttering together, sinking their differences in their common grievance.*

GERVASE (*troubled*)

Master William, is it true, what they say?

WILLIAM

Listen to me, young man. At my age one learns that sometimes one has to damn one's soul for the sake of the work. Trust me, God shall have a choir fit for His service. Does anything else really matter?

[*He and* GERVASE *follow the others out.*

During the singing of the following Interlude, the scene-shifters set the stage to represent the site of the choir. The other three ANGELS *go up and stand above with* GABRIEL.

Every carpenter and workmaster that laboureth night and day, and they that give themselves to counterfeit imagery, and watch to finish a work;

The smith also sitting by the anvil, and considering the iron work, he setteth his mind to finish his work, and watcheth to polish it perfectly.

So doth the potter sitting at his work, and turning the wheel about with his feet, who is always carefully set at his work, and maketh all his work by number.

All these trust to their hands, and every one is wise in his work.

Without these cannot a city be inhabited, and they shall not dwell where they will nor go up and down;
They shall not be sought for in public council, nor sit high in the congregation;
But they will maintain the state of the world, and all their desire is in the work of their craft.

II

About two years have passed since the previous scene. WORKMEN *go in and out, fetching tools and barrows from door, left, which appears to lead to some kind of office or store-room, and carrying out, right, blocks of dressed stone on hand-barrows, etc. About half a dozen* LAY BROTHERS *and* WORKMEN *remain to work on the stage. A general impression of bustle and movement is accentuated by the entrance of a number of respectably dressed* PILGRIMS, *chattering like jackdaws,—right.*

PILGRIMS (*they enter by twos and threes, gape vaguely about and pass on and out by way of the steps*)

Beautiful, beautiful; and everything in such good taste. . . . I wonder what it costs to keep the shrine going in candles. . . . Two years they've been building now—goodness knows how long it's going to take. . . . Dickon, you bad boy, leave that saw alone. . . . Who did you say the architect was? Wilfrid somebody? . . . My poor, dear husband— such a sad sufferer—I was determined to make the pilgrimage. . . . No doubt, it will be all very fine when it's finished, but I don't think it's a patch on Lincoln. . . . Shocking bad dinners they give you at the "Lamb"—you'd better come and have a bite with us. . . . I beg your pardon, madame, was that your foot? Ah, the poor, dear, martyred Archbishop! Such a charming man. I saw him when he came back from France—yes, really, he was as close to me as I am to you. . . . Have you heard the one about the three fat friars and the tinker's widow? Well, there were three begging friars. . . . So I said to her, "Very well, you may take your wages and go." . . . It came to me as I was kneeling there that God would most surely have pity upon my sister. . . . I must say it comes out more expensive than I'd reckoned for. And I was abominably cheated that night we lay at Rochester. . . . The King must be a very naughty man to have killed the poor Archbishop. . . . There! I told you it was only putting ideas into the child's head. . . . Bad business, that fire, and if you ask me, I don't believe the true story ever came out. . . . Yes, darling, ever so sorry—barefoot in a white sheet. . . . Indeed, I have a very great devotion to St. Thomas. . . . This Purbeck marble's all the rage, but I don't care about it myself . . . etc., etc.

[*They trail away, still chattering. During the confusion,* GERVASE *and* WILLIAM *have made their entrances, right,* GERVASE *crossing the stage and vanishing into doorway, left, while* WILLIAM *sits at a trestle-table, centre, and waits resignedly for his workshop to get clear. As the stage empties, the* ANGELS *come down again and take up their former positions.*

CASSIEL

Two years of toil are passed; what shall I write
About this architect?

MICHAEL

A schedule here,
Long as my sword, crammed full of deadly sins;
Jugglings with truth, and gross lusts of the body,
Drink, drabbing, swearing; slothfulness in prayer;
With a devouring, insolent ambition
That challenges disaster.

CASSIEL

These are debts;
What shall I set upon the credit side?

GABRIEL

Six columns, and their aisles, with covering vaults
From wall to arcading, and from thence again
To the centre, with the keystones locking them,
All well and truly laid without a fault.

CASSIEL

No sum of prayer to balance the account?

GABRIEL

Ask Raphael, for prayers are in his charge.

CASSIEL

Come, Raphael, speak; or is thy censer cold?
Canst thou indeed find any grace in William
The builder-up of Canterbury?

RAPHAEL

Yes.

[He swings his censer, which gives out a cloud of incense.

Behold, he prayeth; not with the lips alone,
But with the hand and with the cunning brain
Men worship the Eternal Architect.
So, when the mouth is dumb, the work shall speak
And save the workman. True as a mason's rule
And line can make them, the shafted columns rise
Singing like music; and by day and night
The unsleeping arches with perpetual voice
Proclaim in Heaven, to labour is to pray.

MICHAEL

Glory to God, that made the Firmament!

[Enter GERVASE, left.

GERVASE

Here are the letters for you to sign, Master William. These
to Caen, about the next shipment of stone; these to Dover,
with instructions for the unloading and carriage. I have
mentioned the matter of the damaged crane and told them
it must be made good at their own expense.

[Hands pen and inkhorn.

WILLIAM

Thanks, Father Gervase.

[Signs letters.

GERVASE

This is the invoice for the oak roofing-beams. And there is an enclosure I can't quite understand. Something about the commission.

WILLIAM (*hastily*)

That has no business to be there. Idiots! It refers to a private transaction. Give it to me. I will deal with it myself. Anything more?

[*Taking paper and pocketing it.*

GERVASE

Do you mind looking at this consignment note? We seem to be fifty scaffold-poles short; but I will have them checked again.

WILLIAM

Good. I can trust you to get it put in order. I don't know what we should have done these two years without your vigilant eye and skilful pen.

GERVASE

I wish I could do more to help. But my hands are no good for anything but writing. I should have loved to take a more active part in the work. (*Smiling.*) I must be content to be the man with only one talent, and make it go as far as I can.

[*Enter* HUBERT, *right.*

WILLIAM

If every one would make good use of his own talent and let others do the same, the world would move faster. Well, Brother Hubert, what's the trouble?

HUBERT

Well, sir, if you'd kindly take a look at this here last lot of lime (*presenting specimens of lime and mortar on a shovel*). If lime you can call it. What they've done to it I *don't* know, but it don't seem to have no body in it as you might say. It don't bind right. You should hear what my lads has to say about it.

39

WILLIAM

Yes. Poor slack stuff. Where did this come from?

GERVASE

From Jocelyn's. You remember, the Father Treasurer wanted the order given to them. He said Thomas Clay's price was excessive.

WILLIAM

I wish the Father Treasurer would allow me to know my own job. Tell him—no, don't tell him anything. Order in a fresh lot from Thomas Clay's as before, instructing him to charge it up at Jocelyn's price and send me a private note of the difference. We can adjust it on that timber account. Do you understand? If these timber merchants are knaves enough to offer me a five per cent. commission for giving them the contract and Father Stephen is fool enough to grudge a few pounds extra for first-class material, all right. We play off the knave against the fool, get what we want, and save argument.

HUBERT

Ay, that's so. What the Father Treasurer don't see won't worry him.

GERVASE

But is it honest?

HUBERT

All I know is, this here lime ain't honest. Prior Wibert, him as built the Water-Tower, wouldn't never have asked his masons to put up with cheap rubbish like this here.

WILLIAM (*to* GERVASE)

No, of course it's not honest. And it's not exactly safe. That is, it's liable to misconstruction, if proclaimed upon the housetops. But the Lord commended the unjust steward.

HUBERT

You can't make bricks without straw, nor yet mortar without lime. And if Prior Wibert, rest his soul, was alive, he'd say the same.

40

WILLIAM

Cheer up, little churchman. Take thy bill and sit down quickly and write fifty. Nobody's robbing the Church.

[*Exit* GERVASE, *left, still a trifle unhappy about it.*

H'm. Unfortunate. He'll lie awake all night wrestling with his conscience, and probably let the whole thing out to the Father Treasurer. Can't be helped. Sufficient for the day. . . . How about the new arch? D'you think she's settled in? I'd like to get those supports out to-day.

HUBERT

Been over every inch of her, sir, and I think she'll do. We're getting the tackle up now.

WILLIAM

Let me know when you're ready; I don't want anything started till I come. What do you think of the plan for the roof and clerestory?

HUBERT

Grand, sir, grand. I only wish Prior Wibert, good man, was alive to see it. Always a man for new ideas, was Prior Wibert. Ah! He'd have loved that tall shafting and the way the cross-ribbing is made to carry the span. "Mark my words, Hubert," he used to say to me, "the arch is the secret of building. We ain't half learned yet," he'd say, "what the arch can carry when it's put to it."

WILLIAM

He was right, there. But we're finding out. We're finding out every day. Greece never guessed it; Rome only half understood it; but our sons will know in the years to come. (*With rising excitement.*) We all have our dreams, Hubert. Churches we shall never live to see. Arch shouldering arch, shaft, vault and keystone, window and arcading higher, and wider and lighter, lifting roof, tower, spire, into the vault of heaven—columns slender as lily-stalks—walls only a framework for the traceries—living fountains of stone——

41

HUBERT

That's so, Master, that's so. That's the way to build. Each stone carrying his neighbour's burden, as you might say.

WILLIAM

A triumph of balance, eh, Hubert? A delicate adjustment of interlocking stresses. Look! there was an idea came into my head last night.

[*He sketches on a block of stone.*

Enter STEPHEN *and* MARTIN, *right.*

STEPHEN

Well, I must say, it's rather inconsiderate. Still, we mustn't let the opportunity slip.

MARTIN

Certainly not; rich benefactors have to be humoured. Nobody knows that better than he does. Will you tackle him?

STEPHEN

If you like. Er—Master William!

WILLIAM

What can I do for you, Father Treasurer?

STEPHEN

Forgive me for interrupting you—I know you're very busy, but the fact is, we have a visitor——

MARTIN

Rather an important visitor.

STEPHEN

The Lady Ursula de Warbois——

[*Enter* THEODATUS, *right. He has his sleeves tucked up, and a coarse apron over his habit, and carries a trowel.*

MARTIN

We had been hoping she would come——

STEPHEN

She has just arrived and asked to see the Father Prior.

MARTIN

She is with him now. Father Theodatus, have you heard?
The Lady Ursula is with the Father Prior!

THEODATUS

Indeed?

[*He goes across to speak to one of the* WORKMEN.

WILLIAM

Come, sirs. All this excitement is scarcely becoming to your
cloth. Is the lady young and beautiful? And what is she
doing with the Father Prior, or he with her?

[WORKMEN *snigger*.

THEODATUS

Master William! Pray control your tongue.

WILLIAM

There! you see you have shocked Father Theodatus.

STEPHEN

The Lady Ursula is the widow of an exceedingly wealthy
knight.

MARTIN

She has come to reside in Canterbury; and has several times
expressed interest in the work. To-day she has come and
wants to see over the new choir——

STEPHEN

If she is pleased with what she sees, she will probably be
good for a handsome subscription.

WILLIAM

Oh, very well. Take her where you like. Better stand clear
of the new arch, though. We're going to get the supports
out, and it might come down. You never know—eh,
Hubert?

HUBERT

That's right. You never know.

STEPHEN

Yes—but the point is, she particularly wants to meet the
architect and be shown round personally.

MARTIN

She wants to see the plans, and have everything explained
to her.

WILLIAM

T'cha! women always want explanations. But they never
listen, and wouldn't understand a word if they did. I've no
use for women—not in working hours.

THEODATUS (*gloomily*)

The curse came by a woman.

WILLIAM

Well—if it comes to that, so did *you*, Father Theodatus.

HUBERT

That's right. Women are a curse—but we can't get *into* the
world, nor *on* in the world without 'em.

MARTIN

Well, Master William, I'm sure you will oblige her. People
always like to talk to the architect. The human touch, you
know. It's always good publicity.

WILLIAM

Oh, very well, I suppose one must make one's self a martyr
to publicity. Go and keep an eye on the lads, Hubert; I'll
come as soon as I'm free.

[*Going,* STEPHEN *and* MARTIN *offer to accompany him.*

44

No, thanks. I can find my own way. Don't you run your heads into temptation. *Sed libera nos a malo*—deliver us from the apple and all its consequences.

[*Exit, right, with* HUBERT.

STEPHEN

Dear me! I hope he will behave with discretion.

MARTIN

Never fear. He can bridle his tongue when he likes. He is a politic man. Remember how he persuaded us into the expense of rebuilding.

STEPHEN

Yes—we have had some experience of his policy. Well—he wheedled money out of us; let him now wheedle it out of the Lady Ursula.

MARTIN

At any rate, he is a first-class workman. He gives us good value for our money.

STEPHEN

Does he? I hope he does. Sometimes I have my doubts. From something one of the carriers let fall the other day, I am inclined to suspect him of—some irregularities.

MARTIN

Oh, surely not! The accounts all go through your hands and the correspondence through those of Father Gervase.

STEPHEN

Father Gervase? Do you think a crafty old fox like that hasn't the wit to hoodwink a young and innocent churchman like Father Gervase? Is he in the office, by the way? I am inclined to give him a caution. (*Calling left.*) Father Gervase!

GERVASE (*emerging, left, with letters*)
Yes, Father Stephen?

STEPHEN

Tell me; since you have been handling Master William's
letters, have you ever had any reason to suspect any
financial irregularities?

GERVASE (*taken aback*)

Financial irregularities?

STEPHEN

Tampering with the estimates? Fudging the accounts?
Pocketing commissions and that sort of thing? Doing little
deals on the side?

GERVASE (*recovering himself; with confidence*)

I am quite positive, Father Stephen, that Master William
has never cheated the Church of a single penny, and never
would. He thinks of nothing, lives for nothing, but the
integrity of his work. If you knew him as well as I do, working with him these two years, you would be sure of that.

STEPHEN

I am glad to hear it. But keep your eyes open. I have heard
stories, and I am not altogether satisfied.

GERVASE

Would it not be better to speak openly to Master William
himself?

THEODATUS

Of course it would; but they are afraid to. Why? Because
the man has managed to get the ear of the Father Prior—
and because they don't want him to throw up the job in the
middle—and because, having once put their hands to dirty
tools, they don't know how to draw back. (*To* STEPHEN *and*
MARTIN.) No man can serve God and mammon. God's
House should be built with prayer. You are trying to build
it with worldly wisdom and wordly lucre. Look at all those
pilgrims! How many of them have clean hands and pure
hearts?

MARTIN

We cannot see into their hearts.

46

THEODATUS

Have you listened to their talk? One in ten may be sincere.
The rest are idle men and gadding women, making pilgrimage an excuse for a holiday trip—compounding for old sins
by committing new ones. All they come for is to drink and
gossip in alehouses, tell each other dirty stories, pick up
loose companions, waste their own time and other people's,
and gabble through a few perfunctory prayers at top speed,
so as to have more time for sight-seeing.

GERVASE

Are you not a little uncharitable?

STEPHEN

Most of them are very worthy people. And after all, we
can't do without their money.

THEODATUS

If you had faith, you could. You degrade the Church by
these vulgar and dubious methods of publicity.

MARTIN

Really, Father Theodatus! This is monstrous. The Father
Prior himself entrusted me with the publicity side of the
appeal. I have taken great pains to get these pilgrimages
properly advertised. And this is my reward!

GERVASE

Brethren! brethren! All the workmen are listening to you.

[*Enter* WILLIAM, *right, with* URSULA.

MARTIN

Let them listen!

THEODATUS

I do not care who hears me!

47

WILLIAM

Pray, madam, mind your head—the doorway is rather low. One step down. Allow me. This is just a little corner of our workshop, where—— Walter! Hugh! Simon! Is nobody doing any work to-day? Do you take it for the Feast of St. Lazybones? (*The* WORKMEN *hurriedly return to their tasks.*) Walter—that corner is out of true. And here, you! Is that the way to treat your tools? . . . I beg your pardon, madam. The moment my back is turned, everything seems to come to a standstill.

URSULA

No wonder. Without the heart, how can the limbs do their office? You are the heart of the undertaking.

WILLIAM (*formally*)

It is very good of you to say so. I think you know Father Stephen, the Treasurer? Father Martin, the Guest-Brother? Father Theodatus, the Sacristan? And Father Gervase, who is Clerk and Historian to the Chapter, and is good enough to deal with my correspondence in his spare time. (*To* GERVASE) Have those letters gone?

GERVASE

I am just taking them to the messenger.

[*Exit* GERVASE, *right.*

MARTIN

And what, madam, do you think of our Cathedral?

URSULA

I think it must be the most beautiful in the world. And how glorious the new choir will be when it is finished! Master William has described it all to me and has promised to show me all his plans and drawings. That was a promise, was it not, Master William?

WILLIAM

Certainly—if you are really interested.

48

URSULA

Of course I am interested. I am glad I have come to live in Canterbury. It will be so exciting to watch the work going on from day to day. A widow needs an interest in life. And it will be a great comfort to live under the protection of blessed St. Thomas.

MARTIN

Thousands of the suffering and bereaved have already found healing and consolation by his benign intervention. Only a few weeks ago, out of a large congregation of worshippers who attended a special service——

[*Bell begins to ring.* MONKS *enter, right, and file across the stage and down the steps.* WORKMEN *lay down their tools and go out, right, with dinner-baskets.*

THEODATUS

That is the bell for nones.

[*Exit down steps.*

MARTIN

I will tell you presently about the special service.

[*Exeunt* STEPHEN *and* MARTIN *down steps.*

WILLIAM

Do you propose to attend nones? The lower part of the nave is available for the laity.

URSULA

No; I propose to see those drawings of yours.

WILLIAM

I do not think you came here to see architectural drawings.

URSULA

I came—to see the architect. (*Pause.*) Did you realise that this was not the first time we had met?

WILLIAM

I realised it perfectly. I had the honour to pick up your
glove yesterday in the market-place.

URSULA

I was much indebted to you for the courtesy.

WILLIAM

I was much indebted to you for the opportunity. I am an
opportunist. So, I fancy, are you. We have that much in
common.

URSULA

Is that an impertinence, I wonder?

WILLIAM

Yes.

URSULA

I ought to be offended with you.

WILLIAM

If you are wise, you will be. Let us be plain.
The first time our eyes met, we knew one another
As fire knows tinder. You have seen what havoc
Fire works. Let be.

URSULA

I do not fear the fire.

WILLIAM

My fire should be a lamp to light the world,
Fed with my life, consuming only me;
Will you not learn that it is perilous
To play with fire? That it is death to come
Between the man and the work? In one man's life
Is room for one love and no more—one love;
I am in love with a dream.

URSULA

Tell me your dreams
Sitting by the fire, seeing pictures in the fire,
Visions and dreams.

WILLIAM

Your old men shall dream dreams
And your young men see visions—but not your women.
What use have women for the dreams of a man
Save to destroy them? What does a woman know
Of the love of knowledge, passing the love of women?
The passion of making, beside which love's little passion
Shows brittle as a bubble?—To raise up beauty from ashes
Like the splendour of resurrection; to see the stone
Knit unto stone and growing, as in the womb
Bone grows to bone; to build a world out of nothing—
That is my dream; that is the craftsman's dream,
The power and the glory, the kingdom of God and man—
Of man, never of woman. Women create
Passively, borne on a wind of lust, for a whim,
At the caprice of a man, in a smile, in a spasm
Of the flesh; we, with the will, with the blood, with the
    brain,
All the desire of the soul, the intent of the mind.
Now do you understand what my dreams are
And why they are not for you?

URSULA

I understand.
Knowledge and work—knowledge is given to man
And not to woman; and the glory of work
To man and not to woman. But by whom
Came either work or knowledge into the world?
Not by the man. God said, "Ye shall now know;
Knowledge is death." And Adam was afraid.
But Eve, careless of peril, careless of death,
Hearing the promise, "Ye shall be as gods,"
Seized knowledge for herself, and for the man,
And all the sons of men; knowledge, like God;

Power to create, like God; and, unlike God,
Courage to die. And the reward for her
Was sorrow; but for Adam the reward
Was work—of which he now contrives to boast
As his peculiar glory, and in one breath
Denies it to the woman and blames her for it,
Winning the toss both ways. My simple Adam,
It is too late to scare woman with risks
And perils—woman, that for one splendid risk
Changed the security of Paradise,
Broke up the loom and pattern of creation,
Let in man's dream on the world, and snatched the torch
of knowledge from the jealous hand of God
So that the fire runs in man's blood for ever.

WILLIAM (*carried away*)

So that she runs like fire in a man's blood
For ever! Take what thou wilt—the risk, the sorrow,
The fire, the dream—and in the dream's end, death.

GABRIEL

Thus Eve cast down the gauntlet in God's face:
"My will for Thine; man's purpose against God's;
Slay me and slay the man, slay all my seed,
But let man's knowledge and man's work go on."

MICHAEL

Thus God took up the gauntlet in Eve's face.
Having, like man, courage to look on death:
"My Son for thy sons, and God's blood for man's;
Crucify God, but let the work go on."

CASSIEL

By man came sin.

RAPHAEL

O felix culpa, quae
Talem et tantum meruit Redemptorem!

52

HUBERT (*off*)

Master William! Master William!

WILLIAM

There! that means work. You see what happens when one starts this kind of thing. Go now. They are coming out of church. Quickly—or we shall have Father Martin and the special service all over again. I will come to your lodging after supper.

URSULA (*on the steps*)

Bringing your dreams with you.

[*Exit down steps. Enter* HUBERT, *right.*

HUBERT

Master! The arch is ready when you are.

WILLIAM

I am coming. Work, Hubert, work. Sometimes one persuades one's self that it all means something to somebody.

HUBERT

Do you think the gracious lady will be moved to contribute to the building fund?

WILLIAM

H'm. I had forgotten that aspect of the matter. Yes—I shouldn't be surprised if she did.

HUBERT

The blessed saints be praised for it.

WILLIAM

I wonder!

[*Exeunt* WILLIAM *and* HUBERT, *right.*

The Young Cherub (*suddenly*)

Why did God create mankind in two different sorts, if it makes so much trouble?

[*The* Angels *are inexpressibly shocked.*

Raphael

Hush! you mustn't ask Why.

Michael

Angels never ask Why.

Gabriel

Only men ask Why.

Cassiel

And you see what happened to them, just for asking Why.

Michael

Do you want to eat of the Tree of Knowledge, like Adam and Eve?

Gabriel

And find Michael there, with his big sword?

Raphael

And put our Master to the trouble and pain of another crucifixion?

Cassiel

Or start another war, like that lost brother whom we must not name?

All

Criticising God's creation! I never heard of such a thing!

Choir

Shall we that are but worms, but silk-worms, but glow-worms, chide God that He hath made slow-worms, and other venomous creeping things?

Shall we that are all discord, quarrel the harmony of His creation or His providence?

Can an apothecary make a sovereign treacle of vipers and other poisons, and cannot God admit offences and scandals into His physic?

As soon as He had made light (which was His first creature) He took pleasure in it; He said it was good; He was glad of it; glad of the sea, glad of the earth, glad of the sun, and moon, and stars, and He said of every one, It is good.

III

The scene is as before; two more years have passed; WALTER, HUGH *and* GEOFFREY, *lay workmen, are engaged in polishing marble rather up-stage.*

[*Enter* SIMON, *right, and crosses to door, left.*

SIMON (*sings*)
The animals went in two by two,
  Hey, ho, nonny!
Said the dog, Bow-wow! said the cat, Mew, mew!
  Spring is the time for love!

[*Exit left.*

WALTER
Spring, indeed! I wish the spring were here. It hasn't stopped raining for three months.

HUGH
More like four. We've had vile weather ever since the eclipse last September. What a climate!

WALTER
I knew that eclipse meant bad luck.

GEOFFREY
Well, it's not raining to-day.

HUGH
Bad luck? If we never get worse luck than a bit of bad weather, I don't care how many eclipses we have.

WALTER
We ain't heard the last of the eclipse yet, mark my words.

HUGH

You and your prophecies! What are you grumbling about? Job's going well enough, ain't it? Four years, and here we've finished the triforium and the clerestory, and the key of the great arch will be put in to-day. Not too bad, in four years.

[*Re-enter* SIMON, *left, trundling a coil of rope, wound on a drum.*

GEOFFREY

Ah! he's a good worker, is Master William. And a fast worker. Knows what he's about. He's the sort of master I can do with. Strict, and drives you like the devil, but I don't mind that.

HUGH

That's right. I respect a master that's a good worker. When Master William works, he works.

WALTER

And when he plays (*with a meaning grin*), he plays! Him and the Lady Ursula!

HUGH

Well, I don't mind that, either. That's their affair.

SIMON

Quite right, Hugh. The day for labour and the night for—sleep.

(*Sings*)   Two by two they went into the ark,
            Hey, ho, nonny!
        The doors were shut, they were all in the dark,
            Spring is the time for love!

GEOFFREY

She's somewhere about the place now.

WALTER

Who is? Lady Ursula?

57

GEOFFREY

Yes. Takes a lot of interest. Always putting up a bit o' prayer, or coming to see how the job's getting on, or calling on the Father Treasurer with a little donation to something.

SIMON (*sings*)

But when old Noah opened the door,
    Hey, ho, nonny!
They all came out by three and four,
    Spring is the time for love!

[*Enter* PRIOR *and* THEODATUS, *right.*

HUGH

It's a wonder the good fathers don't see through it.

GEOFFREY

Maybe they do. Maybe it pays them to wink t'other eye. Lady's Ursula's rich. It don't do to offend rich folks.

THEODATUS

You hear that, Father Prior?

WALTER

All the same, mark my words, no good will come of it. That eclipse wasn't sent for nothing.

HUGH

Ah, come off it. You and your eclipse!

SIMON (*sings*)

Who d'ye think had been playing tricks?
    Hey, ho, nonny!
They went in two and they came out six,
    Spring is the time for love!

THEODATUS

For shame, my son, for shame! We cannot have these lewd songs here.

58

[He comes down past SIMON *to the steps, with the* PRIOR.

SIMON

Sorry, Father.

[He goes out, left.

THEODATUS

So it goes on, Father, day after day—
Songs in the workshop, sniggering in the dortor,
Unbecoming gossip among the novices,
Heads wagged in the market-place, and tales going round
In the ale-house, fingers pointed everywhere
At William of Sens, the Cathedral architect—
A notorious evil liver, a seducer of women,
A taker of bribes——

PRIOR (*mildly*)
That was not proved, I fancy.

THEODATUS

A cunning liar, that boasts of pulling the wool
Over the eyes of the fat, innocent monks;
A man without truth, without shame. It is not respectable;
It is not right.

PRIOR
You must not say, without truth,
Lest you should hear the very stones cry out
Against you. Truth is glorious; but there is one
Glory of the sun, another of the moon,
And all the truth of the craftsman is in his craft.
Where there is truth, there is God; and where there is glory,
There is God's glory too.

THEODATUS (*sullenly*)
Craft is the word.
We could do better without William's craft
In more ways than in one. I would rather have
A worse-built church with a more virtuous builder.

PRIOR

Make God the loser for your conscience' sake?
This is God's House, and if on any pretext
We give him less than the best, we shall cheat God
As William never cheated God, nor us.
He that bestowed the skill and the desire
To do great work is surely glad to see
That skill used in His service.

THEODATUS

                    Skill is not all.
The kingdom of Heaven is won by righteousness,
Not skill. He cannot wish His work performed
Save with clean hands and a pure heart.

PRIOR

                                My son,
Will you not let God manage His own business?
He was a carpenter, and knows His trade
Better, perhaps, than we do, having had
Some centuries of experience; nor will He,
Like a bad workman, blame the tools wherewith
He builds His City of Zion here on earth.
For God founded His Church, not upon John,
The loved disciple, that lay so close to His heart
And knew His mind—not upon John, but Peter;
Peter the liar, Peter the coward, Peter
The rock, the common man. John was all gold,
And gold is rare; the work might wait while God
Ransacked the corners of the earth to find
Another John; but Peter is the stone
Whereof the world is made. So stands the Church,
Stone upon stone, and Christ the corner-stone
Carved of the same stuff, common flesh and blood,
With you, and me, and Peter; and He can,
Being the alchemist's stone, the stone of Solomon,
Turn stone to gold, and purge the gold itself
From dross, till all is gold.

60

THEODATUS

     To purge—to burn!
He makes His ministers a flaming fire—
And are not we His ministers? Shall not we
Lay axe to the rotten root, trunk, branch? destroy.
Make bonfire of this scandal in the Church
And burn God's honour clean?

PRIOR

     God is a man,
And can defend His honour, being full-grown
In wisdom and in stature. We need not
Play nursemaid to the Babe of Bethlehem
To shield Him from the harlot and the thief,
Or keep those tender, innocent hands from harm
That bear the sharp nails' imprint, and uphold
The axis of the spheres. He can touch dirt
Without defilement, for Himself hath said,
"What I have cleansed, that call not thou unclean."

THEODATUS

But while His laws are broken in our sight
Must we stand by, and smile, and still do nothing?

PRIOR

Do your own work, while yet the daylight lasts.
Look that it be well done; look not beyond it.
I charge you, on your holy obedience,
Set charity as a bridle on your tongue;
Talk not of William's nor another's faults,
Unless to God, Who hears but spreads no scandal.
Of this be sure: who will not have the Gospel
Shall have the Law; but in God's time, not ours.

[*Enter* SIMON *by door, left, carrying a small windlass.*

SIMON (*bursting irrepressibly into song*)

Every bird had found her mate,
  Hey, ho, nonny!
They all came out by seven and eight,
  Spring is the time for love!

[*He sets the windlass down, centre. Enter* WILLIAM, *right.*

WILLIAM

You are merry, Simon. Is that the rope to rig the travelling cradle?

SIMON

Yes, sir.

WILLIAM

See that every inch of it is well tested before I go up. I'm not as young or as light as I was. Good morning, Father Prior. Ah! Father Theodatus, you are just the man I was looking for. Pray will you help Simon to test that rope? It is to hoist me up to the top of the great arch, and I have a value for my neck.

THEODATUS

Oh, by all means.

[*Moving up, left.*

WILLIAM

Simon is a good lad enough, but I would rather trust your vigilance. Young men's minds are apt to run astray.

[*During the following dialogue,* THEODATUS *takes the free end of the rope and begins to wind it off on to the windlass.* SIMON *stands by the drum, so that, as the rope is slowly wound off, they can both examine it for flaws. They occupy the stage from centre to left.*

PRIOR

Young men are not alone in that, Master William. The talk of the town comes to our ears sometimes, dull-witted old churchmen though we be. It seems that even a master architect may find interests outside his work.

WILLIAM

Outside his working *hours*, Father Prior.

PRIOR

I quite appreciate that. My dear son, as your father in God I might find many things to say to you. . . .

WILLIAM

But as a man of the world you doubt whether I should listen. It is a rare virtue to refrain even from good words.

PRIOR

Then I will speak only as a man of the world and urge the value of discretion.

WILLIAM

Father Theodatus would say, of hypocrisy.

PRIOR

Father Theodatus is not your employer. The Church is your employer, and it is my duty to speak for the Church.

WILLIAM

Very well. As my *employer*, to use your own blunt term, what fault have you to find with my private amusements?

PRIOR

This: that instead of attending to their work, your workmen waste their time in gossip and backbiting about you. If you choose to be damned, you must; if you prefer to make a death-bed repentance, you may; but if an idle workman does an unsound job now, no repentance of yours will prevent it from bringing down the church some day or other.

WILLIAM (*after a pause*)

You are quite right. I congratulate you. You have found the one argument to which I am bound to listen. Were you a diplomat before you were a churchman?

63

Perhaps.

[*Exit, right.*

WILLIAM (*looking after him*)

Or a soldier. The old man's a hard hitter and knows where
to plant his blows. (*He goes up, back, to overlook the work of*
WALTER *and* GEOFFREY, *speaking to* THEODATUS *and* SIMON
as he goes): Test it with the eye and the hand—don't trust
to either alone.

MICHAEL

Are there no fires in Heaven, that every man
With his own hand, upon the anvil of sin
Forges the sword of judgment? Gabriel, Raphael,
There is a sword in the making; look you to it.

[RAPHAEL *goes up and stands near* THEODATUS, *centre, and*
GABRIEL, *near* SIMON, *left.*

℣. The eyes of the Lord are in every place, beholding the
evil and the good.
℞. Shall we continue in sin that grace may abound? God
forbid.
℣. He maketh His sun to rise on the evil and on the good;
℞. And sendeth rain upon the just and unjust.

[*Enter* URSULA, *right.*

URSULA

William!

WILLIAM (*turning quickly and coming to meet her*)

Ah! You have come at a very good moment.

[*He leads her forward to the steps.*

SIMON (*watching them with interest*)

Oho! look at that!

64

WILLIAM

We are just about to put in the key of the great arch.

THEODATUS

Turn away mine eyes from beholding vanity!

WILLIAM

If you will stand here presently and watch, you will see me fly up to the top of the scaffold in a machine of my own devising—and down again, like blessed St. Paul in a basket!

THEODATUS (*hastily reciting with averted eyes*)

Sancta Maria, ora pro nobis;
Sancta Dei genetrix, ora pro nobis;
Sancta Virgo virginum, ora pro nobis.

[RAPHAEL *sets his censer gently swinging.*

URSULA

How amusing! I hope it is safe.

SIMON (*over his shoulder to* GEOFFREY)

More headaches for Father Martin! He don't like these goings-on. Says they look bad, and shock influential patrons.

WILLIAM

Never fear for that. But, hark'ee—we're in disgrace with the Prior.

THEODATUS

Mater castissima, ora pro nobis;
Mater inviolata, ora pro nobis;
Mater intemerata, ora pro nobis.

URSULA

Oh! I ought not to have come.

WILLIAM

That was my fault. I asked you. I wanted you here.

Take care, Simon! There is a flaw in the rope.

[SIMON, *with his eyes on* WILLIAM *and* URSULA, *pays no attention.*

SIMON (*sings*)
> The cat, the rat, the sow, the hen,
> > *Hey, ho, nonny!*
> They all came out by nine and ten,
> > *Spring is the time for love!*

[*The rope runs through his heedless fingers.* GABRIEL *makes a despairing gesture, and looks across at* RAPHAEL. *The scandalised* THEODATUS *continues to pray with his eyes tight shut.*

THEODATUS
> Virgo veneranda, ora pro nobis;
> Virgo praedicanda, ora pro nobis;
> Virgo potens, ora pro nobis.

URSULA
What does the Prior complain of? Scandal in the Cathedral?

WILLIAM
Something like that.

THEODATUS
> Vas honorabile, ora pro nobis;
> Vas insigne devotionis, ora pro nobis;
> Rosa mystica, ora pro nobis.

RAPHAEL
Take care, Theodatus! There is a flaw in the rope.

THEODATUS
> Turris Davidica, ora pro nobis;
> Turris eburnea, ora pro nobis;
> Domus aurea, ora pro nobis.

[RAPHAEL *flings away the censer, which rolls clanging down the steps. The rope, flaw and all, is wound off.*

66

URSULA

At least he cannot say that you think more of me than of
your work.

WILLIAM

No, he has not said that.

THEODATUS

Agnus Dei, qui tollis peccata mundi, parce nobis Domine;
Agnus Dei, qui tollis peccata mundi, exaudi nos, Domine;
Agnus Dei, qui tollis peccata mundi, miserere nobis.

[*The rope is now all wound off.*

URSULA

He will not take the work away from you?

WILLIAM

He is too shrewd for that. Besides, God would not let him;
He has put me here and will keep me here, Prior or no
Prior.

WORKMAN (*putting his head in at the door, below*)

Master Hubert says, is that rope ready?

SIMON

Here you are, mate.

[*He picks up the windlass and takes it down to* WORKMAN, *who
carries it out.*

URSULA

Do we presume too much upon God's mercy?

WILLIAM

We are the master-craftsmen, God and I—
We understand one another. None, as I can,
Can creep under the ribs of God, and feel
His heart beat through those Six Days of Creation;
Enormous days of slowly turning lights
Streaking the yet unseasoned firmament;

Giant days, Titan days, yet all too short
To hold the joy of making. God caught His breath
To see the poles of the world stand up through chaos;
And when He sent it forth, the great winds blew,
Carrying the clouds. And then He made the trees
For winds to rustle through—oak, poplar, cedar,
Hawthorn and elm, each with its separate motion—
And with His delicate fingers painted the flowers,
Numberless—numberless! why make so many
But that He loved the work, as I love mine,
And saw that it was good, as I see mine?—
The supple, swift mechanics of the serpent,
The beautiful, furred beasts, and curious fish
With golden eyes and quaintly-laced thin bones,
And whales like mountains loud with spurting springs,
Dragons and monsters in strange shapes, to make
His angels laugh with Him; when He saw those
God sang for joy, and formed the birds to sing.
And lastly, since all Heaven was not enough
To share that triumph, He made His masterpiece,
Man, that like God can call beauty from dust,
Order from chaos, and create new worlds
To praise their maker. Oh, but in making man
God over-reached Himself and gave away
His Godhead. He must now depend on man
For what man's brain, creative and divine
Can give Him. Man stands equal with Him now,
Partner and rival. Say God needs a church,
As here in Canterbury—and say He calls together
By miracle stone, wood and metal, builds
A church of sorts; *my* church He cannot make—
Another, but not that. This church is mine
And none but I, not even God, can build it.
Me hath He made vice-gerent of Himself,
And were I lost, something unique were lost
Irreparably; my heart, my blood, my brain
Are in the stone; God's crown of matchless works
Is not complete without my stone, my jewel,
Creation's nonpareil.

68

URSULA

Hush! God will hear you—
The priests say He is jealous. Tempt Him not
Lest He should smite and slay.

WILLIAM

He will not dare;
He knows that I am indispensable
To His work here; and for the work's sake, He,
Cherishing, as good masons do, His tools,
Will keep me safe. When the last stone is laid
Then may He use me as He will; I care not;
The work is all; when that is done, good night——
My life till then is paramount with God.

URSULA

You make me shake to hear you. Blasphemy! blasphemy!

WILLIAM

Sound sense. Fear nothing. I must leave you now;
The work waits for me, and that must not be;
Idleness is the only sin. Like God
I must be doing in my little world,
Lest, lacking me, the moon and stars should fail.

[*He goes out down the steps.*

URSULA (*watching him go*)

I am afraid; have mercy on him, Christ!

CASSIEL

Draw thy sword, Michael; the hour is come.

[MICHAEL *follows* WILLIAM *out, with his sword drawn in his hand.*

℣. Except the Lord build the house, their labour is but lost that build it.

℟. Except the Lord keep the city, the watchman waketh but in vain.

℣. The zeal of thine house hath eaten me up; and rebukes are fallen upon me.

℟. For Thou art great and doest wondrous things; Thou art God alone.

[*During the singing of these versicles, the three remaining* ANGELS *stand side by side at the top of the steps, with* URSULA *below them. Now they go up and stand on the plinth at the back of the stage,* RAPHAEL *and* GABRIEL *to right and left, with* CASSIEL *centre.*

CHOIR

The Lord is known to execute judgment; the ungodly is trapped in the work of his own hands.

For he hath said in his heart, Tush, I shall never be cast down; there shall no harm happen unto me.

The snares of death compassed me round about, and the pains of hell gat hold upon me.

I shall find trouble and heaviness, and I will call upon the name of the Lord: O Lord, I beseech Thee, deliver my soul.

[*The stage gradually fills with* MONKS *and* WORKMEN; *among them is a* YOUNG BOY.

MONKS AND WORKMEN

This is a brave day . . . the great arch finished . . . See, they are making ready to drop in the keystone . . . It is wonderful how well Master William's machines work—they have halved the labour of building . . . there's old Hubert—he'll be a proud man to-day . . . Laus Deo! our new choir will be ready for us within the year . . . There it goes! No, they're waiting for something . . . They're waiting for the architect . . . There he is, slung half-way up in the travelling cradle . . . Can't you see? Come on, lad, up on my shoulder . . . There's the keystone slung aloft on the crane . . . Hurray! Master William's up now—just getting to the top of the scaffolding . . . Get ready to cheer, boys. . . .

THE YOUNG BOY (*from his perch on the workman's shoulder, shrilly*)

Oh, look! look at the angel—the terrible angel!

ALL

What's that? An angel? What? Where? Nonsense!

THE YOUNG BOY

High on the scaffold, with the drawn sword in his hand!

URSULA

Mother of God!

[*She falls upon the steps.*
A shout from the stage is succeeded by a heavy crash without from the far end of the building. Men run in, right.

ALL

He's fallen . . . Master William's down . . . He's killed . . . fifty feet at least . . . His foot slipped . . . No, the rope broke . . . What's happened? . . . God have mercy on us! . . . Run for help! . . . Blessed Mary, pray for us! . . . Send for the Prior . . . Fetch a chirurgeon . . . The devil is abroad . . . No, it was an angel . . . Where's that boy who saw the angel? . . . Here, the lady's fainted—give us a hand here to carry her in . . . Come along, let's see what's happened . . .

[*There is a general rush down the steps.*

URSULA (*to the men who are supporting her*)

Take me with you. (*But she is unable to stand.*) No—leave me! Run and bring me word.

[*They leave her crouched on the steps and run out. The three* ANGELS *come down and follow the crowd out. Nobody is left but* THEODATUS, SIMON *and* URSULA.

71

SIMON

The rope! God forgive me—I was talking and laughing.
Father Theodatus, what have we done?

THEODATUS

The rope! God is avenged. But I did not mean—I did not
think—if it had not been for your lewd songs and his own
behaviour with this woman——

URSULA

Could You not break me and not him, O God?

SIMON

We have killed him among us.

CHOIR

Out of the deep have I called unto Thee. O Lord, hear my
voice.
O let Thine ears consider well the voice of my complaint.
If Thou, Lord, wilt be extreme to mark what is done amiss,
O Lord, who may abide it?
For there is mercy with Thee, therefore shalt thou be
feared.
I look for the Lord, my soul doth wait for Him, in His
word is my trust.
My soul fleeth unto the Lord; before the morning watch,
I say, before the morning watch.
O Israel, trust in the Lord, for with the Lord there is
mercy, and with Him is plenteous redemption;
And He shall redeem Israel from all his sins.

[*During the singing of the psalm, the* PRIOR *has re-entered from
the lower end, with* HUBERT, GERVASE *and the* YOUNG BOY.
They mount the steps.

URSULA

Father! Father! In pity, tell me—is he dead?

PRIOR

No, my poor child. But sorely maimed.

HUBERT

He will never be the same man again.

URSULA

Let me go to him.

PRIOR

Presently. The leech is with him now, seeing to his hurts. Trust me, you shall see him presently. (*He goes on up steps and sits, right.*) Now, Hubert, I must know how all this came to pass.

HUBERT

My Lord Prior, there is no doubt at all. There was a flaw in the rope. Just as the cradle came up to the level of the scaffolding, bearing Master William, I saw with my eyes the strands spring asunder. I stretched out my hands to catch him, but I could not reach. If I could have done anything—anything! I would gladly have given my life.

GERVASE

So would I, Hubert.

PRIOR

I am sure you would.

HUBERT

Such a craftsman! such a craftsman! So kind a master! Just, zealous, generous—no fault in him at all.

GERVASE

So faithful a servant of the Church! Who will finish his work now? . . . He was my friend, too.

HUBERT

What I should like to know is—who had the testing o' that there rope?

SIMON (*flinging himself at the* PRIOR's *feet*)

It was I—it was my neglect. I have no excuse. I shall never forgive myself.

URSULA

It was my fault. I was talking to William—distracting the attention of them all. This is a judgment for our sin—his and mine.

THEODATUS

True; it was a judgment. Ask this boy here. Did he not see the angel thrust him down?

PRIOR

Yes, child. What is this about an angel?

THE YOUNG BOY

It is true. I saw a great angel stand between heaven and earth—all in gold and scarlet, with a drawn sword. Oh, and he had great wings, too. He cut the rope and the cradle fell.

THEODATUS

There, you see! it was a divine ʲudgment.

HUBERT

Divine judgment! The boy's dreaming. It was rank carelessness. Simon—who was at the other end of the rope when you tested it? (SIMON *looks round at* THEODATUS, *waiting for him to speak*.) Speak up, man! Who was it?

PRIOR

I was there, Theodatus.

THEODATUS

Well, it was I. But I had nothing to do with it. You heard what the child said. It was a miracle.

PRIOR

I think we sometimes make disasters, and then call them miraculous judgments. Did you at any moment take hand or eye from the rope while you were testing it?

I cannot remember. (*Under the* PRIOR's *eye, he abandons this line of defence.*) *She* was there with William. For my soul's sake I could not look at them. I was saying my prayers . . .

HUBERT

Sayin' your prayers! With the master's safety depending on you!

THEODATUS

God Himself laid the seal upon my eyes. I was His appointed instrument to overthrow the wicked man.

PRIOR

Think what you say, my son. It is not for us
To ordain ourselves the ministers of vengeance;
For it must needs be that offences come,
But woe unto that man by whom the offence
Cometh; 'twere better he had not been born.
This is thy sin: thou hast betrayed the work;
Thou hast betrayed the Church; thou hast betrayed
Christ, in the person of His fellow-man.
What was the prayer wherein thou offer'dst up
Thy brother's life?

THEODATUS
The Litany of the Virgin.

PRIOR

Go to the church; repeat it once again,
Saying at every line: "This was the spear
With which I pierced the body of the Lord,"
Then come to me and ask for absolution.

THEODATUS

I will obey.

[*Exit* THEODATUS, *right.*

PRIOR

For you, my son and daughter,
You see how sin brings its own suffering;
Do not despair; God's mercy is very great. (*He rises.*)
Thou that hast visions of angels, come with me.
I am an old man. Let me have thy shoulder.
So. Thou shalt tell me more about the angel.

[*Exeunt* PRIOR *and* YOUNG BOY, *right.*

GERVASE (*helping* URSULA *to her feet*)

Madam, pray do not weep so. He would be sorry to see it.
I loved him, too. Let us go together to visit him.

URSULA

And supposing he can never work again? What comfort in
this world for him? And what forgiveness for any of us?

[*Exeunt* GERVASE *and* URSULA, *right.*

HUBERT

Well, Simon, you've made a nice mess of it. There, there,
lad, I can see you're sorry. Don't 'ee lose heart, now. It's
a bad business, but we must make the best of it.

SIMON

Oh, Hubert!

[*Exeunt* HUBERT *and* SIMON, *right.*

During the singing of the following hymn, the ANGELS *return
and take up their places as at the beginning of the play.*

CHOIR

Plebs angelica
phalanx et archangelica
principans turma, virtus
Uranica,
ac potestas
almiphona.

Dominantia
numina divinaque
subsellia, Cherubim
aetherea
ac Seraphim
ignicoma,

Vos, O Michael
caeli satrapa,
Gabrielque vera
dans verba nuntia,

Atque Raphael,
vitae vernula,
transferte nos inter
Paradisicolas.

IV

Six months have passed since the preceding scene. During the singing of the interlude, GERVASE, *assisted by a* LAY-BROTHER, *is making up a couch in the centre of the stage. Enter, right,* MARTIN, *carrying a couple of large sheepskins.*

MARTIN

They told me you wanted some extra coverings for Master William's bed.

GERVASE

Thank you, brother. Why, this is very kind! Surely these are the best fleeces.

MARTIN

They are usually kept for distinguished visitors. But Father Wulfram specially asked that you should have them. They will make Master William warm and comfortable—since he has taken this fancy for lying here.

GERVASE

We are in hopes he may sleep better close to his work. He is so restless. Day and night he thinks of nothing but the building, and frets to lie helpless and so far away. From here he can see the sun shine on the arches he has raised; and when he lies wakeful in the early dawn it will comfort him to hear the clink of the mason's trowel and the carver's hammer heralding in the day.

[*The* LAY-BROTHER *sets a stool near the head of the couch, down-stage, and goes out, right.*

MARTIN

Poor soul! Well, let us praise God for this warm and seasonable weather. Now that the summer is come, he will take no hurt from his change of lodging.

[*The* LAY-BROTHER *returns with a jug of water, a horn drinking-vessel, and a candlestick, which he places on the stool.*

GERVASE

May it refresh him, soul and body! But I fear he undertakes
more than his strength will bear. He has insisted to-day on
being carried to view the progress of the roof over the
Choir and Crosses. It is impossible to move him without
causing severe pain—and then he gives orders and excites
himself. Indeed, it is too much for him.

MARTIN (*with some hesitation*)

I suppose nothing would induce him to resign the appointment?

GERVASE

Part him from his work? Oh, no! It would be more bitter to
him than death. And where should we get another like him?

[*Exit* LAY-BROTHER, *right*.

MARTIN

Well, I don't know. It is true he has done magnificent work.
But frankly, dear brother, a sick man with a crippled spine
cannot have his eyes here, there and everywhere, and during
this half-year since his accident things have not gone quite
so well.

GERVASE

You know why that is. Some of the brethren do not work
so loyally for Brother Hubert as they did for him.

MARTIN

Isn't that natural? Hubert is an excellent craftsman, but,
after all, he is only an oblate, and a man of no education.
Now if Master William had appointed, let us say, Father
Hilary——

GERVASE

Father Hilary does fine carving very prettily, but he's quite
out of his depth when it comes to the practical side of building. Now, Brother Hubert understands his job inside out.

MARTIN

Of course, but—— Well, there you are! You can't deny that there has been a certain amount of ill-feeling.

GERVASE (*bitterly*)

Jealousy, vanity, hatred, malice and all uncharitableness! And these are churchmen, vowed to holy obedience and humility.

MARTIN

Beati pauperes spiritu. Beati mites.

GERVASE

Amen! (*He examines the couch critically and gives a punch to the pillows. Re-enter* LAY-BROTHER, *right, with a crucifix in his hand and a large bundle of papers under his arm.*) Ah, thanks, Brother Robert. (*He sets the crucifix on the stool with the other things.*) Better put the papers on that other stool for the moment. (LAY-BROTHER *puts them on stool, right.*) There! I think that is the best we can do.

[*Voices and footsteps off, right.*

MARTIN

I think they are bringing our patient in now.

GERVASE

I hope he is not too much exhausted.

[*Enter, right,* WILLIAM, *carried by* THEODATUS *and* SIMON.

WILLIAM

Ugh! ugh! Gently, you fools, gently. Do you want to kill me? You've had one good shot at it. Jolt, jolt, like a couple of pack-asses. Clumsy idiots.

[*They lay him on the couch, to a running accompaniment of groans and curses.*

THEODATUS

I am sorry. Did I hurt you?

80

WILLIAM

Oh, no! Only jarred me to pieces, that's all.

GERVASE (*arranging pillows*)

Is that a little easier? I'm afraid you have over-tired yourself. Are you in great pain?

WILLIAM

Oh, I daresay it'll be worse in Purgatory.

MARTIN (*pouring out water*)

You have been out too long in the hot sun.

WILLIAM (*drinking*)

Thanks. Sorry, Simon. Don't mind me, Father Theodatus. It's only bad temper. The Prior set you a hard penance when he appointed you beast of burden to a sick man.

[*Exit* LAY-BROTHER.

THEODATUS

No, indeed. There is nothing I would more gladly do. I deserve far more than that for the evil I did you.

WILLIAM

Oh, stop blaming yourself. What's done can't be helped. Blame God, or the devil, or whoever looks after these things. Where's Hubert? I want him here. Go and fetch Brother Hubert, for God's sake, somebody. (*Exeunt* SIMON *and* THEODATUS, *right.*) Why haven't my papers been brought down?

GERVASE (*bringing stool with papers and setting it by the couch up-stage*)

They are all here. I will put them handy for you.

MARTIN

Will you not rest a little first?

WILLIAM

No, I will not. Leave me alone, can't you? Gervase, find me the measurements for those corbels. They've got them all wrong, as I knew they would. (*Enter* HUBERT, *right*.) Just because I'm not there to stand over them all the time—— Oh, Hubert, come and look at this. What did I tell you? I knew it was not my measurements that were wrong. Can't you remember anything you're told?

HUBERT

I am sure, sir, I gave Father Hilary the measurements exactly as you gave them to me. But he would have it as his own way was the right one, and he told the men under him——

WILLIAM

Father Hilary! Why should they pay any attention to Father Hilary? If I had the use of my limbs I'd give them something to remind them who's in charge here. But I have to lie helpless as a log while you make a mess of it among you. Never mind. Not your fault. Gervase, give me pen and ink—I'll show you how you can put it right. (GERVASE *fetches pen and ink from bench, left*.) Lift me up, somebody. (MARTIN *lifts him up*.) Ugh! Now, see here . . . I've got an idea about this. . . .

[*He begins to draw on the plan, but is overcome by faintness.*

HUBERT

Dear master, leave it until to-morrow.

WILLIAM

It looks as though I shall have to. All right, Hubert. Don't worry. We'll put it straight in the morning. (GERVASE *and* MARTIN *take away the drawing materials and settle him back on his pillows*.) Oh, God! Shall I never be able to do anything again?

[*Enter* LAY-BROTHER, *right, with a bowl of soup and a trencher of bread.*

MARTIN (*soothingly*)

You work too hard. You have over-tired yourself. You will feel better when you have eaten. (GERVASE *takes the bowl and hands it to* WILLIAM, *and the* LAY-BROTHER *goes out.*) Come away now, Brother Hubert. He must be persuaded to rest. (*He bustles* HUBERT *away, right, then turns at the door as* ERNULPHUS *and* PAUL *pop their heads round it.*) Here are some visitors for you.

[*Enter* PAUL, *carrying a bunch of roses and something done up in a cabbage-leaf, and* ERNULPHUS, *obviously concealing some offering under his habit. Exeunt* MARTIN *and* HUBERT.

ERNULPHUS

May we come in? Pax tecum, my son, pax tecum.

WILLIAM (*in a dispirited growl*)

Et cum spiritu tuo.

ERNULPHUS

And how do you feel this evening?

WILLIAM (*with a wry face, but not unkindly*)

Horrible!

ERNULPHUS

T—t—t—t—t!

PAUL

It's this dreadful hot weather. Very trying. I don't know when I remember such a trying June. I'm sure we never had such unwholesome heat when I was a boy. I was nearly melted away, working in the garden. And the greenfly gets worse every year. There never was such a year for greenfly. Everything smothered. Still, I've managed to find a few roses (*presenting them*), and see! A dozen or so of the early strawberries. I thought you might like them for your supper.

WILLIAM (*genuinely touched*)

That's very good of you, Father Paul. Are they the first?

83

PAUL

The very first. Nobody else has had any—not even the Father Prior. I hope you will find them sweet. Though I must say, fruit doesn't seem to have the flavour it had in my young days. Still, such as they are, there they are.

[*He puts them on the stool, down-stage.*

WILLIAM

I shall enjoy them immensely. I don't know anything more refreshing than early strawberries.

ERNULPHUS

Oho! don't you? I do. (*He produces a stout little flask from under his habit.*) Just you try this. A reviving cordial water from our own distillery. Not too fiery, and full of healthful properties. Made from herbs, according to our special recipe.

[*Puts it on the stool.*

WILLIAM

Thank you; thank you very much. I will drink it to the healths of both of you.

PAUL

Oh, but it is your own health we must all wish and pray for. We do pray for you, of course. Night and morning. And remember you at Mass. Eh, Father Ernulphus?

ERNULPHUS

Always. All of us. So you mustn't lose heart. Oh, dear, no. Now we had better run away, or we shall tire you out. Good night, my son. May God watch over and restore you!

PAUL

Our Lady and all the blessed saints have you in their keeping.

[PAUL *and* ERNULPHUS *trundle amiably off, right.*

WILLIAM

Good old souls! This is what I have come to, Gervase—to be nursed and coddled, and comforted like a child with strawberries. Ah, well. You can tuck me up for the night and leave me to my own hobgoblins.

GERVASE (*taking the supper things away and helping him to lie down*)

To the holy Angels, rather. There! is that comfortable?

WILLIAM

Yes, thank you, my boy.

GERVASE (*with a little assumption of authority*)

Do not forget your prayers.

WILLIAM

Very well, Father.

GERVASE

Benedicat te omnipotens Deus, Pater, et Filius et Spiritus Sanctus. Amen.

WILLIAM

Amen.

GERVASE (*going out, right*)

Sleep in peace. Hubert and I will be at hand if you should need anything.

[*Exit, left.*

WILLIAM *pulls out a rosary, mechanically counts the first decade, then tosses it away impatiently.*

CHOIR

O lux beata trinitas,
Et principalis unitas,
Jam sol recedit igneus;
Infunde lumen cordibus.

Michael.

GABRIEL

Michael.

CASSIEL

Michael, thou watchman of the Lord! What of the night?
Watchman, what of the night?

MICHAEL

The morning cometh, and also the night; if ye will enquire,
enquire ye: return, come.

CHOIR

Te mane laudum carmine,
Te deprecamur vesperi,
Te nostra supplex gloria
Per cuncta laudet saecula.

[*Enter* THEODATUS, *right.*

THEODATUS

Master William, there is one without would speak with you.

WILLIAM

Who?

THEODATUS

The Lady Ursula.

WILLIAM

What is the use of this? I will not see her. It is always the
same story. She asks to be my wife, my nurse, my servant—
Heaven knows what; to devote her life, make reparation and
all the rest of it. She shall not do it. I will not have people
sacrificing themselves for me. It is monstrous. It is impossible. Tell her so.

THEODATUS

She says she is here for the last time. She is very unhappy.
I think you ought—I beseech you to let her come.

WILLIAM

That is a new tune for you to sing, Father Theodatus.

THEODATUS

I have learnt a little charity of late. Let me beg of you.

WILLIAM

Oh, very well.

[THEODATUS *beckons in* URSULA *and goes out, right.*

URSULA

William, I have come to say good-bye. I will not trouble you
any more. Since I am nothing to you now, and the world
without you is nothing to me, I can but take refuge at the
Throne of Grace and pray for both of us.

WILLIAM

That is folly, my dear. You, in a convent of nuns! Go and be
happy, and forget me.

URSULA

That is the one thing I cannot do. No other man shall have
me, if not you.

WILLIAM

I am not a man, Ursula. I am a cripple with a broken back
—a stock, a stone—I am nothing. A marriage-bond with me
would be a bond indeed. Let the dead past bury its dead.
Our dream is over.

URSULA

"Sitting by the fire, seeing pictures in the fire, visions and
dreams"—do you remember?

WILLIAM

I have no dreams now—only nightmares. Nobody can bring
back my dreams. Some of them even grudge me my work
here—all that is left to me.

URSULA

I have broken what I cannot mend. William, tell me—had I at any time, even for a moment, any part in your dream?

WILLIAM

I hardly know. But once, high in a corner of the clerestory, where none but God will look for it, I carved an angel with your face.

URSULA

Ah, my dear! . . . And you will still have me go?

WILLIAM

Yes; go. I am sorry. Go.

[URSULA *goes without protest.*

Father Theodatus! (THEODATUS *looks in.*) Pray conduct the Lady Ursula to the convent gate and ask the Father Prior if he can come and see me.

THEODATUS

I will, my son.

[*Exit* THEODATUS *with* URSULA, *right.*

CHOIR

My days are consumed away like smoke, and my bones are burnt up as it were a fire-brand.
My heart is smitten down and withered like grass, so that I forget to eat my bread.
For the voice of my groaning, my bones will scarce cleave to my flesh.
And that because of Thine indignation and wrath; for Thou hast taken me up and cast me down.

[*Enter* PRIOR, *right.*

PRIOR

You sent for me, my son?

88

WILLIAM

Yes. I scarcely know why, save that I am in hell and can see no way out.

PRIOR

Is there some sin troubling your conscience?

WILLIAM

All the sins there are—or most of them, any way. Not that they ever troubled me till I was punished for them. But now—they rise up round me in the night and stifle me.

PRIOR

My son, will you not confess them and receive absolution?

WILLIAM

Confess? if I were to confess them all, you would be here till to-morrow. I cannot remember when I last made a confession.

PRIOR (*removing the papers from the stool up-stage and sitting down*)

In general, then, my son, and as well as you can remember them, tell me your sins.

WILLIAM
I do confess to God
The Father and the Son and Holy Ghost,
To Mary Mother of God the ever-virgin,
To the most holy Apostles Peter and Paul,
To blessed Michael and all his angels
And the whole company of Heaven, and thee,
Father, that I have sinned exceedingly,
In thought, in word, in action, by my fault,
By my own fault, my own most grievous fault.
I have lusted as men lust; I have eaten and drunk
With the drunken; I have given way to wrath,
Taking God's name in vain, cursing and smiting;
I have been too much eager after gold

And the brave things of the world, that take the eye
And charm the flesh. Now, smitten in my flesh
My sins have left me, and I see perforce
How worthless they all were. I am sorry for them.
Though yet I think I was not the worse craftsman
Because in me the lusty flesh rejoiced,
Lending its joy to all I did. Some men,
Fettering the body, fetter the soul, too,
So that the iron eats inward; thereof come
Cruelties, deceits, perversities of malice,
Strange twistings of the mind, defeats of spirit,
Whereof I cannot with sincerity
Accuse myself. But if it be a sin
To make the flesh pander to the mind,
I have sinned deep. Of the means, not of the end,
I heartily repent.

PRIOR

Son, they mistake
Who think God hates those bodies which He made
Freedom, not licence, must be given the body,
For licence preys upon itself and others,
Devouring freedom's gifts. Have others suffered
Through lust, wrath, greed of yours?

WILLIAM

I do confess it,
And ask their pardon and God's pardon for it
Most humbly.

PRIOR

In this world as in God's heaven
There is no power to match humility:
It breaks the horns of the unicorns, and makes
The wand of justice flower like Aaron's rod.
Stoop to repent, and God will stoop to pardon.

WILLIAM

I do repent.

90

PRIOR

    Indeed I hope thou dost.
For all these injuries, see thou make amends
So far as may be done; the irreparable
God's grace shall turn to good, since only He
Can lead out triumph from the gates of hell,
As He hath done by thee, using thy faults
To further His great ends, by His sole power,
Not thine.

WILLIAM

    I understand. A year ago
An idle mason let the chisel slip
Spoiling the saint he carved. I chid him for it,
Then took the tool and in that careless stroke
Saw a new vision, and so wrought it out
Into a hippogriff. But yet the mason
Was not the less to blame. So works with us
The cunning craftsman, God.

PRIOR

            Thou hast a mind
Apt to receive His meaning. But take heed:
The mind hath its own snares. What sins of the mind
Trouble thee now?

WILLIAM

I do not know of any.

PRIOR

I cannot read the heart; but I am old
And know how little one need fear the flesh
In comparison of the mind. Think, I beseech thee,
If any sin lie yet upon thy conscience.

WILLIAM

Father, I know of none.

PRIOR

The Tree of Life
Grew by the Tree of Knowledge; and when Adam
Ate of the one, this doom was laid upon him
Never, but by self-knowledge, to taste life.
Pray now for grace, that thou may'st know and live.

WILLIAM

Wilt thou not give me present absolution?

PRIOR

Of all thy fleshly faults, humbly confessed,
Truly repented, I do absolve thee now
In the name of the Father and of the Son and of
The Holy Ghost. Amen.

WILLIAM
Amen.

PRIOR

                    Good night;
Peace be with thee.

WILLIAM
                    And with thy spirit. Good night.

[*Exit* PRIOR. WILLIAM *tosses restlessly.*

℣. The ministers of God are sons of thunder, they are falls
of water, trampling of horses, and running of chariots; and
if the voices of these ministers cannot overcome thy music,
thy security, yet the Angels' trumpets will.

[*Distant trumpet.*

CHOIR

Quantus tremor est futurus
Quando judex est venturus.
Cuncta stricte discussurus.

[GABRIEL *goes up and stands behind* WILLIAM.

Tuba mirum spargens sonum
Per sepulchra regionum
Coget omnes ante thronum.

[MICHAEL *goes up and stands with drawn sword before* WILLIAM.

Liber scriptus proferetur
In quo totum continetur
Unde mundus judicetur

[CASSIEL *goes up and stands at the foot of* WILLIAM'S *bed, with the Book open before him.*

Quid sum miser tunc dicturus,
Quem patronem rogaturus,
Cum vix justus sit securus?

[RAPHAEL *goes up and stands with his censer at the head of* WILLIAM'S *bed.*

WILLIAM

Sleep! while these voices wail through aisle and cloister
Howling on judgment? Cannot Father Ambrose
Keep his monks quiet—let a sick man rest?
I am confessed, absolved. Why think of judgment?
My soul is heavy even unto death,
And something not myself moves in the dusk
Fearfully. Lights! lights! lights!

GABRIEL (*laying his hand on* WILLIAM'S *eyes*)
Let there be light!

[WILLIAM *becomes aware of the presence of the* ANGELS.

℣. Behold, the angel of the Lord, standing in the way, and his sword drawn in his hand.

℞. And he was afraid, because of the sword of the angel of the Lord.

℣. My flesh trembleth for fear of Thee, and I am afraid of Thy judgments.

℞. God is a righteous judge, strong and patient, and God is provoked every day.

93

WILLIAM

So—it is come; first death and then the judgment.
Thou standest there and holdest up the Book
Wherein my sins show black. But I am shriven.
Christ's blood hath washed me white. What then art thou,
Threats in thy hand, and in thy face a threat
Sterner than steel and colder?

MICHAEL

I am Michael,
The sword of God. The edge is turned toward thee:
Not for those sins whereof thou dost repent,
Lust, greed, wrath, avarice, the faults of flesh
Sloughed off with the flesh, but that which feeds the soul,
The sin that is so much a part of thee
Thou know'st it not for sin.

WILLIAM

What sin is that?
Angel, what sins remain? I have envied no man,
Sought to rob no man of renown or merits,
Yea, praised all better workmen than myself
From an ungrudging heart. I have not been slothful—
Thou canst not say I was. Lust, greed, wrath, avarice,
None ever came between my work and me;
That I put first; never by nights of lust
Too spent to labour in the dawning day;
Never so drunken that I could not set
Level to stone or hold the plumb-line true;
Never so wroth as to confound my judgment
Between the man and the work, or call the one
Ill-done because I wished the other ill;
Never so grasping as to take reward
For what I did not, or despised to do.
If I neglected lip-service to God,
My hands served for me, and I wrought His praise
Not in light words puffed from a slumberous mind
Like wind, but in enduring monuments,

94

Symbol and fruit of that which works, not sleeps.
Answer me, Angel, what have I ever done
Or left undone, that I may not repent
Nor God forgive?

MICHAEL

There where thy treasure is
Thy heart is also. Sin is of the heart.

WILLIAM

But all my heart was in my work.

MICHAEL

Even so.

WILLIAM

What, in my work? The sin was in my work?
Thou liest. Though thou speak with God's own voice
Thou liest. In my work? That cannot be.
I grant the work not perfect; no man's work
Is perfect; but what hand and brain could do,
Such as God made them, that I did. Doth God
Demand the impossible? Then blame God, not me,
That I am man, not God. He hath broken me,
Hath sought to snatch the work out of my hand——
Wherefore? . . . O now, now I begin to see.
This was well said, He is a jealous God;
The work was not ill done—'twas done too well;
He will not have men creep so near His throne
To steal applause from Him. Is *this* my fault?
Why, this needs no repentance, and shall have none.
Let Him destroy me, since He has the power
To slay the thing He envies—but while I have breath
My work is mine; He shall not take it from me.

MICHAEL

No; thou shalt lay it down of thine own will.

WILLIAM

Never. Let Him heap on more torments yet——

95

MICHAEL

He can heap none on thee, He hath not borne——

WILLIAM

Let Him strike helpless hands as well as feet——

MICHAEL

Whose Feet and Hands were helpless stricken through——

WILLIAM

Scourge me and smite me and make blind mine eyes——

MICHAEL

As He was blindfolded and scourged and smitten——

WILLIAM

Dry up my voice in my throat and make me dumb——

MICHAEL

As He was dumb and opened not His mouth——

WILLIAM

Cramp me with pains——

MICHAEL

     As He was cramped with pains,
Racked limb from limb upon the stubborn Cross——

WILLIAM

Parch me with fever——

MICHAEL

     He that cried, "I thirst"——

WILLIAM

Wring out my blood and sweat——

96

MICHAEL
                    Whose sweat, like blood
Watered the garden in Gethsemane——

WILLIAM

For all that He can do I will not yield,
Nor leave to other men that which is mine,
To botch—to alter—turn to something else,
Not mine.

MICHAEL

        Thou wilt not? Yet God bore this too,
The last, the bitterest, worst humiliation,
Bowing His neck under the galling yoke
Frustrate, defeated, half His life unlived,
Nothing achieved.

WILLIAM

        Could God, being God, do this?

MICHAEL

Christ, being man, did this; but still, through faith
Knew what He did. As gold and diamond,
Weighed in the chemist's balance, are but earth
Like tin or iron, albeit within them still
The purchase of the world lie implicit:
So, when God came to test of mortal time
In nature of a man whom time supplants,
He made no reservation of Himself
Nor of the godlike stamp that franked His gold,
But in good time let time supplant Him too.
The earth was rent, the sun's face turned to blood,
But He, unshaken, with exultant voice
Cried, "It is finished!" and gave up the ghost.
"Finished"—when men had thought it scarce begun.
Then His disciples with blind faces mourned,
Weeping: "We trusted that He should redeem
Israel; but now we know not." What said He
Behind the shut doors in Jerusalem,
At Emmaus, and in the bitter dawn

By Galilee? "I go; but feed My sheep;
For Me the Sabbath at the long week's close—
For you the task, for you the tongues of fire."
Thus shalt thou know the Master Architect,
Who plans so well, He may depart and leave
The work to others. Art thou more than God?
Not God Himself was indispensable,
For lo! God died—and still His work goes on.

℣. Thou that destroyest the temple and buildest it in three
days, save thyself. If thou be the Son of God, come down
from the cross.
℞. Thinkest thou that I cannot now pray to My Father,
and He shall presently give Me more than twelve legions
of angels? But how then shall the scriptures be fulfilled,
that thus it must be?

RAPHAEL

Lord, I believe; help Thou mine unbelief.

WILLIAM

Lord, I believe; help Thou mine unbelief.

CHOIR

Faithful Cross, above all other
One and only noble Tree,
None in foliage, none in blossom,
None in fruit thy peer may be;
Sweetest wood and sweetest iron,
Sweetest weight is hung on thee.

WILLIAM

O, I have sinned. The eldest sin of all,
Pride, that struck down the morning star from Heaven
Hath struck down me from where I sat and shone
Smiling on my new world. All other sins
God will forgive but that. I am damned, damned,
Justly. Yet, O most just and merciful God,

98

Hear me but once, Thou that didst make the world
And wilt not let one thing that Thou hast made,
No, not one sparrow, perish without Thy Will
(Since what we make, we love)—for that love's sake
Smite only me and spare my handiwork.
Jesu, the carpenter's Son, the Master-builder,
Architect, poet, maker—by those hands
That Thine own nails have wounded—by the wood
Whence Thou didst carve Thy Cross—let not the Church
Be lost through me. Let me lie deep in hell,
Death gnaw upon me, purge my bones with fire,
But let my work, all that was good in me,
All that was God, stand up and live and grow.
The work is sound, Lord God, no rottenness there—
Only in me. Wipe out my name from men
But not my work; to other men the glory
And to Thy Name alone. But if to the damned
Be any mercy at all, O send Thy spirit
To blow apart the sundering flames, that I
After a thousand years of hell, may catch
One glimpse, one only, of the Church of Christ,
The perfect work, finished, though not by me.

℣. Save me from the lion's mouth; Thou hast heard me
also from among the horns of the unicorns.
℞. For why? Thou shalt not leave my soul in hell, neither
shalt Thou suffer Thine holy one to see corruption.

[*Trumpet.*

CASSIEL

Sheathe thy sword, Michael; the fight is won.

RAPHAEL

Close the book, Cassiel; the score is paid.

GABRIEL

Give glory, Raphael; the race is run.

Michael

Lead homeward, Gabriel, the sheep that strayed.

All

Eloi, Eloi, Eloi,
Glory to God in the highest; holy is He!

Michael

How hardly shall the rich man enter in
To the Kingdom of Heaven! By what sharp, thorny ways,
By what strait gate at last! But when he is come,
The angelic trumpets split their golden throats
Triumphant, to the stars singing together
And all the sons of God shouting for joy.
Be comforted, thou that wast rich in gifts;
For thou art broken on the self-same rack
That broke the richest Prince of all the world,
The Master-man. Thou shalt not surely die,
Save as He died; nor suffer, save with Him;
Nor lie in hell, for He hath conquered hell
And flung the gates wide open. They that bear
The cross with Him, with Him shall wear a crown
Such as the angels know not. Then be still,
And know that He is God, and God alone.

℣. Who suffered for our salvation; descended into hell,
rose again the third day from the dead.
℟. He ascended into Heaven, He sitteth on the right hand
of the Father, God Almighty; from whence He shall come
to judge the quick and the dead.

Choir

Eloi, Eloi, Eloi,
Glory to God in the highest; holy is He!

[*While this is sung, the* Angels *go up and stand side by side across the stage behind the couch.*

WILLIAM

I shall not die but live, and declare the works of the Lord.
Who is there? I was dreaming. Gervase! Hubert!

[GERVASE *and* HUBERT *run in, left and right.*

GERVASE

William?

HUBERT

Dear master?

WILLIAM

God hath changed my mind.
I must submit. I must go back to France.
I do but hinder the work, lingering here,
Kicking against the pricks.

GERVASE

Do not say so!

HUBERT

What should we do without you?

WILLIAM

I am not
The only architect in the world—there are others
Will do the work as well, better perhaps.
Stay not to chide me—listen, there is one,
William the Englishman, a little man,
But with a mounting spirit and great vision;
Send now for him. I think we quarrelled once,
Not seeing eye to eye—but that is nothing;
He will respect my work as I do his,
And build a harmony of his and mine
To a nobler close than mine. I'll not dictate
Conditions to the Chapter; but, should they choose
William the Englishman to follow me,
He'll do such work for them as honours God
And them and all good craftsmen. As for me,
My place is here no more. I am in God's hand.
Take me and bear me hence.

HUBERT

Dear master, whither?

WILLIAM

To the Lady Ursula's lodging. If unto her
I can make any amends, then I will make it.
To all of you, I owe a debt of love
Which I will pay with love. Only to God,
That royal creditor, no debt remains.
He from the treasure of His great heart hath paid
The whole sum due, and cancelled out the bond.

GERVASE

Laus Deo!

[GERVASE *and* HUBERT *carry* WILLIAM *out, right.*

CHOIR

O quanta qualia sunt illa sabbata,
Quae semper celebrat superna curia,
Quae fessis requies, quae merces fortibus,
Cum erit omnia Deus in omnibus.

Vere Jerusalem illic est civitas,
Cujus pax jugis est summa jucunditas,
Ubi non praevenit rem desiderium,
Nec desiderio minus est praemium.

Illic ex sabbato succedit sabbatum,
Perpes laetitia sabbatizantium,
Nec ineffabiles cessabunt jubili,
Quos decantabimus et nos et angeli.

[MICHAEL *comes down to the foot of the steps and addresses the*
congregation; the other three ANGELS *standing above him.*

MICHAEL

Children of men, lift up your hearts. Laud and magnify

God, the everlasting Wisdom, the holy, undivided and adorable Trinity.

Praise Him that He hath made man in His own image, a maker and craftsman like Himself, a little mirror of His triune majesty.

For every work of creation is threefold, an earthly trinity to match the heavenly.

First: there is the Creative Idea; passionless, timeless, beholding the whole work complete at once, the end in the beginning; and this is the image of the Father.

Second: there is the Creative Energy, begotten of that Idea, working in time from the beginning to the end, with sweat and passion, being incarnate in the bonds of matter; and this is the image of the Word.

Third: there is the Creative Power, the meaning of the work and its response in the lively soul; and this is the image of the indwelling Spirit.

And these three are one, each equally in itself the whole work, whereof none can exist without other; and this is the image of the Trinity.

Look then upon this Cathedral Church of Christ: imagined by men's minds, built by the labour of men's hands, working with power upon the souls of men; symbol of the everlasting Trinity, the visible temple of God.

As you would honour Christ, so honour His Church; nor suffer this temple of His Body to know decay.

Finis

THE DEVIL TO PAY

BEING the famous HISTORY OF JOHN FAUSTUS the Conjurer of Wittenberg in Germany; how he sold his immortal soul to the Enemy of Mankind, and was served XXIV years by Mephistopheles, and obtained Helen of Troy to his paramour, with many other marvels; and how GOD dealt with him at the last.

A Stage-Play

TO THE INTERPRETER

HARCOURT WILLIAMS

"What I have done is yours; what I have to do is
yours; being part in all I have, devoted yours."

Sound without ear is but an airy stirring,
Light without eyes, but an obscure vibration,
Souls' conference, solitude, and no conferring,
Till it by senses find interpretation;
Gold is not wealth but by the gift and taking,
Speech without mind is only passing vapour;
So is the play, save by the actor's making,
No play, but dull, deaf, senseless ink and paper.

Either for either made: light, eye; sense, spirit;
Ear, sound; gift, gold; play, actor; speech and knowing,
Become themselves by what themselves inherit
From their sole heirs, receiving and bestowing;
Thus, then, do thou, taking what thou dost give,
Live in these lines, by whom alone they live.

PREFACE

In my previous Canterbury play, *The Zeal of Thy House*, the problem was to supply a supernatural interpretation of a piece of human history. In the present play, the problem is exactly reversed: it is a question of supplying some kind of human interpretation of a supernatural legend. This means that the supernatural elements in the two stories have called for quite different handling. In the former case, they affected only the moral, and not the machinery, of the fable; take away the visible angels, and the course of William of Sen's fall and repentance remains essentially unaltered. But in whatever way we retell the tale of Faustus, the supernatural element *is* the story. For the "two-hours' traffic of our stage," we must indulge in the "willing suspension of disbelief." We must accept magic and miracle as physical realities; we must admit the possibility of genuine witchcraft, of the strange legal transaction by which a man might sell his soul to Satan, of the actual appearance of the Devil in concrete bodily shape. The Faustus legend is dyed in grain with the thought and feeling of its period; nothing could be more characteristic than its odd jumble of spirituality and crude superstition; of scripture and classical myth; of Catholic theology and anti-clerical humanism; of the adventurous passion for, and the timorous distrust of learning. We may put what allegorical or symbolical construction we like on this fantastical piece of diabolism; but to enjoy it as drama, we must contrive to put ourselves back in spirit to the opening years of the sixteenth century. Accordingly, the better to induce this frame of mind in the spectator, I have deliberately reverted to the setting and machinery of the early Renaissance stage, with its traditional "mansions," its conventional Heaven and Hell-mouth, and its full apparatus of diabolical masquerade.

The picturesque figure of the Devil has a perennial attraction for the playwright, although, theologically speaking, he is apt to make hay of any story into which he intrudes. The fact is, the Devil is a character of very mixed origin; as Mrs. Malaprop would say, he is, "like Cerberus, three gentlemen at once." There is, to begin with, the "fallen seraph" of ancient Talmudic tradition; the rebel created for better things, and suffering torment in everlasting exile from God's presence. It is his dark angelic melancholy that makes the splendour of Marlowe's Mephistopheles and Milton's Satan. Under whatever name he appears, this personage is but one among an uncounted legion of the lost. Although the existence of a chief devil is postulated (whether called Satan, Lucifer, Beelzebub or what not), each evil spirit is conceived of as being a separate personality, rather than summing up in himself the essence of all evil.

Secondly, and inextricably confused, by name and exploits, with the conception of the fallen angels, we have "the Devil"—the absolute spirit of Evil, set over against God, who is the absolute Good. His origin appears to be Persian, and he properly belongs to that dualistic cosmogony which divides the rulership of the world equally between light and darkness, Ormuzd and Ahriman. In Mediaeval theatrical practice, any devil one may choose to bring upon the stage is apt to assume this generalised character of incarnate Evil, whatever references he may make to his diabolic superiors, and however many demonic companions he may summon to his assistance. For the purpose of dramatic symbolism one has to assume that any devil may symbolise "the Devil," and be treated accordingly. Goethe's Mephistopheles has this universality of evil; and in him the poet typifies his own conception of what Evil is, "*der Geist der stets verneint.*"

Thirdly, there is the "merry devil"—a mocking spirit, who probably derives, complete with horn and hoof, from the classical Pan and his satyrs. This lively personage endeared himself deeply to the Mediaeval playgoer, who, in any performance of religious drama, confidently looked forward to the Devil as the "comic turn." Squibs and crackers and poltergeist antics were always part of "Old Hornie's" repertoire; and thus we find the stately Mephistopheles of Marlowe condescending to play vulgar tricks upon the Pope and souse a Horse-courser in a dirty pond. That kind of thing was expected of the Devil, and, had it been omitted from the play, the pit would no doubt have demanded its money back. Trickery and mischief fit in more appropriately with the character of Goethe's Mephistopheles than with Marlowe's; and indeed, towards the end of the long second part of *Faust*, it becomes difficult to remember that the Devil is the father of all Evil; he bears so strong an appearance of being merely an amiable gentleman with a slightly sardonic sense of humour. But indeed, as Marlowe, Milton, Goethe, and every other writer who has meddled with the Devil has discovered, the chief difficulty is to prevent this sympathetic character from becoming the hero of the story.

It is hopeless, at this time of day, to disentangle the stage presentation of the Devil from its inherited inconsistencies, or to make every detail of it fit neatly into a rigid theological system. Nor is it possible to do away altogether with the inherent unreason that attends the practice of Art Magic. If, as we are so often told, religion and magic were formed out of the same raw material, nothing could be more remarkable and impressive than the difference, in the finished article, between the rational severity of the one and the incoherent irrationality of the other. It must be remembered that the Mediaeval magician did not, generally speaking, set to work to call up devils in the name of Beelzebub; he called them up in the name of the Trinity. However sordid, vile or ridiculous the end for which he summoned the spirits, the ultimate sanction invoked to attain that end was the power of God and His angels. In the very act of denying and defying God, he surrounded himself with every protection that the name of God could afford against the consequences of the act. In their more blasphemous excesses, his conjurations were spells, explicitly compelling God, by the power of His own name, to perform the conjurer's will. It is this curious dissociation of the power from the source of power that characterises magic as opposed to sacrament. The magical power is, in fact, considered to inhere in the divine name itself, and to operate automatically and independently of the divine authority. Thus the ancient manuals of conjuration present us with the somewhat inconsequent spectacle of a magician urgently calling upon God to protect and assist him in the carrying-out of such agreeable little bedevilments as the diseasing of his neighbour's cattle, the debauching of his neighbour's wife, or even the consort and enjoyment of delectable she-devils in bodily form. Whether, indeed, a generation so addicted as our own to the cherishing of mascots and the reckless abuse of ideological formulae is entitled to cast the stone of scorn at its Mediaeval forebears is matter for consideration.

But when we have allowed for all its fantastical trappings and illogical absurdities, the legend of Faustus remains one of the great stories of the world; a perpetual fascination to the poet, whose task it is to deal with the eternities. For at the base of it lies the question of all questions: the nature of Evil and its place in the universe. Symbolise Evil, and call it the Devil, and then ask how the Devil comes to be. Is he, as the Manichees taught, a power co-equal with and opposed to God? Or, if God is all-powerful, did He make the Devil, and if so, why, and with what justification? Is the Devil a positive force, or merely a negation, the absence of Good? In what sense can a man be said to sell his soul to the Devil? What kind of man might do so, and, above all, for what inducement? Further, what meaning are we to place upon the concept of hell and damnation, with which the whole concept of the Devil is intimately bound up?

Questions such as these are answered by every generation in the light of its own spiritual needs and experience. And for each writer, when he has determined his own interpretation of the central mythus, there is, of course, the added technical interest of discovering how many features of the original legend offer themselves as valuable factors in his system of symbolism.

In the true spirit of the Renaissance, the legendary Faustus sells his soul for the satisfaction of intellectual curiosity and the lust of worldly power. Marlowe accepts those inducements as valid, and, though his sympathies are very much with Faustus, does not shrink from the tragical end of the story. Faustus is damned in accordance with the terms of the bond, and the sombre close of the drama is unrelieved by any ray of hope. In this play, there is scarcely any trace of the conventional Mediaeval hell of physical fire and brimstone; the famous speech of Mephistopheles embodies a purely spiritual concept of damnation:

> *"Why, this is hell, nor am I out of it.*
> *Think'st thou that I, who saw the face of God*
> *And tasted the eternal joys of Heaven,*
> *Am not tormented with ten thousand hells*
> *In being deprived of everlasting bliss?"*

For Goethe, it was impossible to accept the idea that desire for knowledge could be in itself an evil thing. Though Faustus signs the bond, Mephistopheles is cheated in the end, and Faustus goes to Heaven. This game of cheat-the-devil is in full accordance with the spirit of the early moralities; these often finish with a judgment scene, conducted by Our Lady in the strictest legal form, in which the Devil is tripped up over the terms of a compact, rather in the manner of Shylock in *The Merchant of Venice*. Goethe conceives of the Devil as a necessary part of God's plan for the world: he is the power *"der reizt und wirkt und muss als Teufel schaffen."* The deadly sin is to give up striving and rest content, and the Devil is the irritant that keeps man at work. Goethe's Faust learns to use his infernal power to a good end, and finds contentment only in devotion to the service of man. It is while busily engaged in a work of public usefulness that he finds himself ready to say to the fleeting moment: *"Verweile doch, du bist so schön"*; and the comment of the angels is:

> *"Wer immer strebend sich bemüht*
> *Den können wir erlösen."*

To endeavour to do again what greater poets have

already magnificently done would be folly as well as presumption; and I have tried to offer a new presentment of Faustus. All other considerations apart, I do not feel that the present generation of English people needs to be warned against the passionate pursuit of knowledge for its own sake: that is not our besetting sin. Looking with the eyes of to-day upon that legendary figure of the man who bartered away his soul, I see in him the type of the impulsive reformer, over-sensitive to suffering, impatient of the facts, eager to set the world right by a sudden overthrow, in his own strength and regardless of the ineluctable nature of things. When he finds it is not to be done, he falls into despair (or, to use the current term, into "defeatism") and takes flight into phantasy.

His escape takes a form very common in these times: it is the nostalgia of childhood, of the primitive, of the unconscious; the rejection of adult responsibility and the denial of all value to growth and time. Time has been exercising the minds of many writers of late. It has been suggested that it is pure illusion, or at most a cross-section of eternity, and that we may be comforted for the failures of our manhood by remembering that the youthful idealists we once were are our permanent and eternal selves. This doctrine is not really even consoling; since, if our youth is co-eternal with our age, then equally, our age is co-eternal with our youth; the corruptions of our ends poison our beginnings as certainly as the purity of our beginnings sanctifies our ends. The Church has always carefully distinguished time from eternity; as carefully as she has distinguished the Logos from the Father. It is true that we must become as little children and that "except a man be born again, he cannot see the kingdom of God." But that is not to be done by attempting to turn time backwards, or deny its validity in a material universe. "How can a man be born when he is old? Can he enter the second time into his mother's womb and be born?" The answer is that he cannot. "That which is born of the flesh is flesh, and that which is born of the spirit is spirit." Time and eternity are two different things, and that which exists temporally must admit the values of time. Against the exhortation to take refuge in infantilism we may set the saying of Augustine of Hippo concerning Christ: *"Cibus sum grandium; cresce et manducabis Me"*—"I am the food of the full-grown; become adult, and thou shalt feed on Me."

Has Evil any real existence, viewed *sub specie aeternitatis*? I have suggested that it has not; but that it is indissolubly linked with the concept of value in the material and temporal aspect of the universe. It is this issue which Faustus refuses to face; rather than grapple with the opposition of good and evil, he dissociates himself from common human experience. The results to his soul of this attempt to escape reality are displayed in a final judgment scene, where (with a rigid legal exactitude which, I feel sure, the Mediaeval mind would heartily approve) the Devil is cheated of his bond, but receives his precise due. The notion of the Devil as being set in charge of the place of purgation, as well as of the place in which all evil is consumed, was familiar enough to the Middle Ages, as is clearly seen in the Wakefield Pageant of *The Harrowing of Hell*, where Christ rebukes Satan in the words:

> *"I make no mastry but for myne,*
> *I wille theym save, that shalle the sow*
> *Thou hast no powere theym to pyne,*
> *Bot in my pryson for thare prow [profit]."*

Of the original Faustus legend, certain episodes are reproduced in some form or another in practically all treatments of the subject: Faustus' raising of Mephistopheles; his "disputations" with him concerning the nature of God; his twenty-four years' bond to Hell; his journeys to Rome, where he plays tricks upon the Pope, and to the Court of Charles V, where he assists the Imperial armies to achieve their victories in Italy; his having Helen of Troy for his paramour; and the final scene in which the Devil comes to claim his own. His servant, Christopher Wagner, is also traditional. One version recounts how Faustus sought to marry "a beautiful servant-girl," but was prevented by Mephistopheles, on the ground that marriage was a sacrament, and therefore an action pleasing to God and contrary to the terms of the bond. This episode forms the basis for the First Part of Goethe's *Faust*.

The central part of the story is chiefly taken up with a long series of disconnected marvels and miracles, mostly of a purely mischievous and puckish sort, as when Faustus swallows a wagon of hay and a span of horses, makes flowers bloom at Christmas, cuts off his own leg and restores it, draws wine from a table, or attends the Pope's banquet invisible and beats the guests about the head. None of this episodic material offers much opportunity to the dramatist for anything but "inexplicable dumb show and noise"; it is the beginning and the end of the tale that constitute its eternal appeal. In a version designed to be played in the restricted period of an hour and forty minutes, it has been necessary to exclude all merely episodic matter, and to concentrate on those incidents which are capable of being compressed into a reasonably coherent dramatic structure.

What Tophet is not Paradise, what Brimstone is not Amber, what gnashing is not a comfort, what gnawing of the worme is not a tickling, what torment is not a marriage bed to this damnation, to be secluded eternally, eternally, eternally, from the sight of God?

JOHN DONNE: Sermon preached to the Earle of Carlisle.

The Devil to Pay was originally produced in the Chapter House at the Canterbury Cathedral Festival, 10–17 June, 1939, under the management of the Friends of Canterbury Cathedral, with the following cast of professional and amateur players:

WAGNER	Philip Hollingworth
LISA	Betty Douglas
FAUSTUS	Harcourt Williams
MEPHISTOPHELES	Frank Napier
CARDINAL	Charles Reeves
PRIEST	William Fordyce
POPE	Geoffrey Keable
HELEN OF TROY	Mary Alexander
YOUNG FAUSTUS	Alastair Bannerman
AZRAEL	Stanley Pine
EMPEROR	William Fordyce
EMPRESS	Vera Coburn Findlay
CHANCELLOR	Sidney Haynes
SECRETARY	Marshall Hughes
SOUL OF FAUSTUS	Max Wood
JUDGE	Raf de la Torre

DEVILS: Nigel Beard, Michael Foster, Anthony Ware, John Williams.

CITIZENS: Paddy Finn, Kathleen Hetherington, Rachael Hubble, Maud Lister, Joan Pollard, Eileen Shipp, Frank Kipps, Howard Overy, Edgar Parker-Pope, Jack Vane.

COURTIERS: Frank Kipps, Jack Vane

PAGE: Donald Foster.

LADIES: Paddy Finn, Rachael Hubble.

The Music for the Songs and Final Chorus composed
by GERALD H. KNIGHT
Singers
String Orchestra
The Play produced by HARCOURT WILLIAMS
Scenery, Lighting and Stage Effects by FRANK NAPIER

The Devil to Pay was first presented in London by the Daniel Mayer Company Limited at His Majesty's Theatre on July 20th, 1939, with the following cast:

WAGNER	David Phethean
LISA	Diana Deare
FAUSTUS	Harcourt Williams
MEPHISTOPHELES	Frank Napier
CARDINAL	Frank Woolfe
PRIEST	Alexander Archdale
POPE	J. Fisher White
HELEN OF TROY	Mary Alexander
YOUNG FAUSTUS	Alastair Bannerman
AZRAEL	John Munn
EMPEROR	Ernest Clark
EMPRESS	Betty Douglas
CHANCELLOR	Frank Woolfe
SECRETARY OF STATE	John Lalitte
JUDGE	Raf de la Torre

FOUR DEVILS: Kevin Keogh, Peter Scott, Peter Graves, Marshall Haley.

PAGE: John Wilson.

CHOIR: Grace Nevern, Peggy Hale, Rae Allan, Gwen Bateman, Betty Douglas, Alexander Archdale, Philip Merritt, Reginald Thurgood, John Lalitte, Murray Davies, Edwin Hill.

Citizens, Courtiers, Ladies, etc., from the members of Choir.

The Play produced by HARCOURT WILLIAMS

PERSONS OF THE DRAMA
in the order of their appearing

CHRISTOPHER WAGNER, Famulus to Faustus
LISA, Maidservant to Faustus
JOHN FAUSTUS, a Conjurer
MEPHISTOPHELES, an Evil Spirit
A CARDINAL
A PRIEST
THE POPE
HELEN OF TROY, a Magical Apparition
JOHN FAUSTUS, in the body of his transformation
AZRAEL, Angel of the souls of the dead
THE EMPEROR
THE EMPRESS
A CHANCELLOR
A SECRETARY OF STATE
THE SOUL OF JOHN FAUSTUS
THE JUDGE
Devils, Citizens, Courtiers, Ladies, etc.

SCENES

I—Wittenberg: Faustus' Study, 1502
II—Rome: The Forum, 1503
III—Innsbruck: The Emperor's Court, 1527
IV—The Court of Heaven: Eternity

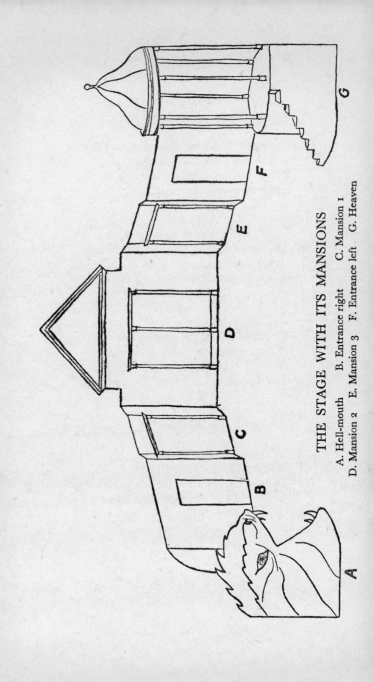

THE STAGE WITH ITS MANSIONS

A. Hell-mouth   B. Entrance right   C. Mansion 1
D. Mansion 2   E. Mansion 3   F. Entrance left   G. Heaven

SCENE I (*Mansion* 1)

WITTENBERG—FAUSTUS' STUDY

[*Lighted candles right and left in sconces. Centre, tall mirror covering entrance to Mansion 2. Left, big chart hung on rollers, showing eclipse of the sun. Right back, between Mansions 1 and 2, trick shelf with bottles, etc. On right wall, stoup of Holy Water. Left centre, chair, and table with books, parchments, flasks and other alchemical and astrological apparatus, together with a wax taper. On floor, down centre, a double circle and pentacle in white chalk. Enter from Mansion 1, WAGNER, carrying a lighted lantern, a long sword, a glass jar, five small lamps tied together, a cabbage and a dried stockfish, and reading a large book by the light of the lantern.*

WAGNER

Oh, dear! Oh, dear! I shall never be ready in time. Lisa! Lisa! (*shuffling to table*). So much to do since my master gave up theology and took to astrology and physic. "Ioth, Agla-nabroth, El, Aniel, Anathiel, Anazim"—what terrible great hard words! (*Sets down lantern, dropping cabbage.*) Alas! what's that? Oh, it's only the cabbage. (*Grovels for it, dropping sword.*) Heaven be praised! I thought it was the precious Holy Water. (*Stands clutching all his parcels and holding book close to lantern.*) "Craton, Muriton, Agarion, Pentessaron"—Bless me! I have forgotten the mandrakes—no, I remember, I put them in my pocket. (*Attempts to verify the mandrakes, dropping stockfish.*) Lisa!

[*Enter* LISA, *left.*

LISA

Oh, my poor Wagner! How dreadfully burdened you are. Here, let me take some of those things. (*Picking up stockfish.*) What's this for? Friday's dinner?

WAGNER

It's a present from the poor fishmonger whose horoscope we cast free of charge. And this cabbage is from the old peasant we cured of the itch. I do hope I've got everything.

LISA (*putting fish and cabbage in her apron*)

I'm sure you have quite enough.

WAGNER

This is a flask of Holy Water from the River Jordan itself. Set it on the shelf. Carefully. It has been blessed by the Pope. And you must take these lamps and fill them with the very best consecrated oil. I'll put the Doctor's sword over here.

[*Wanders away, still clutching book, and leans sword against wall, right.*

LISA (*setting flask on shelf*)

Were there many at his lecture to-night?

WAGNER

Yes, a great many. But I'm sure the most part of them care nothing for the brave things he tells them about Gemini and Capricorn and the movements of the planets. They only want to learn how to get rich, or to beg him to cure their diseases. There was a whole rag-tag and bob-tail besieging him at the door. In his place I wouldn't be troubled with them.

LISA

He is so kind. He will always help them if he can. He can't bear to see any one suffer (*at table, collecting lamps*).

WAGNER

So he sent me on ahead to prepare the room for him. We are to do great things to-night. Don't take the lantern. I need it to study my book.

LISA

But all the candles are lit.

WAGNER (*astonished*)

So they are! I didn't notice. (*Importantly.*) But then, I'm so very busy. Now where in the world did I put the chalk? I'm sure I had a piece somewhere.

LISA

I expect it's in your pocket.

WAGNER

I believe you're right. What a clever girl you are, Lisa, and so very, very pretty.

LISA

Foolish Wagner!

WAGNER

Don't you think you could call me Christopher? (*Pleadingly.*) It isn't a bad name. Do please try. It would make me so happy. I'm very fond of you, Lisa.

LISA

Foolish Christopher (*skipping nimbly out of reach*). Now, you mustn't waste time. Find your chalk and get on with your work, or you won't be ready when Dr. Faustus comes.

WAGNER

The chalk? Yes, I'm sure it's here, but it seems to be mixed up with something. (*Pulling bundle of roots from his pocket.*) Of course—the mandrakes. They must be hung in the chimney to dry.

LISA

What strange-looking things! Put them in my apron. (*He tries to kiss her; she holds the lantern between them.*) Now, be a good Christopher and study your great book.

[*Exit, left, with lantern and lamps.*

WAGNER (*looking after her*)

Sometimes I think she doesn't take me seriously. Well, I must get on. (*Kneels and writes in circle, book in hand.*) The anagrams of God in the five points of the pentacle. IHS, El, Ya, Alpha, Omega. So. And the names of God between the points. Adonai. Emmanuel. Panthon. Tetragrammaton. Messias. So. And between the lamps in the circle, five signs of the Cross. One, two, three——

[*Re-enter* LISA, *with lamps.*

LISA

I have filled the lamps. What are you writing there?

WAGNER

Ah, that is a secret. Give them to me—so, one at each point of the star. These are high and mighty matters, and not for girls to know about. It's all written in this book, that was given to Dr. Faustus by the great conjurer, Cornelius Agrippa. To-morrow, we shall be richer and more powerful than the Emperor. We shall have spirits to fetch and carry for us——

LISA

What? You will not . . . He doesn't mean to . . . Oh, Christopher! There will be no danger to Dr. Faustus?

WAGNER

Of course not. No danger can pass this circle. Besides, I shall be there to protect him. How brave it will be! We shall be masters of all the treasure in the world. We shall heal all the troubles of mankind with a wave of the wand. We shall prank ourselves in costly apparel, and you and I will be married, Lisa, and fly to the court of the Grand Cham on the back of a winged basilisk. Tell me, dear Lisa, tell me——

LISA

I hear the Doctor coming.

[*Enter* FAUSTUS, *Mansion* 1. *He wears a great cloak over his doctor's gown.* LISA *runs to greet him.*

Oh, sir! how late you are! And how wet! Give me your cloak. I'm sure you must be tired to death. Sit down and rest. I will have a fine hot supper ready for you in a moment.

FAUSTUS

Thanks, Lieschen, thanks. But I shall need no supper. I have
work to do.

[*Takes off his cloak and doctor's cap.* LISA *hangs them up.*

LISA

No supper! Why, you have eaten nothing all day.

FAUSTUS

My work must be done fasting. (*He sits on a chair.*) Bring me
a bowl of water, and the robe, slippers and girdle you will
find in my chamber. Is everything ready, Wagner?

[*Exit* LISA, *left.*

WAGNER

Yes, sir. I have this moment finished the circle.

FAUSTUS

See that it is accurately drawn. One of your spelling mis-
takes, or a touch of your usual absent-mindedness, might
land us both in a very queer place. (WAGNER, *alarmed, checks
all his hieroglyphics again by the book.*) Oh, God, I am sick at
heart. When I see how ill this world is governed, and all the
wretchedness that men suffer, I would give my immortal
soul to be done with it all.

WAGNER (*crossing himself*)

Heaven forbid. What a thing to say! When you think how
easily your immortal soul might go wriggling away through
a gap in the circle, like a rabbit through a fence. Or my soul,
for that matter.

[*He carefully touches up a point of the pentacle.*

FAUSTUS

Don't be alarmed. You will be safe enough if you stay where
I put you and don't lose your head and run away.

[*Re-enter* LISA *with slippers, bowl and napkin. She puts the bowl
on the floor while she removes* FAUSTUS' *shoes and puts on his
slippers.*

That will do. Leave it to me. I see you have drawn out the
figure of the sun's eclipse.

WAGNER

Yes, sir. But I don't altogether understand it. The moon gives light to the earth. Why then do we see her black?

FAUSTUS

The moon has no light of herself. When she passes between the earth and the sun she shows but as a mass of dark matter, as your head does, between me and that candle.

[*He washes his hands in the bowl* LISA *holds for him.*

WAGNER

I see. And if the sun were to pass between us and the moon, would he show dark also?

FAUSTUS

No; for he is the very source of the light, and in him is no darkness at all. My robe and girdle, Lieschen.

LISA

Oh, sir! I don't like the look of that robe, and the girdle with all the strange words upon it. They are too much like what you have there upon the floor. I am afraid of them. Will you not sit and have your supper like a Christian, and leave these fearful conjuring tricks to ignorant, unhappy men who know no better?

FAUSTUS

What is all this? Have you been talking, Wagner?

LISA

What do you need with riches and power and the court of the Grand Cham, and wicked spirits and basilisks—you that are happy in your great wisdom and learning?

FAUSTUS

Child, the greater the wisdom, the greater the sorrow. The end of all our knowledge is to learn how helpless we are. Divinity, philosophy, astrology—I have studied them all.

There are no springs of comfort in that barren desert of doctrine. Physic but lays a patch to the old garment; the stuff itself is rotten, warp and woof; the corruption eats deeper than our drugs can reach. (*Violently.*) What is this folly about riches and worldly delights? Do you think I care for such toys? But if magical power can aid me to resolve the mystery of wickedness, lay bare the putrefying sore at the heart of creation, break and remake the pattern of the inexorable stars—— I have frightened you. Fetch me my robe, and do not meddle with what you cannot understand. There, I know you mean well, but do not vex me now.

[*Exit* LISA, *left, removing bowl and shoes.*

Wagner, why do you not attend to your work, instead of chattering to Lisa?

[*Takes off his gown and lays it on the chair.*

WAGNER (*hurt*)

I have worked very hard indeed. I have purchased the lamps, ordered the oil, taken your sword to be ground, brought home the Jordan water, finished the circle and learnt a great many very long and difficult names out of this book. I hoped you would be pleased with me.

[*Re-enter* LISA *with robe and girdle and puts them on* FAUSTUS.

FAUSTUS

Why, so I am. You are an honest, industrious fellow—and if your heart is a better organ than your head, it was not you that had the making of them. Thank you, child. Now run away, and never trouble your pretty head about us. And remember, no matter what you may hear, you must not cross the threshold of this room to-night. On no pretence whatsoever. Do you hear me?

LISA

Yes, sir. May God and His holy angels protect us all.

[*Exit, left, taking* FAUSTUS' *gown.*

FAUSTUS

Now, Wagner, to work! Bring the book to me.

WAGNER (*bringing stoup across from wall and giving it to* FAUSTUS)

This is empty. Will you have the blessed water from the Jordan?

[*He lays the book on the table.*

FAUSTUS

Yes. But make haste; for this spirit will not come save he be called between the ninth hour and midnight.

[WAGNER *brings flask and fills the stoup which* FAUSTUS *holds.*

FAUSTUS (*signing the water*)

In nomine Patris et Filii et Spiritus Sancti, exorcizo te, creatura aquae, ut fias aqua exorcizata ad effugandam omnem potestatem inimici. Amen.

WAGNER

Amen.

[*While* WAGNER *puts back the flask and changes it by means of the trick shelf,* FAUSTUS *sprinkles the water within the circle.*

FAUSTUS

Asperges me Domine hyssopo et mundabor, lavabis me et supra nivem dealbabor. Gloria Patri et Filio et Spiritui Sancto.

WAGNER

Sicut erat in principio et nunc et semper et in saecula saeculorum. Amen. (*He puts back the stoup and now brings the sword, naked, to* FAUSTUS, *who has meanwhile taken the book from the table and opened it.*) Must I put out the lights, Master?

FAUSTUS (*examining the circle*)

Put them all out, and bring me a lighted taper.

WAGNER (*takes taper from table, lights it at one of the candles, and then extinguishes the lights*)

Oh, Master, it's going to be very dark and not at all comfortable. I don't think I care very much about being rich and powerful and riding on b-b-basilisks. D-d-don't you think it would be better to stop all this, and have a nice little astrology lesson or something?

FAUSTUS

Take courage, Wagner. Thou wilt not desert me now? There must be some meaning in this tormented universe, where light and darkness, good and evil forever wrestle at odds; and though God be silent or return but a riddling answer, there are spirits that can be compelled to speak.

[WAGNER *returns, carrying the taper.*

Now follow me into the circle, and see that thou close it well after we have passed over.

[*They step into the circle through a gap left in the figure, which* WAGNER *closes carefully with chalk.*

Light the lamps.

WAGNER

My hand trembles. (*He lights the lamps.*) Oh, dear! what will become of us? Ugh! Something brushed past my face, like a bat. Would I were well out of this.

[*He extinguishes the taper.*

FAUSTUS

Be silent. Stand back to back with me and be sure you let neither hand nor foot stray beyond the circle. Now we begin.

In the name of the most high God, maker of Heaven and earth and of all things under the earth, Ioth, Aglanabroth, El, Abiel, Anathiel, Amazim, Messias, Tolimi, Ischiros, Athanatos, I require of Thee, O Lord, by the seal of Solomon and by the ineffable name wherewith he did bind the devils and shut them up, Adonai, Aglai, Tetragrammaton, grant me Thy virtue and power, to cite before me Thy spirits which were thrown down from Heaven, and in especial that spirit which is called Mephistopheles, that he may come and speak with me, and dispatch again at my command, without hurt to my body, soul and goods, and diligently fulfil the will of me Thy exorcist. Fiat, fiat, fiat. Amen.

[*Thunder.*

[*Here* FAUSTUS *may hand the book to* WAGNER *unnoticed, and so be relieved of it.*

I conjure thee, Mephistopheles, by the unspeakable name of God, and by His virtue and power, and by Him that harrowed Hell; I conjure and exorcise thee, by angels and archangels, by thrones, dominations, principalities and powers, by virtues, by cherubim and seraphim, and by the name of thy master, Lucifer, Prince of the East, that thou do come to us, here visibly before this circle, and that thou do make answer truly, without craft or deceit, unto all my demands and questions.

[*Thunder again, and Hell-mouth opens with a great noise and a red light.*

In the name of Him that liveth and reigneth for ever, and hath the keys of hell and of death, come hither to me, Mephistopheles.

[*Enter* MEPHISTOPHELES *out of Hell, in the form of a lion with the tail of a serpent and the feet of a bull.*

WAGNER (*looking round over* FAUSTUS' *shoulder*)
Oh, help! help! Heaven defend us! We are lost! We're undone. (*He springs out of the circle and runs off, left. Flame and an explosion drive him back. A peal of diabolical laughter is heard.*) Mercy! Help! what shall I do?

FAUSTUS
Spirit, I charge thee, hurt him not.

MEPHISTOPHELES

Enough. Let him go. Away with thee, mannikin! Thy master and I have business together.

[WAGNER *runs out.*

FAUSTUS

And thou, Mephistopheles, put off this ugly shape, fit only to frighten children. Stand before me in the semblance of a man.

MEPHISTOPHELES

With pleasure. Nothing easier. (*He takes off his lion's head and tosses it negligently into Hell-mouth.*) And now, sir, what can I do for you, to justify the expenditure of so many big words and this great exhibition of fi-fo-fum?

FAUSTUS

Answer me truly first concerning thyself. What art thou?

MEPHISTOPHELES

Truly, you should know best, since you called me by name. But indeed, I am not particular. I will answer to anything you like to call me, for my name is legion, and Evil is one of my names.

FAUSTUS

Tell me, then, thou Evil, who made thee?

MEPHISTOPHELES

He that made all things.

FAUSTUS

What? did God make thee? Was all the evil in the world made by God? Beware what thou sayest; I know thee for a false and lying spirit.

MEPHISTOPHELES

That is a most unjust accusation. What lies have I ever told? There is no need for lying, seeing that mankind are such fools.

131

How so?

MEPHISTOPHELES

Why, tell them the truth and they will mislead themselves by their own vanities and save me the trouble of invention. I sat by Eve's shoulder in the shadow of the forbidden tree. "Eat," said I, "and you shall become like God." She and her silly husband ate, and it was so. Where was the lie? Was it my fault if they persuaded themselves that God was everything they hankered to be—all-good, all-wise, all-powerful and possessed of everlasting happiness?

FAUSTUS

Is not God all these things?

MEPHISTOPHELES

Is He these things? Look at the world He made, and ask yourself, what is He like that made it? Would you not say it was the work of a mad brain, cruel and blind and stupid—this world where the thorn chokes the flower, where the fox slays the fowl and the kite the fox, where the cat torments the mouse for pastime before she kills it for sport? Where men, made truly enough in the image of their Maker, rend, ravish and torture one another, lay waste the earth, burn up provinces for a title or a handful of dirty metal, persecute for a pater-noster, and send a fellow-fool to the rack for the shape of his nose or the name of his mother's father? War, fire, famine, pestilence—is He all-good that delights in these, or all-powerful that likes them not and endures them? Ask thyself this.

FAUSTUS

I have asked it a hundred times without thy prompting. It is as though my own heart spoke to me. Man's cruelty is an abomination—but how can one justify the cruelty of God?

MEPHISTOPHELES

Is He all-wise, that had not the wits to keep out of the mess He had made, but must needs meddle with this business of being a man, and so left matters worse than He found them? Why, He could not even speak His mind plainly, but all He said was so fumblingly expressed, men have been by the ears ever since, trying to make out His meaning. And was not that a prime piece of folly, to show up His nature thus—base and ignorant as any carpenter's son, too poor in spirit to argue in His own defence, too feeble to save His own skin from the hangman? Everlasting happiness? What happiness do you find in the history of the Man of Sorrows? By their fruits ye shall know them.

FAUSTUS

It was He that said that.

MEPHISTOPHELES

So He did, in one of His more unguarded moments.

FAUSTUS

And yet, Mephistopheles, His very name has power to conjure thee from the bowels of hell.

MEPHISTOPHELES (*with an almost imperceptible hesitation*)

The power is not in the name. That name is powerful only because you believe in its power. Believe in your own power, and you can command me without any tricks of conjuration.

FAUSTUS

Wilt thou then come when I call? Wilt thou stay with me and be my servant, and do and bring me all things whatsoever I shall desire?

MEPHISTOPHELES

I shall always be with you, John Faustus. You have only to think upon me, and I shall be there.

FAUSTUS

And do my bidding?

MEPHISTOPHELES

With all my power.

FAUSTUS

Not harming me in any manner?

MEPHISTOPHELES

You need have no more fear of me than of yourself.

FAUSTUS

Come hither to me then, and shake hands upon the compact.

MEPHISTOPHELES

By all means—if you will first come out of the circle.

FAUSTUS

How can the circle hold thee back, since it has no power but by me, and I say, Come!

MEPHISTOPHELES (*again embarrassed*)

Very well argued. But the fact is, you and your servant have so drowned the place with Jordan water that I don't care about it. I am very susceptible to chills, and I should infallibly get cramp in my hoofs. Besides, my Master Lucifer forbids me to enter the circle.

FAUSTUS

And wherefore?

MEPHISTOPHELES

For the better encouragement of superstition. But come—command me something. A few sacks of gold, perhaps, or a little supper. You must be famished with all this nonsense of prayer and fasting.

FAUSTUS

Well, then, bring me food.

MEPHISTOPHELES

Ho, there, my merry devils. Food and wine for your master.
Music, ho!

[*Music. Enter, right and left,* DEVILS *dancing, with platters of
fruit, etc., and one with a goblet of wine, which they present to*
FAUSTUS.

Drink, master, drink! What! Does the cursed fruit of the tree
stick in thy throat still? Drink, and drown that devil's gift of
knowledge, from whence spring all the cares that afflict
mankind. Drink—for the kingdom, the power and the glory
are within thy grasp. Only stretch out thy hand and fear not.

FAUSTUS

Spirit, I fear thee not. Give me the cup.

MEPHISTOPHELES

First sheathe that sword; my delicate devils wince
Like women to see cold iron.

FAUSTUS (*sheathing his sword*)
Give me the cup.

[*As* FAUSTUS *stretches his hand beyond the protection,* MEPHIS-
TOPHELES *catches him by the wrist and pulls him out of the circle.
Thunder; and all the lamps are immediately extinguished.*

If God's so harsh a stepfather to His sons
Then must we turn adventurers, and carve out
Our own road to salvation. Here's to change! (*Drinks.*)
O the wine's brave; it dances in the blood
And whirls in the brain, glowing and giving life
As though the vintagers had put in prison
The very sun, and pressed him with the grapes
Till all the vats ran fire.

MEPHISTOPHELES (*aside*)
And so it should,
Seeing what cellars it came from.

135

FAUSTUS

                    God's old realm,
Like an estate farmed by a bankrupt, dwindles
The sluggard way to ruin; her rank hedgerows
Drop down their brambles over the sour ditch;
Bindweed, tough tares, and tangling restharrow choke
Her furrows, where the plough stands idle, rust
Reddening the share; and in her hungry fields
Only the blind mole and the skipping coney
Drive their dark tunnels 'twixt the thistle and thorn.
We'll starve at home no longer. The soul's a world,
And hath her hemispheres, as the world hath,
Where thoughts put forth like galleons, leaving behind
These weedgrown crumbling harbours shoaled with time,
To sail new seas, steer by strange stars, cross over
Unknown meridians, and by pathless coasts
Explore her dusky Indias.

MEPHISTOPHELES

                    Well, well, well—
I have heard young men speak thus.

FAUSTUS

                            Young men speak thus?
I am not old, Mephistopheles. I have grown
A little grey, perhaps, with study and labour,
But I'm not old at all.

MEPHISTOPHELES

Go to, go to.

[*He leads* FAUSTUS *to the mirror.*

You are older than you should be. Mark you, mark
How lean men grow who try to save the world.
That line betwixt the brows—what wrote it there
But squinnying close at books, and frowning down
Your nose at ignorance? And the sour folds
At the corner of the mouth, the virtuous stamp

That Pharisees wear like phylacteries,
Proclaiming at what dear and grudged expense
They are chaste and sober; and the red-rimmed eyes
That weep to see how men enjoy their lusts,
Being so strangely happier than the godly.

FAUSTUS

I have wept for the woes of men, fighting like beasts,
Tortured like helpless beasts.

MEPHISTOPHELES

                    Let that alone,
The remedy makes it worse. Beast wars with beast
And slays and leaves no rancour. Heartbreak comes
With man's self-consciousness and righteous hate,
When one ferocious virtue meets another
As quarrelsome as itself, good savaging good
Like so many angry lobsters in a basket
Pinching each other's claws off. Now, behold
What you now are, and what you might have been
In the innocent world, if man had never meddled
With virtue and the dismal knowledge of God.

[*The image of* FAUSTUS *fades from the mirror and the image of
the* YOUNG FAUSTUS *takes its place. It mimics* FAUSTUS.

FAUSTUS

Is that myself, or the young fair Apollo
Stepped from his golden chariot and new bathed
In springs of Thessaly? It moves like me
And its lips mimic mine with silent speech.
Can it be I indeed?

[*As he turns to question* MEPHISTOPHELES *the image of* HELEN
appears in the mirror behind the image of FAUSTUS *in the place
where* MEPHISTOPHELES *stands behind the real* FAUSTUS.

MEPHISTOPHELES
Look then again.

137

FAUSTUS

O wonder of the world! O soul! O beauty
Beyond all splendour of stars!

[*As* FAUSTUS *moves towards the mirror,* MEPHISTOPHELES
moves to intercept him, and at the same time the image of HELEN
moves, so that as the image of FAUSTUS *clasps* HELEN, FAUSTUS
finds himself clutching MEPHISTOPHELES.

Hence! Let me pass!

[*He breaks from* MEPHISTOPHELES. *As he touches the mirror,
the vision vanishes. Thunder again.*

Hell and confusion! Damned, damned juggling tricks,
Nothing but sorcery!

MEPHISTOPHELES
What did you expect
When you called *me* up?

FAUSTUS
Bring her to me again
In the living flesh.

MEPHISTOPHELES
Fool, she is not for you
Nor any man. Illusion, all illusion!
For this is Grecian Helen, hell-born, hell-named,
Hell in the cities, hell in the ships, and hell
In the heart of man, seeking he knows not what.
You are too careful of your precious soul
To lay fast hold on Helen. She is mirage
Thrown on the sky by a hot reality
Far below your horizon.

FAUSTUS
Can you not bring me
Where Helen is?

MEPHISTOPHELES
I might—but at a cost
You might not wish to pay. In any case
Not as you are. If you would play the lover

138

You must look the part. Throw off this foolish weed!
Lights there!

[*The candles are lit of their own accord.*

Bring forth apparel for your master,
Faustus the conjurer, Faustus the magician,
Faustus the master of the words of power,
Prince of the prince of the air!

[DEVILS *enter and take* FAUSTUS' *robe and apparel him richly.*

And bring him gold
To fill his purse. He must live delicately.

[*Gold brought in a shining dish.*

All the lost treasure of the world is ours,
That men have sweated, toiled, fought, died to gain,
And wasted—the pirate's and the gambler's spoil,
The miser's hoard, the harlot's wage, the grudged
Profits of usury, the assassin's fee,
The politician's bribe, the nation's wealth
Blown from the belching cannon—all flow down
Through veins and vessels of their native earth
In one red stream to the hot heart of hell,
Gushing and hissing—listen!

[*Appropriate noises from Hell-mouth.*

The roar of the furnace!
Hark how the anvils clang in that black stithy
To the hammer-strokes forging the chains of gold
For the neck of the world, bars, ingots, cataracts
Of ringing coin! Power, power, for thy bold hand—
Take it and use it!

VOICE (*without, right*)
Alms, for the love of God,
For sweet St. Charity, pity the poor blind.

[FAUSTUS *stands arrested, with the gold in his hands.*

MEPHISTOPHELES
That is what God allows; will you allow it?

No, by the powers of Hell! If God permits
Such suffering in this damnable world, He's blind,
Deaf, mad, cruel, helpless, imbecile or dead!

[*He rushes to entrance, Mansion* I.

Look, here is gold—gold to thy heart's desire—
No man shall want, if Faustus can prevent it.

[*He flings money out to the beggar. Cries without.*

MEPHISTOPHELES (*at Hell-mouth*)

Lucifer, Lucifer! the bird is caught—
You may turn off the lights and put the cat out
And shut the door and go downstairs to bed.
I shall not be home for supper.

[*Laughter. Hell-mouth closes. Re-enter* FAUSTUS.

These virtuous fools!

FAUSTUS

O, power is grateful to the heart—to change
Sorrow to happiness in a twinkling—blot
The word "Despair" out of life's lexicon,
And make joy blossom in the desert sand.
Bring me swift horses—bring me the wings of the wind!
We'll fly to the wide world's four distracted corners
Like a great gust of laughter, scattering delight.
We'll do—what will we not do, Mephistopheles?
We will forget old sins—we'll break the cross,
Tear the usurper Christ from His dark throne
And this time bury Him deep and well, beyond
All hope of resurrection.

[*Knocking at entrance, left.*

Hush! who's there?

WAGNER (*without*)

O master, dear master, how is it with you? If you are not
carried off body and bones into Hell, speak to me!

FAUSTUS

All's well, Wagner. Wait. I will let thee in presently. Listen, Mephistopheles. You must stay with me, be known as my servant, show yourself only in your human shape, and not alarm my household too much.

MEPHISTOPHELES

I am entirely at your service.

FAUSTUS

Here, take my cloak. (*He puts his cloak on* MEPHISTOPHELES.) Try to look a little more respectable. You would be more convincing in a stout pair of boots.

MEPHISTOPHELES

I will procure boots immediately.

FAUSTUS

And hark'ee. See that you offer no offence to Lieschen. She is a good, modest, virtuous child.

MEPHISTOPHELES

Set your mind at rest. On such as her I have no power.

FAUSTUS

And be gentle with my poor Wagner. So. I will open the door. (*Crossing left, he turns and adds in a fierce whisper.*) Tuck your tail up! (*At entrance.*) Come in, Wagner.

[*Enter* WAGNER.

WAGNER

O Doctor, Doctor, praise God you're safe and sound. Lisa and I have been so frightened. Such dreadful noises—and the thunder—the whole house shook. We've been saying our prayers in the kitchen. Do forgive me for being so foolish and cowardly. I thought you were killed and the devil had eaten you, so I came to see if I could do anything. Has the devil gone away? The room smells shockingly of sulphur.

FAUSTUS

There's nobody here but this—gentleman, whom I have engaged to be my personal attendant.

WAGNER (*to* MEPHISTOPHELES)

How do you do, sir? God be with you. (*Calling off.*) It's all right, Lisa. The devil's gone. (*To* MEPHISTOPHELES.) What a dreadful night to arrive in. Are you wet? Perhaps you would like to change your shoes? I could lend you slippers. It's so unwise to sit in damp feet. What size do you . . .? Oh, I beg your pardon (*to* FAUSTUS). How thoughtless of me. I didn't notice the poor creature was so afflicted.

FAUSTUS

You are too officious.

MEPHISTOPHELES (*to* WAGNER)

It's very kind of you, but I came—by the underground way.

WAGNER

I see. Well (*anxious to do something*), the room is very untidy. Shall I help you off with your robe, Doctor? Dear me, it's off already. What a fine suit of clothes you have got!

VOICES (*without*)

Help! Help! . . . Hand over the money! . . . Thieves! Murder! . . . Strike him down . . . Give me the gold . . . Ah! would you! . . . Down with you! (*Noise of fighting.*)

LISA (*off*)

Help, watchman, help! Watch! Watch!

FAUSTUS

What is all that?

MEPHISTOPHELES

The effects of your benevolence, I fancy.
    [*Enter* LISA, *left.*

142

LISA

Alas! alas! Here's a poor old blind man been set upon and robbed under our windows and a whole crowd of ruffians quarrelling for the money. I saw three men stabbed. (*Noise increases.*) Oh, mercy.

FAUSTUS

Are men mad to abuse the gifts we give them? (*He rushes off, Mansion 1, drawing his sword as he goes.*) What is God about?

WAGNER

I don't understand all this.

MEPHISTOPHELES (*primly*)

Indiscriminate charity is a device of the devil.

LISA (*with a little shriek*)

Oh, Wagner, who's that?

MEPHISTOPHELES

The Doctor's servant, so please you.

LISA (*recoiling against* WAGNER)

I don't like him. I'm afraid of him. Who is he?

WAGNER

Bless me, Lisa, where are your manners? (LISA *drops* MEPHISTOPHELES *a reluctant curtsey and escapes, left.*) You must excuse her. We have all been upset by the thunderstorm. (*With holy-water stoup.*) Oh, dear, this is empty again. (*He hands it to* MEPHISTOPHELES.) Do you mind holding it while I fill it up?

[*Goes up to shelf, back.*

MEPHISTOPHELES

Pray don't apologise. Women have their fancies. I get along very well with them as a rule, but every so often, the nicest girls will take a positive dislike to me. I've no idea why.

WAGNER (*returning with flask*)

Very strange—but as you say, girls are quite unaccountable. Please hold it carefully. This is very special Holy Water from the——

[*Re-enter* FAUSTUS, *Mansion* 1.

FAUSTUS

The watch have arrested them all—Wagner! leave that alone!

[*He is too late. The water steams up and bubbles over the bowl, which* MEPHISTOPHELES *lets fall.*

WAGNER (*crossing himself*)

Holy Mary! Heaven deliver us! Oh, sir, sir; I fear me you are gotten into very ill company.

MEPHISTOPHELES

So that cat's out of the bag!

FAUSTUS

What will you do, Wagner? Will you quit my service?

WAGNER

No, Doctor, no. I'll not leave you alone to face danger again. I'm sorry for what I did. But from henceforth I'll be as brave as a lion.

FAUSTUS

Thanks, my faithful Wagner.

MEPHISTOPHELES (*clapping* WAGNER *on the back*)

Why, that's a bold fellow, to be ready to live cheek by jowl with the devil.

WAGNER

Why, so must every Christian man. And the devil we see is less terrible than the devil we don't see (*shaking* MEPHISTOPHELES *off*). But there's no need to be familiar. (*To* FAUSTUS) And what happens next, if you please?

FAUSTUS

We're off to Rome, to beard God in His own stronghold.

WAGNER (*stolidly*)

Are you going by sea, or—underground?

MEPHISTOPHELES

Through the air, my lad. By enchantment.

FAUSTUS

Those winged dragons you are always talking about.

WAGNER (*drily*)

Just as well. You were always a very poor sailor.

FAUSTUS

You and Lisa can do as you like. Come, Mephistopheles!
[*He goes out, right.*

WAGNER (*going off, left*)

Poor Lisa! She won't like this very much. (*Turning suddenly.*)
Here, you! Clear up all this mess. And look sharp. I'm
going to pack.
[*Exit.*

MEPHISTOPHELES (*staring after him*)

Well, I'll be—blessed!
[*He claps his hands. Music, and enter four* DEVILS, *who clear the stage.* MEPHISTOPHELES *goes out by the same way as* FAUSTUS.

SCENE II (*Mansion 3*)

Rome—The Forum

[*Enter from Mansion 1 (Wittenberg)* WAGNER *and* LISA *in travelling dress, with luggage. They walk all about the stage and come at last to Rome (Mansion 3).*]

WAGNER

Here we are at last—safely in Rome! It has been a long journey from Wittenberg.

LISA

Long and wearisome! I'm so grateful to you, kind Wagner, for coming with me, instead of flying away on the winged dragon with Dr. Faustus and—that other, terrible man.

WAGNER

I shouldn't dream of letting you travel unprotected. Besides, I have thought it all over and decided that winged dragons are all right for learned philosophers, but plain folk like you and me do best on the beaten track. (*Looking about him.*) What a fine city Rome is, to be sure! A hundred times bigger than Wittenberg.

LISA

How shall we ever find the Doctor out, in this great labyrinth of streets and houses?

WAGNER

We shall find him, never fear. During all these months he will certainly have become very great and famous. This wide square must be the market-place. Let's sit down here and rest, and presently we will ask some passer-by to direct us to the Doctor's lodging.

[*They sit down, left. Enter, from Mansion 3, a* CARDINAL *and a* PRIEST *conversing; they come down centre.*

CARDINAL

If such be the case, then His Holiness should be told about it. And in the meantime, by all means speak to the people.

PRIEST

I assure Your Eminence, it is as I say. The whole city is disturbed by the miracles of Dr. Faustus.

WAGNER (*to* LISA)

There! what did I tell you?

CARDINAL

Where does he come from?

PRIEST

From Wittenberg, they say, some twelve months since. His learning is undoubtedly great and his wealth unlimited; though how he came by them, God or the devil knows. He distributes gold to all and sundry, heals the sick, raises the dead, and corrupts the minds of the poor by his vile, atheistical talk. The churches are deserted. Sundays and week-days, the people throng to the lectures of Dr. Faustus.

LISA (*approaching them*)

O Father! If you know Dr. Faustus, pray tell me where he is to be found.

PRIEST

What! Is this another of them? Away, shameless girl.

CARDINAL

The less you have to do with John Faustus the better. His life is scandalous, his followers godless—

PRIEST

Heretical—

CARDINAL

Idolaters—

PRIEST

Sorcerers—

CARDINAL

Whoremongers—

PRIEST

Devil-worshippers—

CARDINAL

Apostate—

PRIEST

Excommunicate—

CARDINAL

And irretrievably damned!

LISA

No, no! if you knew him you would not say such things. He is good and kind.

WAGNER

The most learned man in Christendom.

PRIEST

He is the open enemy of God and Holy Church.

CARDINAL

And known to be in league with the devil. (*As* WAGNER *winces at this home-thrust.*) Will you deny it?

LISA

Alas!

WAGNER (*stoutly*)

If Dr. Faustus commands the spirits it is to a good and pious end. He is very clever, and knows how to bind the devil to the service of God.

CARDINAL

You are sadly deceived. It is forbidden to cast out devils by Beelzebub. Nor will a good end justify such vile and wicked means.

148

WAGNER (*drawing* LISA *away*)

Come away, Lisa. They are jealous of him. We will ask somebody else.

PRIEST (*pulling* CARDINAL *across, right*)

Besides, Eminence, the end he seeks is very dangerous.

[*Various* TOWNSFOLK *begin to drift in, Mansion 3 and left.* MEPHISTOPHELES *enters and stands, right, showing in pantomime that he overhears the conversation of* CARDINAL *and* PRIEST.

He preaches everywhere that he can abolish pain and suffering from the world. And what, pray, would become of religion, if there were no such thing as suffering?

CARDINAL

What, indeed? Who would repent of sin, if he did not fear to suffer in this world. Or if pain and sickness were not there, to put him in mind of his latter end?

PRIEST

Nobody would go to confession, or pay for masses, or indulgences, or prayers for the sick. There would be no pilgrimages, no alms-giving, no thank-offerings, no rich bequests to the Church. And what would happen to us, I should like to know? No sin, no sermon; no cross, no cardinal; no pain, no Pope!

[MEPHISTOPHELES *withdraws again.*

CARDINAL

Quite so; but I should not stress that point in your address. Begin now. I will go and acquaint His Holiness with all this.

[PRIEST *mounts the rostrum, left.*

Give ear, good people. The reverend father has somewhat to say to you.

[*Exit* CARDINAL, *Mansion 3.* FAUSTUS *and* MEPHISTOPHELES *enter unnoticed at back of* CROWD, *who gather right.*

149

Citizens of Rome! Sons and daughters of Holy Church! It has come to the ears of His Holiness the Pope that many among you are led away by the abominable doctrines of one John Faustus—(*cheers for* FAUSTUS)—a charlatan, a sorcerer, a man of lewd and evil life (*cries of dissent*) who would delude you by the promise to do away with toil and labour, with poverty, pain and suffering, and ensure to every man health, wealth and long days upon the earth. (*Renewed cheers.*) Alas, my children, why will you be deceived? Do you not know that toil and suffering were ordained by God for the sins of Adam? And that only by suffering are you made worthy to enter into the joys of Heaven? Do you think there is any way to salvation, except by the cross whereon our Saviour suffered for the sins of all? (*Murmurs of doubt.*) All of you will come to die some day—and how will you answer then for a life spent in sloth and luxury? Will it be easy, think you, to put off that proud and stubborn flesh that no suffering has mortified, no sorrow subdued? Let not the lust of gold corrupt you, for it is easier for a camel to pass through the eye of a needle than for a rich man to enter into the Kingdom of Heaven. Turn away your hearts from idols; embrace the cross and repent; return to the bosom of Holy Church, to whom alone it is given to bind and loose and free you from the domination of evil. If this fellow Faustus seeks to persuade you from your allegiance to the Church, it is that he may destroy your souls. He is a damned soul, burning in a hell of hatred, and would drag you all down along with him to damnation.

FAUSTUS (*leaping upon the rostrum, right*)

That is a lie!

PRIEST

Who dares to say so?

FAUSTUS

I say so. I am John Faustus.

PRIEST

Silence, thou rascal!

FAUSTUS

I will not be silent. I tell you to your face that your Church is corrupt, your doctrine a lie and your God a cruel tyrant.

[*Murmurs among the crowd.* MEPHISTOPHELES *whispers in* FAUSTUS' *ear.*

PRIEST

Out of thine own mouth, atheist! Do you hear this fellow blaspheme against God and His Holy Church?

FAUSTUS

The Church? Hark to the sly priest with his own axe to grind! The Church is rich and you are poor. Her prelates go in rich robes, and you in stinking rags. Wherefore? Ask him that preaches the money out of your pockets to keep him and his greasy brethren in idleness. He cares nothing for your souls, but only for the gold he can squeeze out of you.

PRIEST

It is false.

FAUSTUS

It is true. Ask my servant here, that heard him say as much to the Cardinal.

CROWD

Shame! shame! . . . Down with the idle priests!

FAUSTUS

Why should you slave to enrich these blood-suckers?

CROWD (*rushing towards* PRIEST)

Blood-suckers! . . . Horse-leeches! . . . Down with the priests! . . . Sack the monasteries! . . . Come on! . . . Sack! slay! . . . Away with them! etc.

PRIEST

Beware! Touch not God's anointed!

[CROWD *hesitates.*

Think, before you call down the terrible vengeance of

Heaven. What saith the Scripture? Thou shalt not suffer a witch to live. Faustus is a witch and a sorcerer, and his servant is the devil incarnate. By their fruits ye shall know them. They work the works of darkness, and their gifts shall bring, not blessings, but a curse. Is that not so?

FIRST WOMAN

It is so. We were poor, and Faustus gave us gold. Now my husband has left his home and gone to live wantonly with harlots.

FIRST MAN

I was a cripple and lived by begging. Faustus cured me, and now I must work to live.

SECOND WOMAN

I was barren, and Faustus laid his spells upon me, and now I have borne a child that is possessed by seven devils.

SECOND MAN

I loved my wife, and she died. Faustus raised her from the dead and lo! she is become a shrew, a vixen, the veriest termagant in Rome.

WIFE

Thou art a beast to say so. Take that, coward!
[*She beats her husband. Laughter and commotion.*

FAUSTUS

Ungrateful dogs!—

PRIEST

Hark, how he turns upon you now!

CROWD

Down with him! . . . Sorcerer! . . . Witch! . . . Burn him! . . . Drown him! . . . Tear him to pieces! . . . Witch! Witch! Witch!
[*A rush is made against* FAUSTUS.

152

FAUSTUS (*in a tone of command*)

Mephistopheles!

MEPHISTOPHELES

Back, little men! (*The* CROWD *is frozen into immobility*.) You cannot move hand or foot to harm my master.

CROWD

What's this? . . . I am paralysed . . . I am turned to stone . . . I can't lift my arm . . . I can't put my foot down . . . etc.

MEPHISTOPHELES

A nice lot of fools you look! A most edifying regiment of wax-works! And Master Priest there, fixed on one foot, like an image of Hermes in a garden-pool! Pray, sir, are you afflicted with a sudden cramp? Why not take counsel of Dr. Faustus, that is so eminent a physician? Shall I tickle them for you, master? Shall I twist their bones? Shall I put fire under their tails?

FAUSTUS

Enough! release them, Mephistopheles.

[*The* CROWD *put down their arms and legs again and stand rubbing themselves foolishly.*

O men, men! Why will you quarrel and fight? Why seek to harm me, that have only loved you and laboured for your good? I would free you from the burden of fear and pain and poverty that God has laid upon you. Listen to me. If God made all things, He made the evil that torments you, and why should you serve so cruel a master? If He made not all things, He is not God, and you may defy Him as I do. Be men! Rouse yourselves! Throw off this bondage of super-stition, and learn to know your friends from your foes. I am not your enemy. God is the enemy of us all——

[*Enter, Mansion 3, the* POPE, *carrying a crucifix in his hand, and with* CARDINAL *in attendance.*

POPE

Then learn to face the enemy. Speak on, my child. I stand here for God.

CROWD (*falling to their knees*)
The Holy Father!

FAUSTUS

Stand, then, old man, and hear what I would spit
Into God's teeth, were we set face to face
Even in the Courts of Heaven. God's heart is evil,
Vengeful and tyrannous. He hates the flesh,
The sweet flesh that He made; He treads down beauty
In the winepress of His wrath, pashing it out
To the sour wine of sacrifice; His eye
Is jaundiced to behold such happiness
As men may snatch out of a tortured world.
Look on the symbol in thy hand—the sceptre
Thou rul'st with in His name—it is the yardstick,
The very measure of the devilish hatred
He bears to man, were man His very Son.
Men! I stand here for man, and in man's name

[*He springs upon the* POPE *and snatches the crucifix from him.*

Defy God's rule, break His accursed sceptre
And smite His regent down.

[*He lifts the crucifix to slay the* POPE. *the* CROWD *exhibit horror,
but are held back by* MEPHISTOPHELES.

WAGNER (*throwing himself between them*)
O master, master!

FAUSTUS (*flinging* WAGNER *off*)
You here? Stand aside!

LISA (*catching* FAUSTUS *by the arm*)
Oh, Doctor, dear Doctor! for shame! What! Strike an old
man—helpless—unresisting?

[FAUSTUS *pauses in some confusion.*

Oh, no! how could you dream of it? You will not. I know
you will not. Not the devil himself could change your kind
heart so. And you will not break the image of our dear
Lord, who loved us so well and gave His life for us!

[*During this speech,* MEPHISTOPHELES *retreats and the* CROWD
closes threateningly in on FAUSTUS.

154

FAUSTUS (*letting the crucifix drop into* WAGNER's *hands*)

O Lisa, Lisa!

[*He looks about him, sees the menacing looks of the* CROWD *and goes on in an exhausted voice:*

I too love men; but they are all against me.
They hug their chains; the sacrificial iron
Cankers them at the core. I am not afraid
To suffer; for their sakes I would be damned
Willingly, so I first might do away
Suffering for ever from the pleasant earth.
And here stands power, like a smooth engine, ready
For good or ill alike. Being powerful,
I might be happy—might I not be happy?—
But still the cry of the poor is in my ears
Intolerably. (*To the* POPE): You they call Holy Father—
A kind, compassionate title, "Holy Father"—
Will you be blind to truth? God, having power,
Uses it like a devil; if He were good
He would turn back the ruthless wheel of time
To the golden age again. I am not God,
But can command the devil's power to serve
Good ends. Which is the devil—God, or I?
Do you be judge between us.

POPE

O my poor child,
How much unhappiness is in store for thee!
For thou art taken in the toils of God,
That are more delicate than the spider's thread,
More strong than iron; and though thou wander far
As hell from Heaven, His cunning hand shall twitch
The line, and draw thee home. There is no rest
For such as thee, that bear upon their hearts
The brand of God, and, warring against God,
Make war upon themselves. Thou must be patient,
For God is very patient. Dost thou think
I cannot feel thy griefs? I am the Pope,
Set on a tower above the plains of time
To watch how evil is at odds with good,

And to abide the issue, helpless, save
As prayer and wisdom and the grace of God
Shall give me strength. Hard it is, very hard,
To travel up the slow and stony road
To Calvary, to redeem mankind; far better
To make but one resplendent miracle,
Lean through the cloud, lift the right hand of power
And with a sudden lightning smite the world perfect.
Yet this was not God's way, Who had the power,
But set it by, choosing the cross, the thorn,
The sorrowful wounds. Something there is, perhaps,
That power destroys in passing, something supreme,
To whose great value in the eyes of God
That cross, that thorn, and those five wounds bear witness.
Son, go in peace; for thou hast sinned through love;
To such sin God is merciful. Not yet
Has thy familiar devil persuaded thee
To that last sin against the Holy Ghost
Which is, to call good evil, evil good.
Only for that is no forgiveness—Not
That God would not forgive all sins there are,
Being what He is; but that this sin destroys
The power to feel His pardon, so that damnation
Is consequence, not vengeance; and indeed
So all damnation is. I will pray for thee.
And you, my children, go home, gird your loins
And light your lamps, beseeching God to bring
His kingdom nearer, in what way He will.

[*Exeunt* POPE, CARDINAL *and* PRIEST, *Mansion* 3. CROWD
go out left and right. Manent FAUSTUS, LISA, WAGNER *and*
MEPHISTOPHELES.

MEPHISTOPHELES (*somersaulting across the stage and bowing
derisively after the retreating* POPE)

Go in peace, old gentleman, go in peace! Did ever a man
use so many words to confess his own incompetence? That
fellow has no business in Peter's seat—he ought to be in
Parliament. Come, Master—will you take the road to
Calvary, and sup at the Skull-and-Crossbones?

FAUSTUS

I am tired, tired, Mephistopheles. Follow Christ? That way is too long and too uncertain.

MEPHISTOPHELES

His way was folly and failure. I told you so, and now the Pope confirms it. Take your own way, in the devil's name, and shake a little sense into mankind.

FAUSTUS

My way frightens them. They have not even the heart to be grateful for my gifts.

WAGNER (*simply*)

Well, they are the devil's gifts after all. Perhaps it's true that they don't turn out very well. I'm sure people were very grateful in Wittenberg. Don't you remember? All those presents of fish and vegetables? I had hard work to carry them home.

LISA

Won't you come back to Wittenberg and heal the sick with your drugs and simples as you did before? Indeed, indeed you were happier then.

FAUSTUS

Much happier, Lisa.

MEPHISTOPHELES

If you were happy, why did you send for me?

WAGNER (*threatening* MEPHISTOPHELES *with the crucifix*)

Will you kindly go away and stop interfering?
  [MEPHISTOPHELES *retreats*.

LISA

They are waiting for you, Doctor, and longing for your return—all the poor and the sorrowful, and the mothers with their sick children. They love you so much—we all love you in Wittenberg.

FAUSTUS

Do they love me, Lisa? Do you think that is happiness, after all? To take the easy way—to love and be beloved, and not trouble to understand or get things altered? Perhaps. Every day the same sun rises, and year by year the spring returns. Have the swallows built again under the eaves of my window?

LISA

Oh, yes! Before we left home there were five speckled eggs in the nest.

FAUSTUS

There is peace in those quiet streets, cool and deep beneath the leaning gables. Let us go home, and find a little love before we die. They love me in Wittenberg. . . . Do you love me, Lisa?

LISA

Alas! I think I have loved you all my life.

WAGNER

Oh, God!

MEPHISTOPHELES

Didn't you know that? Any fool could have seen it.

FAUSTUS

Poor child! You should find a better lover. I am growing old, Lisa. I have forgotten how to love.

WAGNER

I am a fool indeed. But that's nothing new.

LISA

You are the most wonderful man in all the world—far too great and good for me.

FAUSTUS

Hush! that is foolishness. But a very sweet foolishness. Look at me. Your eyes are like quiet pools with the stars reflected in them.

158

MEPHISTOPHELES

Cheer up, fool. I know how to deal with this.

WAGNER

I don't want any of your help.

MEPHISTOPHELES

But *she* does. Do you think he cares twopence for her?

FAUSTUS

My head aches. I am homesick. Take me in your arms and comfort me.

LISA

With all my heart.

MEPHISTOPHELES

Hush-a-bye, baby, on the tree-top! Do you call this love?

WAGNER

What else do you call it?

MEPHISTOPHELES

Childishness. All men are fretful children when they can't get their own way. Love? Fiddlesticks!

LISA

Does it ache much?

FAUSTUS

Not now. There is rest in your presence, because there is rest in your soul.

MEPHISTOPHELES

Rest, indeed? We'll see about that. Sacripant! Belphegor!
[*Calling off.*

FAUSTUS

What was that song you used to sing while the bread was a-baking? All about Kings and Queens?

LISA

That little, nursery song?

MEPHISTOPHELES (*calling off*)
Here's a soul drowsing into Paradise. Whips! Whips!

LISA (*sings*)
Five silver fishes swimming in the sea,
Five gold birds in a sycamore tree,
[*Enter* HELEN, *right, with* DEVILS *attending her.*
Five red deer running over the land,
Five jewel-rings upon my hand.

MEPHISTOPHELES (*in the ear of* FAUSTUS)
Master, where are your eyes?

FAUSTUS
Gadfly! Let me sleep.

LISA (*sings*)
When trees grow tall and leaves grow green
You shall be king and I shall be queen.

MEPHISTOPHELES
Nay, dream on if you will. Sloth is a sin and serves my purpose; though there are merrier ways to be damned.

FAUSTUS (*freeing his eyes from* LISA's *hand and sitting up*)
Away with you to hell. Be off, I say. (*He sees* HELEN.) O my soul!

HELEN
John Faustus!

FAUSTUS (*leaping to his feet*)
Call me across a void of empty stars
And I shall hear.

HELEN
O love, hast thou forgotten?

FAUSTUS
Not till the seas run dry; not till the centre
Kiss the circumference, and time's iron hand
Crack the great axle of the world asunder!
O Helen, Helen, Helen, I have loved thee
Before time was.

160

LISA
Come back, sweet love, come back!

WAGNER
Master, beware! 'Tis witchcraft.

FAUSTUS
It is the voice
Of all the world's desire.
LISA
Oh, he is lost.
[*She falls into the arms of* WAGNER, *who helps her off.*

FAUSTUS
In what miraculous dream, in what far land,
Under what magic boughs, did thou and I
Lie once, and watch the sun shift through the leaves
Glinting the golden apples, when Troy town
Was yet unbuilt, that now is but a song
Almost beyond all memory? When did we learn
Immortal love? What unimagined page
Of scripture holds our legendary names,
Faustus and Helen?

HELEN
My name is Helen now;
God's wrath, and ruin of distressful stars
Have made me so accurst. But once, ah, once
Adam lay on my breast and called me Lilith—
Long, long ago, in the old, innocent garden
Before Eve came, bringing her gift of knowledge
And shame where no shame was. The sons of Eve
Are all ashamed of me.

FAUSTUS
Are all athirst
For thee, thou star of more than mortal hope
To men!

Shame and desire eat out their hearts,
For they are Adam's seed. And thou wast Adam,
Whose boyhood love was mine. So, when I call,
Thou canst not choose but turn to me again
From the very arms of Eve. Bone of thy bone
Is she, earth of the earth; she gives thee rest,
As the kind earth shall rest thy bones at last.
I am the fire in the heart, the plague eternal
Of vain regret for joys that are no more.

FAUSTUS

Wherefore no more? I have returned to thee
Across the barren ways of world and time;
My soul is in thy breast. Take me to thee,
That we may love and laugh in innocence
With the everlasting gods! Devils, stand back!
I will to Helen. In the tremendous name
Of power ineffable, by the seven-fold seal
Of Adonai, back!

[*The* DEVILS *restrain him still.*

What barrier's here
My witchcraft cannot break?

HELEN

The bitter knowledge
Of good and evil. None may touch my lips
While on his own hangs still the fatal taste
Of Eve's sharp apple.

FAUSTUS

Paris had thy kiss.

HELEN

Paris cast back the apple to the gods,
Whose ringing discord jarred the towers of Troy
In ruin down.

FAUSTUS

And so will I; let ruin
Roar like a cataract and drown the world!
Knowledge, begone! All part and lot in Eve
I here renounce. Thou, Mephistopheles,
Serpent of Eden, take thy curse again,
Undo the sin of Adam, turn the years
Back to their primal innocence. By thine oath
Sworn in the mouth of hell, and by the power
Of all my magical art, I do command thee!

MEPHISTOPHELES

Softly, softly. What a hurry you are in! You impetuous
young lovers want everything done in a moment. Take
away the knowledge of good and evil? That's rather an
unusual order.

FAUSTUS

Can it be done, or no?

MEPHISTOPHELES

Oh, it can be *done*. Everything can be *done*. But we have to
charge a price for that sort of thing.

FAUSTUS

Quick. Name it. What price?

MEPHISTOPHELES

The usual price. Your soul.

FAUSTUS

Take it. Sin and soul together.

MEPHISTOPHELES

And we can't sell you eternal youth upon freehold. I could
manage a twenty-four years' lease if that would suit you.

FAUSTUS

It would be worth it, were it twenty-four hours or twenty-
four minutes.

163

Very well. It's a bargain. (*Calling off towards Hell-mouth.*)
Ho, there! Bring me the bond.

[HELEN *vanishes, the stage darkens.*

Drawn in the name of John Faustus and of me, Mephistopheles. He to abjure and renounce the worship and service
of God, and to enjoy in exchange eternal youth and primal
innocence for four-and-twenty years; at the end of which
term he, the said John Faustus, shall become forfeit to the
Devil, and be carried away, soul and spirit, body and bones,
to Hell.

FAUSTUS

Quickly! Where is Helen gone? The air grows thick. My
senses swim. The walls of Rome swoon into darkness about
me.

MEPHISTOPHELES

Walls of Rome? Nonsense! You are in your own study at
Wittenberg. See! There are the lit candles (*the candles on the
walls are lit*). And your magic mirror (*the mirror becomes
luminous*). And your servants about you.

[WAGNER *and* LISA *creep in to stand beside* FAUSTUS.

FAUSTUS

Where is the bond? I will sign it with my blood.

WAGNER

Master, think again.

LISA

For thy dear soul's sake, take Christ's way, not this way.

[*The image of* HELEN *is seen in the mirror.*

FAUSTUS

I come, I come, sweet Helen. Mephistopheles! The bond!
Make haste.

[*Hell-mouth opens. Enter a* DEVIL *with the bond.*

MEPHISTOPHELES

It is here.

164

FAUSTUS

A pen—give me a pen. Where is the table?

MEPHISTOPHELES

Here.

[*Two* DEVILS *enter, bearing a board, which they offer to* FAUSTUS, *kneeling, as though for a table.*

Pluck forth thy dagger. Prick thine arm. Write.
[FAUSTUS *pricks his arm.* MEPHISTOPHELES *puts the pen into his hand.*

FAUSTUS

See how the red stream runs upon the table like letters written in fire. *Homo, fuge*—Flee, O man. What, shall I turn back now? (*Thunder.*) A dreadful voice cries in my ear: Flee from the wrath to come! O, whither shall I fly?

LISA

Fly to the arms of God.

FAUSTUS

To the arms of love. Sweet Helen, receive my soul. (*He signs the bond. Thunder again.*) So, it is done.

MEPHISTOPHELES

Done! And so clap hands on the bargain. (*Diabolic laughter.* MEPHISTOPHELES *tosses the bond to the* DEVIL, *who returns with it to Hell. Hell-mouth shuts.*) Come now, go to thy Helen as a new-made man.

FAUSTUS

How now? What wilt thou do to me?

MEPHISTOLES (*leading him to the mirror, where the image of the* YOUNG FAUSTUS *now appears beside* HELEN)

Have courage, my master, my bold conjurer, my masterful great magician. See, it's as simple as walking through a mirror. In with you, in with you!

[MEPHISTOPHELES *pushes* FAUSTUS *before him into the mirror, and* HELEN *and the* YOUNG FAUSTUS *walk out of it.*

165

FAUSTUS

Oh, I am free!

YOUNG FAUSTUS

I am free! Come, Helen, to my arms!

[*As* YOUNG FAUSTUS *embraces* HELEN *and carries her off, right,* MEPHISTOPHELES *carries away the old body of* FAUSTUS *behind the mirror, which grows dark.*

LISA

He has fled from us into a dream. He has left the world empty. I am afraid of this thing that looks with his eyes and speaks with his voice.

WAGNER

It is Faustus and not Faustus. A stranger—yet I feel as though I had known him a long time.

LISA

It is the shadow of an imagination. . . . How still the town is! No stir of wheel or footfall; no chime of the clock; no watchman's voice.

WAGNER

And how dark! but not with the darkness of night. It is like the dusk and silence that creep before an eclipse.

LISA

My sun is eclipsed for ever.

WAGNER

Poor Lisa! I know by my own heart how sorrowful you must be.

LISA

And I know by mine how bitterly I have hurt you. Forgive me, Christopher. We cannot help ourselves.

WAGNER

Please don't trouble about me. It really isn't worth it. It was presumptuous of me to set my hopes so high. One must expect disappointment in this world. (*Stoutly.*) And you know I am very absent-minded. I shall quite often forget to be miserable.

166

LISA

Dear, good Christopher. What a comfort you are! . . . I'm sorry. I feel so desolate. I can't help crying.

WAGNER

There, there!

[*He puts his arm round her and pats her shoulder consolingly.* MEPHISTOPHELES *slithers in and speaks in his ear.*

MEPHISTOPHELES

Christopher, Christopher! Shall I bring her to your bed?

WAGNER (*whisking round*)

What the devil? . . .

[LISA *sees* MEPHISTOPHELES *and springs away with a faint shriek.*

So it's you again!

MEPHISTOPHELES

Clever lad! Now's your chance. Say the word, and I'll tumble her into your arms like a ripe plum.

WAGNER

Don't be disgusting.

MEPHISTOPHELES

Oh, but you want her, Christopher.

WAGNER

No, I don't. Not if she doesn't want me. You needn't think she'd listen to you. Anything *you* brought me wouldn't be Lisa at all, but something nasty in her shape. I know your tricks by heart. They're all in the conjuring book.

LISA

What's he saying, Christopher?

WAGNER

A lot of filthy nonsense. Don't mind him.

I've been thinking what to do. Since our dear master is out of his mind, we must stay close to him and perhaps find some way to restore him.

WAGNER

To be sure we will.

LISA

And we will try and do his work—help the poor and heal the sick with the remedies he taught us. And when God sees what we are doing, He will say: That is the real Faustus; that's what he really meant to do. Faustus is still doing good by his servants' hands.

WAGNER

I always said you were clever. I should never have thought of that.

LISA

So you see, our work will plead for our master's soul.

WAGNER

Of course it will.

MEPHISTOPHELES

You flatter yourselves. I can't understand how men can be such fools.

WAGNER

Very likely not. There's a great deal you can't understand, you nasty, ignorant, dirty-minded demon. So hold your tongue and be damned to you!

MEPHISTOPHELES (going)

That is a very superfluous wish. Good evening.

WAGNER

Hi! Stop! What have you done with Dr. Faustus?

MEPHISTOPHELES (airily)

We are just starting on a grand tour of the world. The Duchess Helen accompanies us. You might call it a little

honeymoon trip. Constantinople. The Pyramids. Morocco.
Persia. The Caucasus. The Earthly Paradise. All carried out
in first-class style; a chariot-de-luxe with six dragons——

WAGNER

You don't say so. Then you can saddle me a chimaera—two
chimaeras; and see that one of them is trained to carry
a lady.

MEPHISTOPHELES

Certainly, certainly. Shall I charge them to your account,
or the Doctor's?

WAGNER (*firmly*)

You will include transport and service under your all-in
terms. Did you bring our baggage from Rome?

MEPHISTOPHELES

I'm afraid it was overlooked in the hurry.

WAGNER

Then fetch it. At once. Do you hear, you lazy devil?

MEPHISTOPHELES

Immediately.

[WAGNER's *and* LISA's *baggage is wafted in from the direction
of Rome. Noise of wheels and trampling, off, right.*

Excuse me, the chariot is at the door.
[MEPHISTOPHELES *hurries off, Mansion* 1.

WAGNER

Come, Lisa. Dry your eyes. Be brave. Needs must when the
devil drives. (*Cracking of whips, with snorting and trampling, off,
right.*) There's no time to waste in virtuous foot-slogging.
Come Heaven, come Hell, we'll follow our Master Faustus.
[*Exeunt* WAGNER *and* LISA, *Mansion* 1.

169

FAUSTUS (*off, right*)

Stand back, there. Give them their heads.

WAGNER (*off, right*)

Up with you, Lisa. My stirrup, Mephistopheles.

MEPHISTOPHELES (*off, right*)

To the four winds—away!

[*The infernal cavalcade is heard to rise in the air and fly off.*

SCENE III (*Mansion 2*)

INNSBRÜCK—THE EMPEROR'S COURT

[*Enter from Heaven, the Angel* AZRAEL. *He turns, as though answering someone inside.*

AZRAEL

Yes, sir. Certainly, sir. No difficulty at all, sir. Everything is quite in order.

[*He comes down and on, left, and walks briskly across to Mansion 2, sorting a sheaf of papers as he goes. At the entrance to the Mansion, he bumps, in a preoccupied way, into* MEPHISTOPHELES *coming out, and apologises without looking at him.*

Sorry; my fault.

[*Exit into Mansion.*

MEPHISTOPHELES (*looking after him*)

Stuck-up snob! Can't even recognise an old companion who's come down in the world. (*Coming down-stage; in the voice of an impatient man summoning a waiter.*) Demons! demons! . . . the service is getting very slack. . . . Oh, for Satan's sake, hurry up there!

[*Enter a* DEVIL, *right.*

The fool wants another job done. A trifle for the Empress. Flowers out of season with ripe fruit and blossom on the same branch. Fetch it and look sharp. . . . Where from? How the devil should I know? Try the Hesperides. (*Exit* DEVIL, *left;* MEPHISTOPHELES *sits down and registers fatigue.*) This is the worst term of hard labour I ever undertook. If my four-and-twenty years were not up to-night, I should go on strike.

[*Re-enter, Mansion 2,* AZRAEL, *with a baby in his arms.*

Good morning, my lord Azrael.

171

AZRAEL

Why, it's Mephistopheles! Good morning. And how's the world with you? You're looking a little exhausted.

MEPHISTOPHELES

Yes, I dare say. What's that you've got there? Contraband?

AZRAEL

No, no. Nobody you've any claim on. A sweet and pious soul, born anew as a little child into the Kingdom of our Father. Do you want to see her papers? (MEPHISTOPHELES *extends his hand in grim silence.*) Suspicious old devil, aren't you?

MEPHISTOPHELES (*examining papers*)

So that's who it is.

AZRAEL

One of your failures, Mephistopheles. Nothing for you there at all. Not so much as a whiff of Purgatory fire. Only a brief educational course in the heavenly kindergarten. Satisfied?

MEPHISTOPHELES (*returning papers with a grunt*)

All right. Just as well. We're run off our hoofs already. My client Faustus——

AZRAEL

Yes. You've been keeping our department pretty busy too. We were working overtime to deal with all those poor souls parted from their bodies at the battle of Pavia. That was your show, wasn't it?

MEPHISTOPHELES

And a damned good show, too. I had fifteen legions of devils fighting on the Emperor's side, to say nothing of a magical tempest and a great quantity of heavy artillery forged in our own works. To-day, we propose to sack Rome, with lavish accompaniments of loot, rape, and carnage. All this, if you please, by the orders of Faustus, who was once so tender-hearted, he would rescue the fly from the spider. What do you think of that?

AZRAEL

A truly remarkable exhibition of primal innocence.

MEPHISTOPHELES

Primal innocence? Primitive brutishness. The fellow's grown mischievous as an ape, lecherous as a goat, giddy as a peacock, cruel as a cat, and currish as a cross-bred tyke. Since first man fell into sophistication I have found no way to ruin him so effective as his restoration to a state of nature.

AZRAEL

Indeed? Most interesting.

MEPHISTOPHELES

It's the greatest discovery of the age. Though the work it entails is apt to be a little trying.

[*Enter* DEVIL, *left, with flowering and fruited branch. He hands it to* MEPHISTOPHELES, *and exit.*

This kind of nonsense is merely trivial. But when Faustus takes a fancy to do vulgar conjuring tricks——

AZRAEL

Such as?

MEPHISTOPHELES

Such as swallowing a load of hay and a span of horses; or breaking off his own limbs and strewing them about the place like a dissipated daddy-long-legs; or drawing wine from the table-top, to astonish a parcel of drunken louts in a beer-cellar—well! I do feel the whole thing's rather *infra dig.*

AZRAEL (*amused*)

You are of Lucifer's household. Your professional pride must sustain you.

[MEPHISTOPHELES *gives a short, vexed laugh. Enter, from Mansion 2,* FAUSTUS, *in the body of his transformation, and* WAGNER *reading a book.* WAGNER *has aged considerably in the intervening twenty-four years.*

Here comes your master, all agog for fresh marvels.

Hey, Mephistopheles! Why are you idling there? How fare our troops? Is the siege well begun?

MEPHISTOPHELES

It is begun.

WAGNER (*sitting apart and reading abstractedly*)

Fumitory mingled with treacle, and tormentil, to allay the fever.

FAUSTUS

With what success?

MEPHISTOPHELES

Already the walls of Rome totter at the blast of our cannon. By every gunner stands an able fiend to aim the shot and set hell-fire to the match. From the bottomless pit, our sappers delve their way deep below mine and counter-mine.

FAUSTUS

Ha!

WAGNER

Herb of grace is a mithridate to combat the plague.

MEPHISTOPHELES

The Emperor's army go to the assault as though the devil were in them.

FAUSTUS

So they ought, so they ought. What forces have you dispatched?

MEPHISTOPHELES

Halphas, the mighty earl, strides like a stork before his six-and-twenty legions of the damned. And Salmack, lord of corruption, marquess of hell, whose throne is in the sepulchre; where his strokes light, the maggot and the worm make holiday.

WAGNER

Hoarhound, pimpernel and pellitory are good for stinking sores.

MEPHISTOPHELES

Procell, the strong duke, is there, with eight-and-forty legions; Haborim and Labolas and all the captains of destruction.

FAUSTUS

Brave, brave! This news delights me. What joy can equal the swift tumult of war—shock of arms, shouting of men, crash of cannon, the whole world piled together pell-mell in a quick confusion! We must behold it, Mephistopheles. The Emperor is coming. I have promised that thou wilt show him all manner of fine things in a vision.

AZRAEL

So. There will be more work for me and my people.

FAUSTUS

Who is that? Send him away, Mephistopheles. I am afraid of him. The smell of death is upon his garments.

AZRAEL

I am Azrael, angel of the souls of the dead; and where war goes, I must follow.

FAUSTUS

Don't talk about death. I don't like it. What are you doing here?

AZRAEL

I am carrying to Heaven a soul that once was dear to thee.

FAUSTUS

Whose soul?

AZRAEL

Hast thou forgotten Lisa, the little maid that loved thee?

FAUSTUS

Lisa? Is Lisa dead? Wagner, do you hear this?

WAGNER (*quietly*)

I know it, master. She died in my arms but now.

FAUSTUS

What killed her?

AZRAEL

She went in thy name into all the plague-stricken quarters of this city, nursing the sick with the skill that Faustus taught her, when Faustus felt pity for men. The sickness took her and she died, and her last prayer was for thee.

FAUSTUS

Alas, alas! Poor Lisa. Oh, Wagner, I can never be happy again. Why am I so vexed and thwarted? I gave all I had for happiness. I gave—what was it I gave? I have forgotten . . . I only sought to be happy, and how can I be happy now that Lisa is gone?

WAGNER

She brought happiness to all who knew her, and that was her happiness and mine.

MEPHISTOPHELES (*to* WAGNER)

All the same, you would have done better to take my advice.

WAGNER

Art thou an authority upon happiness, thou shadow of an immortal grief? Master, I was never wise; but age and time have instructed me. To aim at happiness is to miss the mark; for happiness is not an end at all. It is something that comes of itself, when we are busy about other matters.

FAUSTUS (*without heeding him*)

Poor, pretty Lisa. She was kind to me. She looked after all my wants. What will become of me now?

AZRAEL

Thou wilt go to thine own place, Faustus. But her place is with the angels in Heaven.

[*Exit up to Heaven.*

WAGNER (*suddenly recalled to himself*)

I must work, I must work. So much to do, and so little time, now that I am all alone to do it. (*He wanders away, right, reading his book.*) Yarrow for green wounds; master-wort is a sovereign remedy for all diseases. . . .

[*He sits down and remains, absorbed in his studies.*

FAUSTUS (*inconsolably*)

My heart is broken. Nothing is left in all the world but sorrow. (*His eye lights on the branch* MEPHISTOPHELES *is holding, and his wandering fancy flits off in a new direction.*) That's pretty. What is it?

MEPHISTOPHELES

Surely you remember. It is the present you wanted to give to the Empress.

FAUSTUS

Oh, the Empress? She will be here presently. Hark'ee, Mephistopheles, the Empress is a fair woman, a blithe and buxom lady. She must be mine, d'ye hear me? I must and will possess her. Thou shalt bring her to me to-morrow.

MEPHISTOPHELES

To-morrow?

FAUSTUS

Yes, to be sure. I say, thou shalt bring her to-morrow.

MEPHISTOPHELES

There will be no to-morrow for you, master.

FAUSTUS

What's that?

MEPHISTOPHELES

Must I remind you of the terms of our bargain? I have served you diligently these four-and-twenty years. To-night the compact ends.

FAUSTUS

What then, devil, what then?

177

Why then you must die, and be forfeit, body and soul, to hell.

Death and hell? Death and hell? Don't speak those words. They madden me. I'll not hear them.

Stop your ears and welcome. But die you must and be damned.

Never believe it. There's no such thing as death, nor hell neither—save for a few such lubber-fiends as thou, to do the bidding of Faustus. Sin, death, age, sorrow—all that was a foolish dream, and fled like a dream for ever. Death comes with creaking bones and a sick carcase. Look at me, Mephistopheles. Have I aged a hair in four-and-twenty years? Not I. Then what's all this talk of death? It touches me not. I am the everlasting youth of the world. I am John Faustus. (*Flourish without.*) Here comes the Emperor, with my lady the Empress. Give me that bough. Make haste.

[*Enter the* EMPEROR *and* EMPRESS, *attended.*

Is Dr. Faustus of Wittenberg here in presence?

Good morrow and good fortune to your Imperial Majesties. Health, wealth and honour attend your Grace. And on you, most exquisite, beautiful and benign lady, may Venus bestow the plenitude of her favours. Be you ever fair and fruitful as this golden bough, fresh-plucked for your delight from the garden of the Earthly Paradise.

Thanks, gentle doctor.

We are much beholden to you. Tell us now. Is this promised spectacle ready, whereof you have reported such marvels?

MEPHISTOPHELES

Whenever you will. Command my master, and he shall command me.

EMPEROR

We know thee, Mephistopheles, as a cunning artificer and a spirit of great ingenuity. What are you able to show us?

FAUSTUS

Whatsoever you please to desire, of things near or far; past, present, or things to come.

EMPEROR

Then let us see and speak with Socrates, the wisest sage of antiquity.

EMPRESS

Oh, no! Socrates was an elderly, ugly monster, with a snub nose and a scolding wife. Show us rather Adonis; or Apollo singing to his lyre, and attended by the nine Muses.

EMPEROR

Nay, madam; I am neither Adonis nor Apollo. Would you make a jealous husband of me?

EMPRESS

Give me leave, I pray you. Indeed, my good lord, I insist.

EMPEROR

Do you so? Then will I demand to look upon fair Helen of Troy, whose beauty set fire to the world. That is a fair revenge, is it not, Dr. Faustus?

FAUSTUS

Your Majesty is more beautiful than ever Helen was.

EMPRESS

Fie, fie, sir. The flattery is too gross.

MEPHISTOPHELES

The truth is, madam, that by a delicate sorcery my master hath had the fair Helen to his paramour. But he grew weary and left her twenty years since, and now has no value for her.

FAUSTUS

Value? What does that mean? Helen was a troublesome baggage.

MEPHISTOPHELES

Man's delight is ever in the unattainable. When he is innocent, he longs for knowledge; when he is grown wise, he hankers after innocence. Between Lilith and Eve, Adam is unfaithful to both, and there is no contenting him.

FAUSTUS (*suddenly aggressive*)

But, mark you, Helen is mine for all that.

EMPEROR

We would not for the world offend you. Say no more.

MEPHISTOPHELES

Yet your Majesty shall have his will; for every man is fated, once at least in his life, to look on Helen.

WAGNER

Plantain or rosa solis—what herb shall we lay to a corroding ulcer?

EMPEROR

Enough. We will think upon some other device.

EMPRESS

Do you choose, my lord. But I will not hear of Socrates or Diogenes, or any such old, crabbed philosopher.

EMPEROR

Why then, since I am Emperor and hold half the world in fee, let me see Alexander the Great, weeping because he had no more worlds to conquer.

FAUSTUS

Tush, these are trifles. Alexander is dead and his conquests forgotten. I have better than that to show you.

[*Enter a* SECRETARY OF STATE, *with a letter.*

EMPEROR

Anything, so it be diverting. (*To the* SECRETARY.) How now?

SECRETARY

Here is urgent news, sire, from Rome. Your Imperial armies, leagued with the Constable of Bourbon, have this night attacked the city, with intent to seize the Vatican and overthrow the Pope.

[*Sensation.*

EMPEROR

To overthrow the Pope?

EMPRESS

Alas! this is sacrilege!

EMPEROR

How came the news so soon?

FAUSTUS (*eagerly*)

Sire, this is what we would show you. My couriers, sped by a magical device, have brought the message on the wings of the wind. My arms, my arts are at your service. We shall have as merry a battle as ever we had at Pavia.

EMPEROR

This will not do. Who writes the letter?

SECRETARY

The captain of your lanskers.

EMPEROR

Read what he says.

SECRETARY (*reads*)

"The Pope is the Emperor's worst enemy. This war is of his making, and the insult to our master must be avenged. For the honour of God he must be hanged, though I have to do it with my own hand."

EMPRESS

Worse and worse.

EMPEROR (*as though persuading himself*)

True; the old fox has brought it upon himself. He has intrigued against me with France, with Venice and with Milan. He has roused up the Holy League to oppose me—me, that have ever been the champion of the Church. Nevertheless——

FAUSTUS

Why do you hesitate? Sweep him out of the way. You have the power—take all you can and keep it.

EMPEROR

We have never sought for conquest. Yet what is our own by right and inheritance we must and will defend.

MEPHISTOPHELES

Sire, if a poor ignorant devil may venture an opinion, there is but one question here. Who is to be master of Europe? Germany is yours; Spain and the Netherlands are yours. England is rotten with decay; she will truckle to the stronger power. France alone is your foe, and you cannot control France while your hands are tied by Rome. Crush the Pope and make Germany secure against France, and you may be sovereign of the world.

EMPEROR

Security? Yes. Chancellor, what do you say? The Pope is our spiritual sovereign?

CHANCELLOR

Then, sire, let him not meddle with the temporal arm. That belongs to Caesar, and the Emperor is Caesar's heir. The Church that appeals to Caesar's weapons is sold to Caesar already, and must abide the arbitration of Caesar.

MEPHISTOPHELES

Excellent, excellent. "Render unto Caesar——" I couldn't have quoted Scripture better myself.

EMPRESS

Yet how can we prevail, if God be not on our side?

WAGNER

Are we so sure that God takes sides? He sits in the centre like the sun and rules our orbits whether we will or no.

MEPHISTOPHELES

Well spoken, Wagner. God will not care, He makes His profit either way.

WAGNER

We may dwell on the light side or the dark side. That is all.

FAUSTUS (*contemptuously*)

Here's a wealth of my astronomy at second-hand.

EMPEROR

Right or wrong: if we attack the Pope the world will condemn us. And how then?

MEPHISTOPHELES

Use policy, sir, use policy.

FAUSTUS

I am weary of all this. Let's have the show.

MEPHISTOPHELES (*to* FAUSTUS)

Master, you are very right. (*To the* EMPEROR). Say nothing, know nothing, watch how the battle goes. If your armies are defeated, hang your generals. If they are victorious, rebuke them in public and reward them secretly. Deny the deed and wink at it. Learn to be ignorant, for ignorance is the master-weapon of policy.

FAUSTUS

You are tedious with your policy.

MEPHISTOPHELES

As to the outcome of the fight, I will answer for it. Dr. Faustus will assist you by his art. (*Aside to the* CHANCELLOR.) And what better ally can you have in war than a profound scientific knowledge coupled with a total innocence of all moral responsibility?

CHANCELLOR

You may think such things, but not say them.

EMPEROR

There to the South, under the sun, lies Rome—
Would that the sun's rays, journeying hence, could show us
What his bright eye beholds!

FAUSTUS

           Why, so they can,
My magical arts to aid.

WAGNER

           The camomile
Was consecrate in Egypt to the sun;
It cureth ague and the melancholy.

MEPHISTOPHELES

Turn your back to the light, and look up northward,
Where the pale clouds lie like a silver screen.
See where the shadows waver, cast by the sun,
As spectres move on the Brocken.

EMPEROR

I see! I see!

ATTENDANTS

O wonderful!

EMPEROR

The ramparts of a city—
The tumult of armed men—banners and lances—

FAUSTUS

Now they advance—now they retreat—the gunners
Stand to their cannon—

MEPHISTOPHELES

They touch the linstock now—

EMPEROR

The brazen mouths belch fire—

EMPRESS

The smoke rolls over—

FAUSTUS

Up, winds, and send the echo! Let us hear
The terrible voice, the glorious voice of war!
   [*Confused noise, and chambers shot off within.*

EMPEROR

The wall is breached! Our lanskers storm the gap,
Crying, God save the Emperor!

CHANCELLOR

Stones and chains
Are hurled upon them!

FAUSTUS

Haro! still they go forward—

No, they give ground!

EMPRESS

Locked to and fro they sway—

EMPEROR

They are repulsed again.

CHANCELLOR

The town's defenders
Make sortie through the breach.

FAUSTUS

Now, now our hosts,
The hosts of hell stride out between the armies!

EMPEROR

A smother of smoke hides all.

FAUSTUS

They march, they march,
The tall, infernal seraphim! O brave!
Raim, that once ruled as a throne in Heaven
Now like a raven spreads his sable pinions
And drives all backward.

MEPHISTOPHELES

Focalor the duke
On griffin wings hovers before the Romans,
And by his art calls up the inky Styx
Bubbling about their feet; bogs of delusion
Snare them about.

FAUSTUS

They stumble and go down
Held in the stinking marsh. The water drowns them!

EMPEROR

I see not this—only a mist of blackness
Shot through with flame.

CHANCELLOR

    Ha! the defenders rally!
Rank upon rank they crowd the wall. Our armies
Falter—

EMPEROR

  The day is lost!

MEPHISTOPHELES

    Strike, Halphas, strike,
Lord of the legions, builder and destroyer
Of towers!
 [*A great explosion.*

FAUSTUS

  Well done! well done!

EMPEROR

     A monstrous mine
Bursts in the breach, and blows them all to pieces!
Arms, bodies, stones and fragments, nightmare faces,
And shattered engines tumbled together, falling—

EMPRESS

O, fearful!

CHANCELLOR

  In! in! in! the town is taken!

EMPEROR

Our hosts rush on—they carry all before them—

FAUSTUS

Swords out and forward pikes! The streets run blood,
The horses trample the fallen!

MEPHISTOPHELES

    The Pope is fled
To the castle of Sant' Angelo—

187

EMPEROR

     They surround him—

FAUSTUS

Brands! brands! and fire in the city!

EMPRESS (*covering her eyes*)

     Enough! no more!

MEPHISTOPHELES

Visions away! The Emperor's arms prevail.

CHANCELLOR

Congratulations to your Majesty;
You are master now of Europe.

FAUSTUS

     Is the show ended?
I was enjoying myself. Begin again.

MEPHISTOPHELES (*briskly*)

Nothing more is needed. Your Majesty knows exactly where
you stand. Write quickly now to your general, forbidding
him to attack, and to all your brother sovereigns, explaining
that the thing was done without your knowledge.

EMPEROR (*to* SECRETARY)

Put the letters in hand immediately.

MEPHISTOPHELES (*aside*)

Innocence and ignorance, most ravishing and blessed
qualities, what should we do without you? If we have not
set Europe at odds for four hundred years, my name is not
Mephistopheles.

EMPEROR

Will not the Pope take vengeance for this?
188

MEPHISTOPHELES

Never fear it. He is bound hand and foot. See where he
stalks, a pallid phantom, the sport and puppet of Empire.
[*The Phantom of the* POPE *appears, led in chains by* DEVILS.

POPE

John Faustus! John Faustus!

FAUSTUS (*shrinking like a whipped cur*)

Touch me not. Spare me. Let me go.

MEPHISTOPHELES

Courage, master. He cannot harm you. . . . There was a
Pope once, scourged Faustus to the heart. He carries the
sting in his memory. . . . Up, I say! What are you grovelling
for?

POPE

Thou fool! This night shall thy soul be required of thee.
[*The* PHANTOMS *pass away.*

FAUSTUS (*laughing wildly*)

Aha! did you hear that? The old fool dares to threaten me!
Punish him, Mephistopheles! Away, old rogue! I will have
you beaten, tortured, smothered in sulphur! Up, devils, and
after him!

MEPHISTOPHELES

Master, be quiet.

EMPRESS

Poor soul! he is distracted.

MEPHISTOPHELES

Leave him to me. (*He shakes* FAUSTUS *into subjection as one
would shake a dog.*) Come now. What will your friends think
of you? Never mind the Pope. (FAUSTUS *growls angrily at the
name.*) I say, be quiet. Never mind him. (*To the* EMPRESS.)
Fear nothing, madam. This fit takes him at times, but his
bark is worse than his bite. (*To* FAUSTUS.) Peace, now. Consider. Is there no other entertainment we can show the
Emperor? Some handsome compliment? Some pageant of
victory?

FAUSTUS (*all eagerness*)
Yes, yes. I am ready. What would your Majesty like to see?

MEPHISTOPHELES
Master, we will show him the thing he asked for, the longing
of his inmost heart. Music, strike up!

[*Music plays.*

The sun is fled, and darkness folds the earth
Like the chill shade that steals before the eclipse.

[WAGNER *springs to his feet, dropping his book with a crash.*

Rise up, thou star of evening, called by night
Hesperus, but in the morning, Lucifer,
And sometimes Venus, lady of love.

WAGNER
                    O master,
Look to thy soul, the sands are all run out.
    [*Enter the vision of* HELEN, *veiled and carrying a wreath of
    laurel.*
EMPEROR (*rising*)
What wondrous shape is this, that gliding moves
So like a goddess, and in her hand holds forth
The glittering laurel?

MEPHISTOPHELES
                    Learn and mark well her name.
She is all things to all men; and unto thee
The spirit of power, that like the will o' the wisp
Flits on the waters of time, and lures men on
To victory or to death. She is the promise
Of golden phantasy, the worm in the brain,
The song in the soul; she is the world's desire.
Gaze on her face, for men have died for her,
Great cities perished, gallant ships gone down,
Thrones and dynasties crumbled away to dust
For a glance of her eye. She is the unattained,
The unattainable.

HELEN (*standing high in the* EMPEROR'S *seat*)
> Crowns for the victor, crowns,
Riches and wisdom, honour and glory and blessing.

EMPEROR

O, my heart burns. Unveil, thou wonder of women.

WAGNER

Beware, beware! It is glamour!

MEPHISTOPHELES (*throwing back* HELEN'S *veil*)
> Have thy will.
Behold the face of Helen.

FAUSTUS (*as the* EMPEROR *springs forward*)
> Keep off! She is mine!

EMPEROR

Stand back and let me not!

WAGNER
> Master, forbear!
[FAUSTUS *throws* WAGNER *down. Exit* MEPHISTOPHELES, *back.*

EMPEROR

Give place, I say!

EMPRESS

O Heaven!

FAUSTUS (*drawing his sword*)
> Look to thyself!

CHANCELLOR

Will you lay hand upon the Emperor?
Treason! treason!
[CROWD *rushes in and surrounds them. In the confusion,* HELEN

is carried up back-stage by the EMPEROR *and the* CHANCELLOR, *and held in one of the entrances, with her back to the audience. As she goes, she drops the laurel wreath near* WAGNER. EMPRESS *in the arms of her ladies, left.*

A COURTIER
Vile sorcerer!

SECRETARY
Murderous dog!

CROWD
Down with him! Down!

FAUSTUS
Help, Mephistopheles!
[*His cry momentarily arrests the action.* MEPHISTOPHELES *reappears above Hell-mouth, right, flourishing the bond.*

MEPHISTOPHELES
Faustus, the four-and-twenty years are past,
My service done. The devil claims his own.

FAUSTUS
Hell and damnation!
[*He is dragged down upon the fore-stage.* AZRAEL *comes down out of Heaven and enters, left, bearing a black pall.*

Wagner! Lisa! Christ!
Save me! Have pity!

CROWD
Strike now!

MEPHISTOPHELES
Bondsman of hell,
Die and be damned!

CROWD
Take that!

FAUSTUS

O I am slain!

[*As* FAUSTUS *falls among the* CROWD, *there is a loud cry up-stage.*

EMPEROR

She's fled! Helen is vanished! Melted away
Clean from our hands—only her garments left!
O sorcery!

[*He comes down a little, holding* HELEN'S *cloak.*

AZRAEL (*he is now on the fore-stage, with his back to the
audience, and holding the pall spread out*)

Princes and earthly powers
Pass like a pageant, and make room for death.
Cover the face of Faustus.

[AZRAEL *and* WAGNER *cover* FAUSTUS *with the pall, and*
AZRAEL *kneels beside the body, still with his back to the audience.*

WAGNER (*rising*)

O dear master,
Now art thou gone to find reality.
May God remember all thy willing manhood,
Not thy refusal. This thy golden dream
Shall dwell with me; and I will be thine heir,
Hoping that hope may yet outdo despair.

[*Exit* WAGNER *carrying the laurel wreath. The stage empties of
all except* AZRAEL *and* MEPHISTOPHELES, *who now comes down.*

MEPHISTOPHELES

Thank you, Azrael. I will trouble you for that soul. You
needn't think you can sneak off with it. I saw you. It's
bought and paid for. Here is the bond. Be good enough to
hand it over.

AZRAEL (*who has the soul of* FAUSTUS *in his arms,
concealed in a bag*)

Just a moment. Things must be done in an orderly way. The
man is dead, and I have taken his soul in charge. That is my

office. If you think you have any claim on the property, produce your evidence.

MEPHISTOPHELES (*producing the bond*)

There you are. Laugh that off.

AZRAEL

It appears to be properly executed. Always supposing your client's soul was his to sell.

MEPHISTOPHELES

And whose else should it be?

AZRAEL

God's, Who redeemed it.

MEPHISTOPHELES

Nonsense. You can't get away with a legal quibble like that. The deed's watertight, and you know it.

AZRAEL

Well, you can take the soul on the security of the bond. But I shall enter a caveat, and appeal to the High Court.
[*He hands the bag over.*

MEPHISTOPHELES

You can enter anything you like. Come now, my little master, my high-and-mighty magician, let's have a look at you. You've given me trouble enough. Let's see how you like it when *I'm* the master! Believe me, my friend, I'll make it hot for you. (*He opens the bag and pulls out a* BLACK DOG.) Here! What's this? What's happened to it? You rascally, cogging angel! You cozening celestial sharp and shyster! This isn't the right soul!

AZRAEL

It's all the soul he's got.

194

It's a fraud! I've been tricked! That damned charlatan Faustus has cheated me. What's the use of a thing like this?

AZRAEL

That's your affair. *Caveat emptor.*

MEPHISTOPHELES

It was a perfectly good soul when I bought it. And now, look at it!

AZRAEL

It does seem to be rather out of repair. What have you been doing to it?

MEPHISTOPHELES

Great Lucifer! I like that. *I* been doing to it?

AZRAEL

You've had it these twenty-four years. If that's the way you treat the King's property——

MEPHISTOPHELES

I'll not stand it. God never plays fair. But I've got a clear case. I'll have the law of you——

AZRAEL

I'll sue you for damages——

MEPHISTOPHELES

I'll have my rights, I tell you. I will have justice!
  [*Without pause or shift of furniture, the action passes to the next Scene.*

SCENE IV

THE COURT OF HEAVEN

[*Heaven opens, and the* JUDGE *appears above.*

JUDGE

Who calls on justice?

MEPHISTOPHELES

    I, Mephistopheles.
I am defrauded of my rightful due,
Payment for four-and-twenty years of hard
Devoted, scrupulous, vigorous, swift, exacting,
Skilled and assiduous labour, by John Faustus
The conjurer of Wittenberg, and this
Smug-faced angel of yours.

AZRAEL

    Sir, I protest!
The fraud is all the other way. This fellow
Contracted with John Faustus for his soul,
Payable in exchange for value received,
The bond, post-dated, falling due to-day;
Which soul, I took in charge at Faustus' death
In execution of my official duty,
Lock, stock, and barrel as it stood. He claimed
The same upon his bond, which seemed in order
So far as such things go. I handed over
The goods to him, entering a caveat
In the King's name, as to the ownership,
Since it might well appear the vendor had
No title to give, barter, sell, exchange,
Mortgage or pawn or otherwise dispose of
Crown property. Well and good. But in the interim
(To wit, the four-and-twenty years expired)
This Mephistopheles, by his own act——

196

That I deny. It was the act of Faustus
Or Azrael, or God, or all of them——

AZRAEL

Had so deformed the soul that it is useless
To God or him, Faustus or any one.
Therefore he claims: and first, against myself
That I did not deliver the true soul
But something substituted; or if I did,
Then against Faustus, for a wilful damage
Executed upon the soul, whereby
He should escape the explicit provision
Made by the bond; lastly, against the Crown,
That if it prove that Faustus or myself
Were acting in this matter as the King's agent,
The Crown may quit the claim. To all of which
I answer by a counter-claim for damage
Done to the goods by Mephistopheles—
A wrong to Faustus, and a clear offence
Against God's peace, His crown and dignity.

JUDGE

Set up my chair of justice in the court
Below there; I will give the cause prompt hearing.

[*The* JUDGE *comes down.*

MEPHISTOPHELES

Olimoth! Belimoth! (*To* AZRAEL.) Don't you trouble, sir,
I'll see to this. Lymeck! Bealphares!

[*Enter* DEVILS *both sides.*

A seat for Justice!

[*Exeunt* DEVILS *and re-enter with a chair, etc.*

(*To* AZRAEL.)   This is nothing at all
To all the fetching and carrying, running about,
Materialising and dematerialising
This and that and the other, I've had to do

197

For Faustus—and of all the troublesome clients
Commend me to him.

 [*The* JUDGE *enters.*

       Pray, sir, take your seat.
There is the body of the said John Faustus,
This is the bond, and this the soul in question.

 [*When the* JUDGE *has inspected the* SOUL, *the* DEVILS *take it
into the wings.*

JUDGE

Show me the paper.

MEPHISTOPHELES

    Here. (*Fussily.*) You see it says
"I give my soul"—and "soul" in that connection
Must mean a human soul. I have been in business
Upon this planet several million years,
And it is always so interpreted.
But this alleged——

JUDGE

    Stop talking, Mephistopheles.
Give me a moment to peruse the terms.
Why! What is this? "Agree to take away
The knowledge of good and evil"? Come now, my poor
Deluded and benighted imp of darkness,
What did you think would happen to the soul
When you did that to it?

MEPHISTOPHELES

    I did not know;
How should I? Never before, in all my long,
Industrious, strictly dishonourable career,
Have I been put to such a task as that.
It was hard work, but still, I did it.

JUDGE

      Yes;
Your zeal is your undoing. If I say
"Here is a sword of steel; I give it you

198

On one condition—that you treat it first
With the most powerful corrosive known
To alchemy"—what will the sword be like
By the time you claim it?

MEPHISTOPHELES

Well, but if in good faith
I take and treat the sword as you require,
Not knowing how corrosive acts on steel,
Which yet you knew before you gave the order,
Is that an honest bargain?

AZRAEL

And suppose
The sword was borrowed, and belongs in fact
To the armoury of God, what will God say?

JUDGE

You have been swindled, Mephistopheles,
By accident, or by design, your own
Contributory negligence assisting.
Where were your wits? 'Tis true, the foes of God
Are not at any time remarkable
For logic or for common-sense. However,
There must be justice; and the point you urge,
Azrael, is well taken, since all souls
Are God's indeed. Therefore these charges come
To rest on Faustus, who to you, and you,
And to God chiefly, is responsible.
We'll hear the prisoner in his own defence.

MEPHISTOPHELES

Faustus hath made himself into a beast
And has no wit to answer more than a beast.

JUDGE

Truly; but since, in this high court of Heaven
Where time is not, the present, past and future

Are all as one, and answerable together
Eternally to Him that is eternal,
I call the prisoner. Wake, thou that sleepest!
Not as thou art, but as thou wast, John Faustus,
Rise up and answer at the bar of judgment.

[*They take away the pall.* FAUSTUS *wakes in his own body.*

FAUSTUS (*as one dreaming*)
Whither away, love? O return, return!

MEPHISTOPHELES
What? Dreaming still on Helen?

FAUSTUS
                              Christ! Christ! Christ!
They have taken away my Lord these many years,
And I know not where they have laid Him. Sir, if you know,
Tell me, for I denied Him, and just now
I heard the crowing of the cock. How long
The night has been! And now the dawn is red
And a great storm coming . . . Hush! for I remember.
I bartered away my soul for ignorance,
In ignorance, not knowing what I did.
There has been cheating somewhere. I was not happy
Those four-and-twenty years. Something was lost
That makes for happiness. Yet I seemed to know
Pleasure of a sort, and pain too—but they slipped
Like water through my fingers, neither perceived
Fully, nor remembered fully, nor assessed
At any quotable value.

JUDGE
                        Value exists
Not in the object, but the valuing mind;
The soul's choice makes the value. Therefore ask
This poor brute soul thou madest for thyself
How it doth reckon value.

[*Here a* DEVIL *shall show* FAUSTUS *the* SOUL *and retire again.*

I was cheated;
I did not bargain for a soul like this,
But for the primal innocence that was Adam's
Before he fell to knowledge. Is it sin
To cancel out a sin? Does God love sin
To set such value on it? Or is He helpless
To undo the past; and did the devil speak truth?

JUDGE

All things God can do, but this thing He will not:
Unbind the chain of cause and consequence,
Or speed time's arrow backward. When man chose
To know like God, he also chose to be
Judged by God's values. Adam sinned, indeed,
And with him all mankind; and from that sin
God wrought a nobler virtue out for Adam,
And with him, all mankind. No soul can 'scape
That universal kinship and remain
Human—no man; not even God made man.
He, when He hung upon the fatal tree,
Felt all the passion of the world pierce through Him,
Nor shirked one moment of the ineluctable
Load of the years; but from the griefs of time
Wrought out the splendour of His eternity.
There is no waste with God; He cancels nothing
But redeems all.

FAUSTUS (*to* MEPHISTOPHELES)

Serpent, thou didst deceive me!

MEPHISTOPHELES

So Adam said, and Eve; but I spoke truth
To them and thee. I warned thee that the truth
Would but beguile thee, as it beguiles all fools.
Thou askedst, What was I? and I spoke truth;
And who made evil? and I spoke the truth;
And what God was? and there I turned the question
Back upon thee, and thou didst answer it
According to thine own folly; but I spoke truth.

The truth, but not the whole truth, Mephistopheles.
The whole truth is the perfect sphere of Heaven;
The hollow half-truth is the empty dome
That roofs the hall of hell, mocking with echoing
Shards of distorted speech and the fiends' laughter.

Mephistopheles

Laughter! I tell you I have split my sides!
These wiseacres, that are too clever to see
A plain fact in broad daylight. Up they come,
Sidling and bridling like a fretful horse,
Showing the white of the eye. "What, that a fact,
That tall, black, ugly fence? It can't be true,
There must be some way round—the gate, if you please."
And I am there—Oh, I am always there
To bow, and touch my hat, and take my fee
And open the gate that leads them into the circle,
The ring with the barriers, the closed ring, the place
From which there is no way, no way, no way out.

Faustus

Love would have found the way, if way there were:
"Father, if it be possible, let this cup
Pass from Me." But it was not possible, never
Has been nor will be possible. Over the fence
Is the only road. For all the by-ways run
Down to the circle, the closed circle of self
From which there is no way out.

Judge

                    There is no way out.

Mephistopheles (*sings*)

Jump little man,
As high as you can;
The way across
Is by thorn and cross;

But the only way round
Leads into the pound,
So hey, so ho,
And over you go.

AZRAEL

You are too noisy. Silence in the court
The prisoner waits for judgment.

MEPHISTOPHELES

                                Yes, and I
Wait for my fee, which has been tampered with.
Here is the bond: "I, Faustus, give my soul
For such and such considerations"—all
Duly fulfilled by me; but where's the soul?
That thing there, which you flatter by the name,
I have no use for; it is not as specified.
If there is justice in this court at all
The devil must have his due.

JUDGE (*to* FAUSTUS)

                                You hear the charge
Preferred against you, on two counts. Imprimis:
That you did sell a soul for which Christ died;
A crime against God's crown. Next, that the price,
Promised in God's true gold, was paid in fact
With coin debased and worthless; a civil trespass
Against this gentleman. What have you to say?

FAUSTUS

I must admit the trespass, and the crime
That caused the trespass. I have no defence
Save ignorance; yet ignorance was itself
The very prize for which the crime was done;
Nor yet is ignorance a defence in law.
Speak thou, O righteous judge, for I am silent.

JUDGE

Poor, empty vessel whence the wine was spilt,

What shall we do with thee? Listen to judgment.
For this last time, God gives thee back again
The power to choose, weighing the good and evil—
A fearful option; yet no other course
Can justice take, since here thou standest bound
In thine own blood, and no remorse of thine
Can raze one jot or tittle from the law.
Hear, then, the dread alternative of choice;
And first, wilt thou, with that dumb changeling soul,
Incapable alike of hell or heaven,
Wander for evermore between the worlds
Unblest, undamned, unknowing?

FAUSTUS

Nor blest nor damned?
Merciful God, what kind of doom is this?

JUDGE

A gentle doom; sorrow shall never touch thee,
Nor pain, nor any question vex thee more;
Yea, though thy loss be wider than the world,
Or than a thousand thousand worlds at once,
Thou shalt not feel nor know it.

FAUSTUS

O, what loss?

JUDGE

A loss beyond all loss: to live content
Eternally, and never look on God;
Never behold the wonder of His face
Fiery with victory, bright above the burning
Wings of the cherubim; never to hear the loud
Exultation of trumpets shatter the sky
For the Lamb's marriage-feast; nor drink the wine
Of God; nor feel the glad earth thrill to the tread
Of the tall, strong, unresting angels' feet;
Nor know the dream of desire, that is beyond

All happiness; nor ever more to find
Beauty in sunlight, or the flowery fields,
Or in man's heart; nor ever laugh again.

FAUSTUS

No, no, no, no!

JUDGE

Does ignorance not suffice thee?
Wilt thou have knowledge after all, John Faustus?
Take back thy soul, then, and fulfil the bond;
Go down with Mephistopheles to hell,
And through the bars of those relentless gates
Gaze on the glory of the Lord far off
And know that He is terrible and just.

FAUSTUS

No choice but this?

JUDGE

No other choice at all.

FAUSTUS

Either to lose God and not know the loss,
Nor even to remember God exists;
Or see the glories that I may not share,
And in the sharp hell of a lost desire
Burn on unquenchably.

JUDGE

So stands the choice.

FAUSTUS

O lost, lost, either way!

MEPHISTOPHELES

Excuse my laughter;
Justice hath pinned thee now in a cleft stick.
Writhe, my good friend, my toad beneath the harrow;
'Twill serve thee little, but no matter—squirm
For my amusement. How do you like this game?

You're playing with cogged dice, cully—all sides alike.
Lend me an angel, we'll toss for it; heads I win
And tails you lose. If you call "God!" and win,
Then I win you; and if you lose the throw,
Then you lose God; why then, call "tails," and get
The tail of the dog there. Maybe this will teach you
To play chuck-farthing with your soul!

FAUSTUS

                                    I stand
Between the devil and the deep seas of God
On a road that leads nowhither. This is strange—
The love of God urges my feet towards hell,
The devil that seeks to have me flings me back
Into God's arms. Are you two allies, then,
Playing into each other's hands, and grinning
Friendship across my frontiers? I will have
The truth of this, although the stink reek up
And blast the airs of Heaven! Thou, Mephistopheles,
Answer again, and this time all the truth,
Art thou God's henchman or His master? Speak!
Who made thee?

MEPHISTOPHELES
God, as the light makes the shadow.

FAUSTUS
Is God, then, evil?

MEPHISTOPHELES
God is only light,
And in the heart of the light, no shadow standeth,
Nor can I dwell within the light of Heaven
Where God is all.

FAUSTUS
What art thou, Mephistopheles?

MEPHISTOPHELES
I am the price that all things pay for being,
The shadow on the world, thrown by the world

Standing in its own light, which light God is.
So first, when matter was, I was called Change,
And next, when life began, I was called Pain,
And last, when knowledge was, I was called Evil;
Nothing myself, except to give a name
To these three values, Permanence, Pleasure, Good,
The Godward side of matter, life and knowledge.

FAUSTUS

Thus far, then, have I come to learn the truth
I taught my servant, many years ago:
"The sun can cast no shade; only the dark
Dead body of earth or moon can make eclipse
Of his perpetual radiance." Thus I told him,
Being blind to my own parable; but he,
Knowing no syllable of sun or moon,
Walked in the light of the true innocence
To the end I sought for. Pity my blindness, sir,
For His dear sake that healed the blind and cast
The devils out——

MEPHISTOPHELES

        Hast thou learned nothing yet?
He'll not reverse the past. The past is here
And thou must answer it.

FAUSTUS

        O, by the Name
And power of Him that harrowed hell——

MEPHISTOPHELES

                Thou fool!
Thou juggling sorcerer! Thinkest thou with those
Same words wherewith thou once did'st conjure me
To conjure justice?

FAUSTUS

        Devil, thou didst speak truth,
And with thine own truth will I choke thee now
To the deep of thy false throat. Not in the words

Is power, but in the faith of him that speaks,
And in the person of the very Christ
In Whom stands all the meaning of creation.
Words? They are rags, tags, fluttering remnants blown
Along the winds of fancy; only in Him
Is neither variableness nor shadow of turning.
Sir, I beseech thee, as thou art all truth,
Answer me truly; in this desperate choice
What would God have me do?

JUDGE

I may not tell thee.
Only the knowledge of the good and evil
Gained once by sin, by double sin rejected,
Restored again by grace, is granted thee
For guidance. Thou must choose and choose alone.

MEPHISTOPHELES

Why, this is better than a circus! Round
And round again till you're giddy, faster and faster
Round the closed circle. I met you first in a circle——
You should know something of circles. You're well inside,
Dodging the ring-master there, with the hoop in his hand
And the lash at your heels. Faster and faster, Faustus,
Round and round, and then—the crack of the whip
And through the hoop you go. So, Faustus, choose
In the devil's name.

AZRAEL

In the name of the most high God
Choose, Faustus, and for ever.

FAUSTUS

I have chosen.
I will go down with Mephistopheles
To the nethermost pit of fire unquenchable
Where no hope is, and over the pathless gulf
Look up to God. Beyond that gulf I may
Never pass over, nor any saint nor angel

208

Descend to me. Nevertheless, I know
Whose feet can tread the fire as once the water,
And I will call upon Him out of the deep,
Out of the deep, O Lord.

JUDGE

Art now so bold
To call down God, thou that aforetime didst
With cowardly conjurations call up devils?
Then tell me: art thou able to be baptised
With Christ's most bitter baptism, or to drink
The cup that all His shuddering mortal flesh
Shrank from, yet drank, down to the dark dregs, driven
By the strong spirit?

FAUSTUS

I dare not say I am able.
Yet I say this: that nothing thou canst do
Shall threat me from the quest of Christ eternal.
Yea, though thou stand with thy keen sword made bare
To keep me from Him, and have at thy command
In ninefold rank the terrible hosts of Heaven,
Yet will I seek Him. If I go down to hell
He is there also; or if He stand without,
My hands shall batter against hell's brazen gates
Till the strong bars burst asunder and let Him in.
Then will I seize Him, then fall down before Him,
Cling to His garments, hold Him fast by the feet,
Cry in His ear, "I will not let Thee go
Except Thou bless me. Even the unjust judge
Heard the poor widow, and Thou shalt hear me!
Spare not Thy rod, for Thou hast borne the rod,
Quench not Thy fire, for Thou didst pass through fire,
Only be with me!"

MEPHISTOPHELES

This is brave indeed!

FAUSTUS

Mock me not, nothingness; I have found courage

In Him that never feared to look on sorrow,
And though He slay me, I will trust in Him.

MEPHISTOPHELES

Then, Faustus, thou art mine!

FAUSTUS

Thine here and now,
But wheresoever and whensoever, God's.
Sir, I am ready.

MEPHISTOPHELES

Come on, my violent friend.

JUDGE

The kingdom of Heaven suffereth violence,
And violent men may take it by assault
In the last breach of despair. Thus all things come
To their own place at last, the tares to the burning
And the good grain to God.
(*To* MEPHISTOPHELES.)   Thou hast claimed thine own,
It is thine. Burn it. Touch not my good grain,
I shall require it at thy hand some day;
And for thou knowest that thy time is short,
Be diligent.

MEPHISTOPHELES

I'll warrant thee for that.
Open the gates there!
    [*Hell-mouth opens.*

JUDGE

Faustus, look on me;
Through the harsh mask of judgment read my soul,
And when I meet thee at the gates of hell,
Know me again.

FAUSTUS

Slay me, but leave me not.

JUDGE

Lo! I will never leave thee, nor forsake thee

Even to the world's end. Take him, Mephistopheles,
And purge him throughly, till he find himself,
As I have found him mine. God is not robbed;
And I will bring mine own as I did sometime
From the deep of the sea again.

FAUSTUS

From the deep of the sea.

[FAUSTUS *is led away by* MEPHISTOPHELES *to Hell,* AZRAEL
and the DOG *accompanying him. The* JUDGE *goes up into Heaven.*

DEVILS (*below*)

Deep calleth unto deep with the noise of the cataracts.

AZRAEL

ut of the deep have I called unto Thee, O Lord; Lord,
hear my voice.

DEVILS (*below*)

Sheol is naked before Him, and Abaddon hath no covering.

AZRAEL

O let Thine ears consider well the voice of my complaint.

DEVILS (*below*)

They lie in the hell like sheep, death gnaweth upon them;
their beauty shall consume in the sepulchre.

AZRAEL

But God hath delivered my soul from the place of hell, for
He shall receive me.

[*The* JUDGE *being now come up into Heaven, the gates are opened
with a great light.* FAUSTUS *at Hell's mouth sees the glory of
Heaven.*

ANGELS (*above*)

Return, return, O Shulamite; return, return, that we may
look upon thee.

AZRAEL

If any man's work shall be burned, he shall suffer loss.

DEVILS *(below)*

Where their worm dieth not, and their fire is not quenched.

ANGELS *(above)*

But he himself shall be saved, yet so as by fire.

[FAUSTUS *follows* MEPHISTOPHELES *into Hell, and the* DOG *with him. Hell-mouth is shut upon them.*

CHORUS *(while* AZRAEL *returns into Heaven)*

Multitudes, multitudes in the valley of decision; for the day of the Lord is near in the valley of decision.

That which the palmer-worm hath left hath the locust eaten; and that which the locust hath left hath the canker-worm eaten.

A fire devoureth before them, and behind them a flam burneth.

Multitudes, multitudes, in the valley of decision.

Rend your heart and not your garments, and turn unto th Lord your God;

And I will restore unto you the years which the locust hath eaten.

Multitudes, multitudes—I beheld, and lo! a great multitude

Ten thousand times ten thousand, and thousands o thousands.

Worthy is the Lamb that was slain to receive power, and riches, and wisdom, and strength, and honour, and glory, and blessing;

Blessing and honour, and glory, and power, be unto Him that sitteth upon the throne, and unto the Lamb, for ever and ever. Alleluia. Amen.

FINIS

HE THAT SHOULD COME

A Nativity Play in One Act

NOTE TO PRODUCERS

He That Should Come was originally written for broadcasting, and its adaptation for the stage has presented
certain difficulties, owing to the difference between the two
media. The main dialogue seemed to require little altera-
tion; the trouble begins with the background and subsidiary
characters.

The intention of the play is to show the birth of Christ
against its crowded social and historical background, and
for that purpose it was necessary to make real to the audience the bustling and variegated life of an autonomous
province in the great, sprawling, heterogeneous Roman
Empire of the first century. The inn was to be shown
crowded with as many and various types as possible—the
orthodox Pharisee, with his rigidly national religious views;
the Hellenised Jew, with his liberal outlook influenced by
contact with Rome; the Greek, with his intellectual pli-
ability and sceptical detachment; the trader, treading warily
on thorny political ground and anxious to give offence to
nobody; the peasant, earning a precarious livelihood amid
the hurly-burly of conflicting forces perpetually threatening
his small security; behind them all, the ruthless tyranny of a
self-made Oriental despot, ruling a strange mixed province
of strict Jews in the south and fierce heathen tribes in the
north; and behind him again, the iron strength of Rome,
legal, military, and imperial, caring nothing for internal
politics or religious disputes so long as her tributaries kept
the peace and paid the taxes.

To obtain this effect, the scene was laid, not with particular reference to the traditional cave at Bethlehem, but in
an Oriental inn of the usual kind, consisting of a two-storied
rectangular building surrounding an open courtyard, somewhat after the style of a college quadrangle. In the centre of
the courtyard was a raised platform, on which the travellers

sat or lay, surrounded by their luggage. The ground floor of the building consisted of a series of vaulted stables carrying the chambers on the first floor, over which was a flat roof. The inn had a gate, which was barred at night against marauders. The inn is supposed to be situated on the road going up from Bethlehem to Jerusalem.

It thus became possible to introduce all the necessary characters quite plausibly into this common courtyard. For the purpose of a broadcast, the crowded condition of the inn was sufficiently indicated by introducing a few allusions to the throng of travellers and by fading in a babble of voices at appropriate points in the dialogue. Attention was easily focused on one point or another of the scene by conveying the suggestion of the character picking his way among the assembled travellers, and by inserting a line to announce his arrival at the gate, the stable, the Centurion's post, and so forth.

This scene, so excellently suitable for a broadcast, at once offers difficulties in the theatre, where the crowd of travellers has not merely to be indicated, but to be seen in action and kept continually on the stage. Having once introduced the characters, you cannot move them off and leave the stage clear, because it is the whole point of the story that the inn was crowded to suffocation and that there *was* no clear space. In consequence, the stage being thus crowded and obliged to remain crowded, it becomes very difficult to move the actors naturally from one point to another, or to give the "background characters" anything sensible to do without distracting attention from the speakers. A subsidiary difficulty was to bring the various groups, as they became important to the action, into a sufficiently commanding position and not leave them isolated up-stage or blocked in inconvenient doorways to right and left.

I have coped with these difficulties as well as I could, bearing in mind that the play may be acted by repertory or amateur companies having at their disposal stages of widely varying dimensions and lighting equipment. The play as here arranged allows for the largest stage and the largest company that are likely to be available. There are fifteen characters necessary for the performance of the dialogue; to these I have added nine subsidiary characters to bring the cast up to twenty-four. These, with a proper allowance of baggage and other properties, should be enough to produce a quite convincing crowd on a stage of reasonable dimensions. The actual "crowding-space" of the stage will be governed by the size of the central rostrum, where this is available, and the scenery or curtains can be brought in accordingly.

Where the stage is insufficiently large to accommodate the full cast, the minor characters can be cut down at will, and the "background" dialogue altered to fit the situation. The guiding principle to be taken is to ask: How many people will give an effect of real crowding on this particular stage? and to work from that figure. Where the smallness of the stage or of the available company requires the cast to be limited to the fifteen principal characters, the Landlady's call for a midwife can be answered from off-stage, as though from the upper storey of the inn.

In the absence of built scenery, the play can very suitably be performed in curtains; an inner set of these can be bunched so as to suggest the archways alluded to in the text. The stage directions allow for either one or two archways on either side, according to the depth of the stage. Where there are two, the directions "right" and "left" should be taken to refer to the lower entrances and the directions in brackets (R.U.) and (L.U.) to the upper entrances.

If the play is performed in a church without scenery or curtains, it is suggested that the entrance to the choir should be screened off and opened to display the tableau of the Holy Family. The exits right and left can then be suitably made into the aisle or transept as the case may be, whose arches will supply the appropriate suggestion.

What is done with the Kings during the main action of the play depends upon the means at the producer's disposal. I have made one or two suggestions, according as the building is furnished with one or more sets of front curtains and with more or less elaborate front-of-house lighting. If the play is given in a church without curtain, the Kings might very suitably enter from the west door, through the darkened nave, and be lit by a single spot or a strong electric torch till the time comes to light the whole scene. It would then be symbolically appropriate that they should make their exit eastward, if possible, up either side of the choir towards the Sanctuary, with the light of a torch going before them to represent the Star.

The action of the play should take about an hour. If it is found too long, the Greek Gentleman's Song and the second verse of the Soldiers' Marching Song may be cut. In the original broadcast the long speeches of the Kings were also omitted; but this cut is not recommended. As accompaniment to the songs, a harp, lute, guitar (if that is the best available), or other *plucked* string instrument will give the right effect; orchestral or organ accompaniments are quite unsuitable. A piano would do at a pinch; a harpsichord still better.

The whole effect and character of the play depend on its being played in an absolutely natural and realistic style. Any touch of the ecclesiastical intonation or of "religious unction" will destroy its intention. The whole idea in writing it was to show the miracle that was to change the whole course of human life enacted in a world casual, inattentive, contemptuous, absorbed in its own affairs and completely unaware of what was happening: to illustrate, in fact, the tremendous irony of history. It may be found advisable to make this point clear to the actors before they start, lest some preconceptions as to what is or is not "reverent" in a Nativity Play should hamper the freedom of their performance. I feel sure that it is in the interests of a true reverence towards the Incarnate Godhead to show that His Manhood was a real manhood, subject to the common realities of daily life; that the men and women surrounding Him were living human beings, not just characters in a story; that, in short, He was born, not into "the Bible," but into the world. That an audience will take the play in this spirit is proved to me by the various letters I received after the first broadcast. As one man in a country village put it, "It's nice to think that people in the Bible were folks like

us." And another correspondent: "None of us realised before how much we had just *accepted* the story without properly visualising it. It . . . brought home to us as never before the *real* humanity of Jesus." There will always be a few voices raised to protest against the introduction of "reality" into religion; but I feel that the great obstacle in the path of Christianity to-day is that to so many it has become unreal, shadowy, "a tale that is told," so that it is of the utmost importance to remind people by every means in our power that the thing actually happened—that it is, and was from the beginning, closely in contact with real life.

I found that the broadcasting company really enjoyed playing in this little piece of "real-life" drama, and hope that it will prove itself "good theatre" in a different medium. Since I have had no chance to try out the adaptation with actors upon a stage, I shall be very glad if producers will let me or my agents know how it works out in practice, and what devices their ingenuity has used to get over the obvious "snags" in presentation, so that, if necessary, I may revise the text in the light of their experience.

DOROTHY L. SAYERS.

He That Should Come was first performed in the original broadcast version on the London National Transmission from Broadcasting House on Christmas Day, 1938, with the following cast:

CASPAR	Harcourt Williams
MELCHIOR	William Devlin
BALTHAZAR	Robert Adams
MERCHANT	Henry Longhurst
GREEK GENTLEMAN	Robert Farquharso
PHARISEE	Alan Wheatley
CENTURION	Gordon McLeod
LANDLORD	Philip Wade
LANDLADY	Marjorie Fielding
JOSEPH	Patrick Curwen
MARY	Gwen Catley
JEWISH GENTLEMAN	Raf de la Torre
1ST SHEPHERD	Wallace Evenett
2ND SHEPHERD	Frederick Peisley
3RD SHEPHERD	Pat Laffan

Barry Faber, Angela Kirk and the B.B.C. Singers

The Music composed by ROBERT CHIGNELL

Producer: VAL GIELGUD

The present version has been adapted for Stage Performance by the author. The music may be had on loan from Dorothy Allen, 32 Shaftesbury Avenue, W.1 (acting in association with Messrs. Pearn, Pollinger & Higham Ltd.), to whom all applications for performing rights should be addressed.

DRAMATIS PERSONÆ

Persons of the Prologue and Epilogue

CASPAR, King of Chaldea, an aged man.
MELCHIOR, King of Pamphylia, a man in the prime of life.
BALTHAZAR, King of Ethiopia, a young negro.

Persons of the Play

THE JEWISH MERCHANT, a stout man with a plummy voice.
THE PHARISEE, a tall, thin and severe man.
THE YOUNG GREEK GENTLEMAN, a suave young man, with a foreign accent.
THE JEWISH GENTLEMAN, the "Oxford Graduate" of the period.
THE ROMAN CENTURION, the very best type of non-commissioned officer.
THE LANDLORD, a square-built, husky-voiced person, with a wholesome terror of the law.
THE LANDLADY, a harassed woman with a shrill voice.
JOSEPH, a mild, courteous man, with the plain dignity of the skilled artisan.
MARY, a serene, sweet-voiced woman, with an air of great stillness about her.
1ST SHEPHERD, an elderly peasant.
2ND SHEPHERD, a middle-aged peasant.
3RD SHEPHERD, a young peasant.

MINOR PERSONAGES

Two Roman Soldiers—A Husband and Wife—A Father, Mother and Little Boy—A Manservant—A Maidservant.

PROLOGUE

[The Prologue is played upon the fore-stage. If there is a front
curtain as well as tableaux curtains, it rises to discover MELCHIOR.
If not, MELCHIOR *should enter in darkness before the curtain, and*
a steel spot be gradually turned up to reveal him, sitting left of stage.

MELCHIOR (*sings to the tinkling of a lute*)
High upon the holy tree
    (*Whither away, love?*)
Dragon-guarded ceaselessly
    (*Whither away?*)
There hangs the splendour sought of old,
The lamb, the ram, the fleece of gold
    (*Colchis, O Colchis,*
    Give me my heart again!)
[*Enter* CASPAR. *He speaks out of the darkness, right.*

CASPAR
What traveller is that,
Sitting and singing beside the desert fountain,
Challenging with his frail music
This blinding silence of silver midnight,
Brighter than moonlight, whiter than sunlight,
This unaccustomed miracle of sevenfold starlight?

MELCHIOR (*rising*)
I am a Greek,
Born in the West, on the shores of the Mediterranean,
A European, in fact. I am not afraid of a thing
Merely because it is unaccustomed. Our instinct
Is to challenge destiny. That is why I am here.
There is a muttering among the oracles,
A song in the poets' mouths. They tell of a child
That shall shake off the iron yoke of necessity,

Bring back the golden age and the brave Saturnian reign.
He hath set up his sceptre in the sky; very well;
It is my duty to find out the truth about this;
I am a ruler, I owe my people the truth;
And on my people's behalf I have ridden hither,
Melchior, King of Pamphylia, surnamed "the Just,"
Following the Star.

CASPAR (*coming forward into the light*)

I am an astrologer; I have watched from the high towers
Nightly the signs of heaven stride
Through the houses of fate in the turning horoscope.
I have seen this new star turn and burn
Slowly out of the east, leaping from cusp to cusp,
Till now it sits ruling the house of life;
And I have asked myself what god should be born
From this astonishing conjunction. Therefore am I come,
Caspar, King of Chaldea, surnamed "the Wise,"
Following the Star.

MELCHIOR

Listen! the sound of bells—
Another traveller comes, riding upon a camel,
With a train of swift camels. His face is as the night,
His eyeballs glint white in the night of his face. Who's there?
   [*Enter* BALTHAZAR, *right, and speaks out of the darkness.*

BALTHAZAR

Out of the darkness, out of the desert,
Beyond the secret springs of the Nile
I have seen the fire of desire flare in the zenith
Scaring the crocodiles under the shadow of the pyramids.
The dusky gods have trembled, the witch-dancers are struck
      down
In the midst of their dances.
A cry is gone up in the halls of the dead, from the seven
      gates of the dead,
The cry of Isis over Osiris slain,
The birth-cry of Horus.

224

This is the end or else the beginning of all things,
And sorrow either way, between a cry and a cry;

[*He comes into the light.*

Therefore I come, seeking the soul of sorrow,
Balthazar, King of Ethiopia, surnamed "the Servant,"
Following the Star.

MELCHIOR

Yonder it stands, and yonder, by my reckoning,
The City of Jerusalem, a twelve-days' journey hence.

CASPAR

Strangely are we met, Wisdom, Justice, and Service,
Following the Star, seeking we know not what.

BALTHAZAR (*standing between them*)

Magi, my brothers, let us take counsel of the crystal—
I hold it in my dark hand, shining against the darkness of
    my hand;
Let the crystal display to us what shall be the end of the
    journey.

[*He kneels down.*

CASPAR

Will he come, will he speak at last, the ultimate wisdom,
The unalterable truth behind and above the appearance?
I have studied all the philosophies, and now I am old;
Every day I care less about life and death, sorrow and
    happiness—
I ask only that what we see shall correspond to something,
Beautiful or terrible, but constant in some way or other.
We build the house of thought, stone upon stone,
And just as we have finished the topmost pinnacle
There comes a grinning doubt and pulls away the founda-
    tion.
One has to assume something before one can think at all,
If it is only the validity of one's own thinking,
Or one's immediate perceptions,
Or the numerical proposition that two and two make four.

Give me a single integer and I will build up the universe
Star upon flaming star, and the singing orbits of planets,
And the springing sap, and the life in the blood, and
    splendour,
Beauty and love and grief and the promise of immortality—
Only, it is from the universe that I deduce the integer
From which to deduce the universe again;
And thus all knowledge is only a vicious circle
Ceaselessly spinning upon the axis of nothing.
Nor can I even be sure that everything,
Including myself, is nothing,
Since it is in myself that I find the all and the nothing;
And it may be that nothingness is in itself an illusion,
The last illusion of all.

   [CASPAR *kneels*.

MELCHIOR

I will accept the illusions;
I do not mind whether they are illusions or not,
I am not interested in dogma, I want a religion that works
What I look for is good government,
A reasonable way of life, within the terms of the illusion.
If there is nothing at the end of it, be it so—there is nothing
But in the meantime, can we not achieve a little decency
A little dignity,
A pattern of some kind, such as we make so easily
For a curtain or a cornice, which does not matter at all,
But cannot make for our lives, which matter a great deal
Or, at any rate, seem to matter? Always we hope for a
    formula,
The master-word, the philosopher's stone, the elixir of life,
The abracadabra that settles everything—
The formula of empire, the formula of liberty,
The formula of isolation, the formula of collective security
The formula of discipline, the formula of self-expression,
And all the rest of it.
Always we are disappointed, always there are complica-
    tions,
There does not seem to be any simple rule
To make things go smoothly.

We have wasted too much time in quarrelling and asking
    questions;
Let us put our trust in a personality
Capable of commanding our loyalty—strength
And leadership, and calm hands ordering everything,
And the government shall be upon his shoulder, lord of
    lords, and king of kings.
    [MELCHIOR *kneels*.

BALTHAZAR

how much you need to content you!
The wisdom that sets the soul beyond the reach of suffering,
the power to abolish suffering. I am more humble;
do not mind being ignorant and unhappy—
All I ask is the assurance that I am not alone,
Some courage, some comfort against this burden of fear and
    pain.
I am a servant, born of the seed of Ham,
The oppressed, the accurst;
My skin is black with the punishing fury of the sun.
About my palaces the jungle creeps and whines,
Famine and plague are my fireside companions,
And beyond the circle of the fire, the glare of hungry eyes.
The lion sits by the water-hole, where the women go down
    to wash,
In the branches crouches the leopard.
I look out between the strangling branches of the vine and
    see
Fear in the east, fear in the west; armies
And banners marching and garments rolled in blood.
Yet this is nothing, if only God will not be indifferent,
If He is beside me, bearing the weight of His own creation;
If I may hear His voice among the voices of the vanquished,
If I may feel His hand touch mine in the darkness,
If I may look upon the hidden face of God
And read in the eyes of God
That He is acquainted with grief.

CASPAR

Gather the rays of the Star into the crystal.

Melchior

Look, and see the shape of things afar off.

Balthazar

Listen, and hear the shadows speak in the crystal.

[*A murmur of movements and voices behind the tableaux curtains or gauzes.*

Caspar

See! the light stirs and blurs to a pale cloud in the crystal

Melchior

Like an opal, with green fire darting and parting at the cor

Balthazar

Look and listen! the life of the world is born in the heart ⟨ the crystal.

[*The spot is gradually dimmed down upon the Three Kings who may then make their exit in the black-out, or, if preferred, the may remain upon the stage throughout the action of the play.*

If gauzes are available, the lights behind them will be brought u slowly on the dimmers as the spot fades during the Kings' las three lines, and the gauzes taken up in succession during the opening conversation in the inn.

Where there are no gauzes, the tableaux curtains will be opened a cue on the fully-lit scene.

Suggested Lighting: *Steel in the front spots; blue and white in No. 3 batten; steel arena flood on check centre for star over stable; amber flood shining down staircase left (L.U.) and steel flood through doorway to gate, right; red light in braziers, reinforced by spots if necessary. The impression to be conveyed is of an unroofed courtyard on a brilliant star-light night.*

The Stable of the Nativity can be lit by a white batten, or by couple of baby spots centred upon the Holy Child.

[*The voices of the travellers are heard before the curtains ar opened. The four following pages must be played at top speed.*

Merchant

Landlord! Landlord!

228

ANOTHER VOICE (*fading off, left*)

Three of us and six servants, and see that the brown mule
gets a good rub down.

PHARISEE

Landlord! Landlord!

MANSERVANT

T'ch, t'ck! Git over there!

MERCHANT

Held up twice between here and Jericho. What the Government thinks it's doing. . . .

1ST SOLDIER

Best of three!

2ND SOLDIER

My belt against your Persian dagger.

JEWISH GENTLEMAN

Look sharp, my lad, with that jug of wine.

MANSERVANT

Yes, sir! Yes, sir! Coming in a minute.

WIFE

Really, Ezra, am I to stand here all night?

[*The curtains open. The centre of the stage is occupied by a rectangular platform, its down-stage edge lying just behind the curtain
line. A passage runs round the back and both sides at stage level. At
the back are three archways, leading to the stables; their entrances
(R.B., C.B. and L.B.) are concealed by rough hangings of sacking. Similar archways, at the sides of the stage, lead, on the right to
the gateway of the inn, on the left to a staircase going up to the roof.
(*NOTE.—If the depth of the stage permits, there may be two of these
entrances either side, in which case the lower right entrance will lead
to the gate, and the upper left to the stairs. See p. 217.) Behind the*

229

centre archway at the back is the Stable of the Nativity, the floor of which is raised somewhat above the level of the platform. Both platform and passage-way are obstructed by baggage of every description —mattresses, saddle-bags, saddles, cooking utensils, and so forth. On the right, the GREEK GENTLEMAN *has just entered, and is working his way centre. Near right entrance sprawl a couple of* ROMAN SOLDIERS, *entertaining themselves with a dice-box and a large pot of beer. Well down, and a little right of centre, the* PHARISEE *is sitting, with the* LANDLORD *in attendance. Just above centre, a* PEASANT FATHER *and* MOTHER *have established themselves with their* LITTLE BOY; *a* MAIDSERVANT *is filling their pitcher with water and giggling at* FATHER. *Right of centre the respectable* HUSBAND *and* WIFE *are standing surrounded luggage, and looking rather helpless. Above and left of them stan the* MERCHANT, *and a little above between them and the fami party stands the* ROMAN CENTURION, *checking over the papers the* JEWISH GENTLEMAN. *Right back a* MANSERVANT *is carryi a bundle of fodder into the stable. All through the opening dialog the* PHARISEE *sits severely silent, reading a scroll.*

HUSBAND

Of course not, my dear. (*He beckons to the* MAIDSERVANT. Here, girl, here! (*The* GIRL *is being chucked under the chin by th* FATHER, *and pays no attention.*)

MAIDSERVANT

Give over, now, do!

LANDLADY (*entering left (L.U.), shrilly*)

Now then, you lazy baggage! Water and towels for the party upstairs.

MAIDSERVANT

Yes, madam. (*She hurries off, left (L.U.).*)

HUSBAND (*trying in vain to detain her*)

The service in these inns is disgraceful!

WIFE

Is there nobody here to attend to a lady?

230

LANDLORD (*coming up-stage*)

Wife, here's a lady wants you.

LANDLADY

Gentleman upstairs wants these cleaned. (*She dumps a cloak nd a pair of boots into his arms. He takes them off, right (R.U.).*) ?es, madam? (*She attends to* WIFE.)

MANSERVANT (*coming down to* JEWISH GENTLEMAN *with wine*)

rry to keep you waiting, sir. We're run off our feet with e rush.

BOY

other! Mother! I want a piece of cake.
[CENTURION *goes centre and speaks to* GREEK GENTLEMAN.

MOTHER

ake, indeed! You'll wait till supper's ready.

GREEK GENTLEMAN

Jative of Bethlehem? Heaven forbid! We're going on to erusalem. (*He comes down to* MERCHANT.)

FATHER (*catching* MANSERVANT *as he returns centre*)

Give us a hand with the pack-saddle, can't you? (*They go up owards stable, back (L.B.). The* CENTURION *has meanwhile rossed right, and is watching the* SOLDIERS *at their game.*)

1ST SOLDIER

The gods to aid! (*Throws dice.*) Venus, by Bacchus!

2ND SOLDIER

Curse it! You've cleaned me out. (*Drinks.*)

1ST SOLDIER

That's no reason to swill all the beer. (*Snatches pot from him. Scuffle.*)

231

Find us a nice quiet spot, away from those drunken soldiers.
 [*Her* HUSBAND *leads her across left, above* MERCHANT *and his baggage.*

MANSERVANT (*off, back*)

Steady, hoss, steady. So-ho there!

JEWISH GENTLEMAN

Hey, you! Take those damned camels where my horse can'
wind 'em! (*He dashes out (R.B.).*)

MERCHANT (*down, left*)

Taxes! that's what it means, more taxes! Why else shoul
they take a census? Just idle curiosity on the part of th
Imperial Government?

GREEK GENTLEMAN

Well, sir, I imagine they must find occupation for the staff ·
the Home Office. Besides, the Emperor takes a great interes
in vital statistics.

MERCHANT

Vital statistics my foot! They mean to clap on a poll-tax, yo
see if they don't. As if we weren't squeezed and badgere
enough already, what with Imperial taxes and the King
taxes, customs, excise, land-tax, house-tax, and now thi
monstrous new stamp-duty on sales. Trade, sir, trade is th
life-blood of the country, and they're strangling it, deliberately doing all they can to strangle it, with these iniquitous
exactions. But there! I can tell by your speech you're a
foreigner. Perhaps they manage things better where you
come from. (*Sits on* HUSBAND's *baggage, left.*)

GREEK GENTLEMAN

I am a Greek, sir; Philip is my name. I am travelling t
Jerusalem with letters of introduction to the King's historian. I dabble a little in letters—oh, very amateurishly,
I assure you—and have foolishly undertaken to write a
trifling study of social and economic conditions in th
232

Roman provinces. Anything I can learn about the effect of legislation on commerce is of great assistance to my ignorance.

[LANDLORD *re-enters right (R.U.) and checks papers with* CENTURION; *they move up back.*

MERCHANT

Well, you can put it in your book, sir, that the effect of this kind of legislation is disastrous. I don't mince words, I say disastrous. Between the King and the Emperor, we're between the upper and the nether millstones. The King hampers the labouring classes at the expense of respectable citizens, and the Emperor makes it his business to thrust a crowbar into the wheels at every opportunity. . . .

HUSBAND

Confound you, sir, that's my bag you're sitting on. (*He jerks his luggage away and returns up left.*)

MERCHANT

. . . It's a scandal to disturb honest tradesmen at the busiest time of the year, and send them trapesing up and down the country, just to get themselves registered at some infernal village where they had the misfortune to be born. Here's weeks of valuable time wasted—not to mention the peril to life and limb.

[LANDLADY *works up and off, left (L.U.).*

GREEK GENTLEMAN

Certainly the roads are in a shocking state—and terribly congested.

[JEWISH GENTLEMAN *comes out of stable (L.B.) and goes in again (R.B.).*

MERCHANT

Congested? That's nothing. They're not safe, my good sir, they're not safe! Bandits and revolutionaries lurking in every thicket. My heart was in my mouth all the way, and we

233

passed some most ruffianly-looking characters in the hill-country near Beth-Horon. I suppose, by the way, you don't know anybody who's travelling back in that direction, and would permit me to join his company?

GREEK GENTLEMAN

I'm afraid not. I'm a stranger here myself, you know. But we might ask the Roman centurion over there. He seems to be checking up on the arrivals.

MERCHANT

Thank you, thank you, that's an excellent suggestion. Wi you add to your kindness by accompanying me? I don't lik the look of some of these people—I'm sure they'd pick you purse as soon as look at you. (*They move up centre. To* WIFE Excuse me, madam, I wish to speak to the Centurion. (*T* HUSBAND) Allow me, sir. (*They grudgingly make way for him.* This place is dreadfully overcrowded. (*He encounters* MAN SERVANT *and* FATHER, *returning from the stable, their shoulder laden with a pack-saddle, goatskins, cooking utensils, etc.*) Pray let me pass, my good fellows. (*They shove past him, thrusting him aside upon the* BOY, *who utters a sharp yell.*) Oh, I beg your pardon, I didn't see your little boy; I hope I've not hurt him.

MOTHER (*venomously*)

Some people want all the place to themselves!
[*In the meantime, the* CENTURION *has moved across with the* LANDLORD *to the left upper corner of the stage, and is as far off as ever. The* MERCHANT, *with a despairing cry, darts after him in this new direction, and becomes involved with the* LANDLADY *and the* MAIDSERVANT, *who enter left* (*L.U.*), *bringing some cooked food to the* HUSBAND *and* WIFE.

MERCHANT

Dear, dear, I'm sorry. How clumsy of me! Pardon, pardon.

LANDLADY (*looking daggers*)

Granted, I'm sure.

234

[*The* CENTURION *and* LANDLORD *come halfway down by passage, left; the* MERCHANT *following. The* GREEK GENTLE-MAN, *smiling imperturbably, insinuates himself neatly through the crowd in the* MERCHANT'S *wake, and everybody thinks him charming.*

MERCHANT (*arriving at last*)

Good evening, Captain. Can you spare me just a moment of your time?

CENTURION

In one minute, sir. Here, landlord, all these papers seem to be in order. I shouldn't think there'd be any more arrivals now. You'd better close the gates.

LANDLORD

Yes, Captain. Thank you, Captain. I don't see how we could take anybody else if they did come. (*Shouting.*) Porter, bar the gates!

PORTER (*shouting off, right*)

There's another party here wants to come in.

LANDLORD

What's that?

PORTER

There's a party here with a donkey. I've told 'em there ain't no room.

LANDLORD

All right, I'll come myself. (*He comes down left and starts to cross behind* PHARISEE, *turning as he goes to speak to the* CENTURION.) There wasn't anything further, was there, Captain?

CENTURION

No, that's all right. Carry on.

[*Exit* LANDLORD, *right.*

Now, Master Merchant, what can I do for you?

MERCHANT

I was wondering, Captain, whether you knew of anyone who would be returning by way of Beth-Horon?

235

CENTURION

Well, let me see, now. Why, yes, there's a young gentleman going through that way to-morrow as far as Lydda. I forget his name, but you'll find him somewhere about, wearing a Roman dress and a green cloak.

MERCHANT

Thank you, Captain, thank you. I am going to Lydda myself.

[*Re-enter, right,* LANDLORD. *He backs in, making expostulatory gestures.* JOSEPH *follows, pleading with him.* MARY *comes quietly behind* JOSEPH.

Is he a wealthy gentleman, with plenty of armed servants? Do you think he would permit me to join his party?

LANDLORD

No, no, no, I tell you.

JOSEPH

Yes, but do listen a moment . . .
  [LANDLADY *works across to them.*

CENTURION (*to* MERCHANT)

Couldn't say, I'm sure, sir. You'd better ask him. (*His eye has been caught by the little disturbance on the other side of the stage.*) Excuse me, the landlord seems to be having a spot of bother over there. I'll have to go and keep an eye on it. Now then, good people, out of my way, please! (*He strides unceremoniously across the centre of the stage.*)

MANSERVANT (*obsequiously*)

Clear the way for the Captain!

MOTHER (*snatching her* BOY *out of the way*)

Look out, here's the Centurion coming.

FATHER (*finding himself accidentally blocking the* CENTURION'S *path and being unceremoniously shoved aside*)

Beg your pardon, Captain. (*Aside.*) Damn your Roman insolence!

236

CENTURION (*whisking round*)

Hey?

FATHER

Nothing, Captain.

[*Meanwhile the* MERCHANT *and the* GREEK GENTLEMAN *have wandered off left to look for the* JEWISH GENTLEMAN.

LANDLORD

I'm sorry, my good man, I tell you it's absolutely impossible.

JOSEPH

implore you, good host, in the name of all the Prophets . . .

LANDLORD

e reasonable, man. I don't mean it unkindly. It can't be one, that's all. We're packed right out—aren't we, wife?

LANDLADY

Packed out? I should think we were. I'm sure I don't know how we shall manage as it is. Not an inch of space down here, as you can see for yourselves, and they're sleeping on the roof head to tail like herrings in a basket. Indecent, I call it. The Government's got no right to land poor innkeepers in such a pickle.

CENTURION

Now than, ma'am. What's the trouble here?

JOSEPH

Good soldier, can you help us to find a lodging for the night? We have sought everywhere in the town, and this is our last hope.

LANDLORD

And I'm telling him, Captain, we haven't so much as a corner. They'll have to push on to Jerusalem.

LANDLADY

It's only five miles, and it's a big place.

237

JOSEPH

Alas! sir, it's very late and a bad road. Will you not persuade this worthy couple to give us a shake-down somewhere? We are not particular. As you see, we are humble folk, and there are only the two of us.

LANDLADY

Yes, and like to be three of you before long, I reckon.

JOSEPH

Indeed, that's true. My wife is in no fit state to travel farther. Besides, our journey ends here.

LANDLORD

Captain, you can see we are not to blame——

CENTURION

Wait a bit, wait a bit. Let's get this straight. You, good master, what's your name?

JOSEPH

I am called Joseph ben Heli, and this is Mary, my wife.

CENTURION

Trade?

JOSEPH

Carpenter.

CENTURION

Place of residence?

JOSEPH

Nazareth in Galilee.

CENTURION

Lineage?

JOSEPH

Of the house and lineage of David.

CENTURION

Of David, eh? And this is the city of David?

Yes, Captain.

CENTURION

And therefore the proper place for you to get yourselves registered?

JOSEPH

Yes, Captain.

CENTURION

I see. Well, it does seem a bit hard to move you on, especially as your good lady is so near her time. What do you say, landlord? Can't you shift some of the baggage and give them shelter under the arches?

[*During the following conversation,* MANSERVANT *and* MAIDSERVANT *bring in three braziers, placing one for the* MOTHER, *who uses it to cook supper, one just below the* HUSBAND *and* WIFE, *and the third near the* PHARISEE.

LANDLORD

Don't see how we can, sir. We've got all the servants of these ladies and gentlemen bedded down there as it is. You couldn't put a pin between 'em. It's not my fault if people will travel with such a lot of attendants. Inconsiderate, I call it, but there you are.

CENTURION

How about the stables? Is there any room there?

LANDLORD

Well, I dunno about that. Let me see now—it means getting their ass in as well. Could you lie along of the ass, mistress?

MARY

Yes, indeed we could. She's a quiet good creature and gives no trouble, does she, Joseph?

JOSEPH

None whatever. Thank you kindly. A stable would be far better than nothing.

LANDLORD

I haven't promised anything yet. Let me put on my thinking cap. We can't move the camels, nor yet put the young gentleman's stallion in with the mares. Perhaps we could—— No! that won't work.

LANDLADY

Could we make room for the captain's gelding along of the merchant's she-asses—if you didn't mind, sir—

CENTURION

Not in the least. By all means.

LANDLORD

That's a good idea. Then we could put these people an their donkey in with old Ibrahim's draught-ox. How woul that suit you?

JOSEPH

Excellently. We are greatly obliged to you.

MARY

It is most kind of you. We are sorry to be putting you to all this extra trouble on our account.

LANDLORD

That's all right. Don't like to think of you with nowhere to lay your heads. Especially under the circumstances, eh, wife?

LANDLADY

It's not that anybody *wants* to seem disobliging——

CENTURION

Of course not, of course not. Well, that's all settled. I'm sure you'll manage capitally. Good night to you. (*He joins the* SOLDIERS *and confers with them.*)

MARY *and* JOSEPH

Good night, Captain.

[*Here the* MERCHANT *reappears, left* (*L.U.*), *followed by the* GREEK GENTLEMAN. *They move along the passage-way at the back.*

LANDLORD

Now you come along with me. I'll have some clean straw put down for you. (*Calling off right.*) Take the ass round to the stable! (*Hoofs heard off right and round to centre back.*) Mind how you go; you'll have to pick your way a bit. (*They move up back and across among the piled-up baggage in the passage-way.*) It's just across here and under the——

[*The* MERCHANT *falls over a pack-saddle, into the* LANDLORD'S *arms.*

Ouf! you might look where you're going, sir!

MERCHANT (*panting*)

I'm extremely sorry, Landlord. Could you tell me . . . Oh, ear! (*He is out of breath.*)

GREEK GENTLEMAN

Landlord, we are looking for a young gentleman in a green cloak. Have you by any chance seen such a one?

[JEWISH GENTLEMAN *emerges from stable, R.B.*

LANDLORD

This'll be him, sir, just coming through the archway.

MERCHANT

Oh, thank you, thank you!

LANDLORD

Don't mention it. (*He enters the centre stable with* MARY *and* JOSEPH.)

[LANDLADY *has meanwhile worked away left.*

MERCHANT

Sir! Pray, one moment, young gentleman!

JEWISH GENTLEMAN

Hullo!

GREEK GENTLEMAN

Your pardon, sir. This good merchant wishes to ask you—
(*with a change of tone*) Now, by all the gods of Olympus! If it
isn't my old friend Yussuf!

JEWISH GENTLEMAN

Philip! by all the Prophets! What on earth are you doing
here? (*They come down right.*)

GREEK GENTLEMAN

Just travelling about. Studying social history and all that.
Writing a little verse, and tinkering about with a magnum
opus that will never get finished.

JEWISH GENTLEMAN

The same old Philip. Not changed a bit since college days.
I'm delighted to see you. Come and sit down and let's have
a yarn.

MERCHANT (*panting after them*)

Forgive me, sir, but I——

GREEK GENTLEMAN

Oh, yes, I forgot. This honest merchant wants to know if he
may have the protection of your company as far as Lydda.
[*Meanwhile* LANDLORD *may be seen taking straw in to stable,
C.B.;* MAIDSERVANT *may take in water, etc., and fasten curtain
of sacking across entrance.*

JEWISH GENTLEMAN

Certainly, by all means. The more the merrier. I hope, sir,
you'll join us in a cup of wine.

MERCHANT

I am very much obliged, sir.

JEWISH GENTLEMAN

Here's a good place to sit in, near this worthy Pharisee.

(*They all sit by* PHARISEE.) I trust we do not disturb you, sir. Thank you. Shockingly crowded this place is to-night, and I entirely agree with you, merchant, that travelling's no joke these days.

MERCHANT

Terrible, sir, terrible! Times are hard enough, goodness knows, without Caesar taking it into his head to number the people. Apart from everything else, look at the interruption to business. It's a sin and a shame——

PHARISEE (*interrupting*)

It is a sin indeed to number the people. It is the sin of King David, to which Satan provoked him. Is it not written in the Book of the Chronicles of the Kings of Israel?

GREEK GENTLEMAN

I have not studied the work in question, but I'll take your word for it.

JEWISH GENTLEMAN

You may take his word for it, Philip. He is a learned Pharisee, and he ought to know.

PHARISEE

Judging by your dress, gentlemen, and by the speech of one of you, you are Romans.

JEWISH GENTLEMAN

My friend is Greek, but I am as good a Jew as yourself, sir. I was educated in Rome, certainly, and prefer to dress in the fashion.

PHARISEE

God deliver us from the fashions of Rome—where they teach our Hebrew youth to sneer at God's word and bind a foreign yoke and a pagan custom upon our necks in flat defiance of the Law of Moses.

[*Throughout this conversation, the* LANDLORD, LANDLADY, *and* SERVANTS *move unobtrusively about, looking after the travellers, who eat their supper and prepare for the night. Some of this action*

*can be supposed to take place off, left, in attendance on people
upstairs; and the* MANSERVANT *can go in and out of the stables.
The* CENTURION *goes centre and stands behind the brazier warm-
ing his hands.*

JEWISH GENTLEMAN

Nonsense, sir! Surely one can be a sincere Jew and still live
like a gentleman?

PHARISEE (*contemptuously*)

Like a gentleman!

JEWISH GENTLEMAN

Yes, sir. I come of a good house; my father is a magistrate.
I shall probably end up as a member of the Sanhedrim
myself when the time comes. And when I'm there, be sure
I shall press for a more enlightened and cosmopolitan
policy.

PHARISEE

Indeed, sir! Well, I am Zadok the Pharisee, a follower of
Judas the Gaulonite, and I say that your godless Roman-
ising policy is bringing upon this nation the curse due to
the backslider and the apostate.

JEWISH GENTLEMAN

Upon my soul, sir——!
  [*This little passage of arms attracts the attention of the* CEN-
  TURION. *Seeing that it quiets down, he takes no action, but he
  keeps his eye on it.*

MERCHANT

Pray, gentlemen, don't quarrel. I'm a man of peace. I quite
see your point, good Master Zadok. You're bound to look at
things from the religious side. But I'm a plain man, and
what I object to is the inconvenience. Here I am, torn from
my home, put in peril of my life, and goodness knows what's
happening to my business all this time! That scoundrelly
Greek—Oh, I beg your pardon, noble sir—that manager of
mine is probably making hay of the accounts, and I shall

lose all my best customers. I'm a spice-merchant, gentle-
me, Aaron ben Isaac is my name, in a pretty big way down
at Joppa.

PHARISEE

I'm glad you stick to the old-fashioned native name.

MERCHANT

Did I say Joppa? I meant Caesarea, of course. Caesarea we
call it now, since Herod rebuilt it and made all those
modern improvements. A heathen name, of course, but
what's in a name?—and I must say, the King has succeeded
in putting the town on the map. Here's my card, by the way,
if you should happen to be requiring pepper, or perfumes, or
anything in that line. I have the honour to supply nutmegs
to the Imperial Household.

[*The* LANDLORD, *with a jug of wine in his hand, is now centr*
of stage. He serves HUSBAND *and prepares to go off left.*

JEWISH GENTLEMAN

Thanks very much. I'd be glad to know of any one who can
supply bath-unguents and toilet-waters reasonably. The
prices in Jerusalem are positively outrageous. Landlord!
bring us some wine here!

[LANDLORD *returns with a jar of wine.*

PHARISEE

Bath-unguents, indeed! That's all you young men think
about. It was a black day for Jewry when King Herod built
the public baths for the corruption of our young men.

[*The* CENTURION, *smelling trouble, wanders casually up to the*
back of the group, with the detached air of a London policeman
patrolling a public meeting.

You loll about there all day, oiling your bodies and anoint-
ing your hair, reading lascivious heathen poetry, talking
blasphemy, and idling away the time with Greek slaves and
dancing-girls. May the curse of Korah, Dathan, and Abiram
light on King Herod and his baths too! May the earth open
and swallow them up!

LANDLORD

Your wine, gentlemen. (*Whispering.*) Sir, I implore you not to talk so loudly. King Herod's spies are everywhere. And the centurion is standing just behind you.

JEWISH GENTLEMAN

Serve to the gentlemen. Your health, sirs. Personally I'm all for King Herod. He may be a bit of an autocrat, but he's done a lot for the country. How about his big housing schemes in Samaria, and Caesarea with its great new harbour and up-to-date drainage system?

MERCHANT

That's a fact. You wouldn't know the old place.

GREEK GENTLEMAN

I must make a point of visiting it.

JEWISH GENTLEMAN

Look at the Jordan Valley Waterworks. Look at the Temple in Jerusalem. Look at the theatres and amphitheatres the King has built and endowed——

PHARISEE

Nothing would induce me to look at them. Play-acting and wild-beast shows are an abomination in the sight of the Lord. Immoral, irreligious, and thoroughly un-Jewish.

JEWISH GENTLEMAN

Yes, they *are* un-Jewish. Our national attitude to the Arts is deplorable. King Herod is the only Jew in the country who cares twopence about cosmopolitan culture.

PHARISEE

Thank God for it. Nothing is so demoralising as art and culture. As for Herod, he is no true Israelite. He is an Edomite, a son of Ishmael, and, what's more, an unbeliever. He

246

breaks the Law of Moses by letting the barbarians in the provinces put up graven images to him. And you, Aaron ben Isaac, who complain of the Imperial taxes, have you forgotten that it is unlawful to pay tribute to Caesar?

[*The* CENTURION *at this point really does take notice.*

LANDLORD

Hush, hush, sir, for Heaven's sake!

MERCHANT (*alarmed*)

Here, I say! Hadn't you better be careful?

PHARISEE

You have no spirit. You are slaves, sold by Herod into the bondage of Rome—and all you can do is to sit there grumbling feebly about taxation and interruptions to business. What room will there be for such as you in the great day of redemption when the Lord's Messiah comes?

CENTURION

And what will your Messiah do when he does come?

LANDLORD

God of Abraham! I knew there'd be trouble. I'm sure, Captain, the gentleman means no harm. Don't hold it against me. This is a respectable house.

MERCHANT

Of course, of course, Captain. And anyway, I wasn't saying anything. I swear I haven't uttered a syllable against the Emperor or King Herod either. I never suggested the taxes were illegal. I only said they came heavy on a man, and so they do—but there's nothing treasonable in that.

JEWISH GENTLEMAN

That's what taxes are for—to give us something to grumble about. Eh, Captain? Sit down, man, and have a drink.

247

GREEK GENTLEMAN

That's right, Captain. Fill for the Captain, landlord.

CENTURION

Thank you kindly, sir. I don't mind if I do. Cheer up, land-lord, we're not going to crucify you yet awhile.

LANDLORD (*pouring wine for* CENTURION)

No, sir. Thank you, sir. (*He retires, left.*)
  [*Sound of singing and marching off, back.*

CENTURION

Your health, sir! The gods be favourable to you. Cheer up, Master Merchant. So long as the taxes are paid, Rome can put up with a grumble or two.

MERCHANT (*with a wry face*)

Yes, yes, of course——

CENTURION

And, after all, we do give you something to show for the money.

PHARISEE (*sarcastically*)

Undoubtedly. Baths and theatres and drainage systems, and other worldly luxuries that our fathers did very well without.

CENTURION

Better than that, sir. Peace and security. Listen!

SONG OF THE LEGIONARIES (*as they pass the inn*)
  Bread and cheese, bread and cheese
  Marching through Spain, boys,
  With a sackful of loot
  And a hole in your boot
  At the end of the long campaign, boys;
  Bread and cheese, bread and cheese.
  [*The* ROMAN SOLDIERS *join in for a bar or two.*

248

Early and late, boys,
For we'll get no cheer
Of beef and beer
Till we see the Julian gate, boys.
Beef and beer, beef and beer, etc., etc.

[*The song dies away off right, past the gate.*

CENTURION

Those are the lads of the Sixth, going up to keep order in
Jerusalem. Good luck to 'em. And to King Herod too, say I.
Regular good army man, is King Herod.

[*The* MERCHANT *endorses these sentiments with eager nods.*

Judaea was in a pretty mess till he took it over. He and the
Emperor together have kept order these thirty years. No
invasions, no civil wars, peace and prosperity and a reasonable check kept on bandits and insurgents. What more do
you want?

PHARISEE (*with dignity*)

Peace is not everything. Prosperity is not everything. (*The*
MERCHANT *tugs anxiously at his sleeve, but he continues.*) We
want liberty for our nation and liberty for our religion.

CENTURION

Bless my heart, what do you think liberty means? Liberty to
cut one another's throats—as you were doing before Rome
stepped in and put a stop to it? There's no liberty in civil dis-
order. Liberty means freedom to go safely about your business and behave yourselves like good citizens. And you'll
only get that under a strong central government. Do you
think your Christ or Messiah or whatever you call him is
going to beat Rome at that game?

PHARISEE

When the Messiah comes——

JEWISH GENTLEMAN

Need we argue about the Messiah?

249

MERCHANT

No, no, of course not. Let's keep clear of politics.

GREEK GENTLEMAN

Yes, but what is the Messiah?

PHARISEE

When the Messiah comes, he will restore the kingdom to Israel and smite the heathen with a rod of iron.

[MERCHANT *groans*.

CENTURION

I can't understand you Jews. Can't you live and let live? Nobody minds your worshipping what you please and how you please. The Emperor's very keen on religious toleration. We've got temples in Rome to all sorts of odd foreign deities, you'd be surprised; and if you liked to put one up there to your Jehovah, or whatever you call him, there's no reason why he and our Jove shouldn't get on capitally together.

PHARISEE

The Lord God of Heaven is One God and One alone. We can make no compromise with idols.

CENTURION

It seems to me you want all the religious liberty for yourselves and none for other people. Well, it's no affair of mine. But if your Messiah is proposing to start a war of religion——

MERCHANT

Really, now, really. *Do* let's leave the Messiah out of it. So far as I know, he isn't even born yet.

CENTURION

Very sensible of him. If he takes my advice he'll put off being born for quite a little bit. King Herod has done a very tidy job keeping order in this province and he has no use at all for Messiahs and insurrections. Good evening. (*He marches off left, and is seen to speak to the* LANDLORD, *who follows him off.*)

[LEGIONARIES *heard again, singing:* "*Beef and beer.*"

MERCHANT

Heaven preserve us! my heart was in my mouth. All this treasonable talk——

JEWISH GENTLEMAN

Zadok, do you never think that this stiff-necked resistance may end by destroying our nation?

PHARISEE

Your easy toleration will end by destroying our souls. How long, O Lord, how long? (*He stalks stiffly away, and settles down left.*)

SONG OF THE LEGIONARIES

[*As the* LANDLADY *passes on some errand, the* 1ST SOLDIER *puts his arm round her. She pushes him off. Laughter.*

Beef and beer, beef and beer
Sitting at home, sweet home, boys,
With a wench in your arm
To keep you warm,
O take me back to Rome, boys!

MERCHANT

Men like that are a public danger.

[*Knocking off, right, and sounds of argument with the* PORTER.

Oh, dear me! Are the soldiers coming in? Bear witness, gentlemen, I never saw him before.

[LANDLADY *extricates herself from the* SOLDIERS *and hurries off, right.* MERCHANT *retires to remote corner down left, below* PHARISEE.

251

Beef and beer, beef and beer,
And cram your bellies tight, boys,
For it's starve and freeze
On bread and cheese
When the eagles take their flight, boys.
Bread and cheese, bread and cheese, etc.

LANDLADY (*shrilly; backing in, right*)

Now then, now then, what do you want at this time of night? It's no good, I tell you, my man. We're full up. Can't take anybody else. You needn't start arguing. We're full up.

1ST SHEPHERD

Excuse me, ma'am. My mate and me only looked in to se if we could buy a drop o' beer.

LANDLADY

Beer? Good gracious me, what next? This is an inn for travellers, not a jug-and-bottle department. You must go to the wine-shop in the next street.

[SHEPHERDS *edge in after her*.

1ST SHEPHERD

The wine-shop's shut, ma'am, and we thought if you'd be so good as to oblige us——

LANDLADY

Nonsense. You must knock the wine-merchant up—or go without, much better for you. Get along now and don't hang about the doorway. You smell of the sheepfolds. Be off with you!

JEWISH GENTLEMAN (*calling up-stage*)

Oh, for Heaven's sake, woman, stop screaming!

LANDLADY

Oh, dear! That's the young gentleman from Rome. Now he'll be vexed. (*Coming down.*) I'm sure I'm very sorry, sir

252

it's these common shepherds, pushing in here, wanting to buy beer, as if this was a vulgar alehouse. I've told them as plain as I could——

Jewish Gentleman

I heard you. Your voice, sweet hostess, goes through my head like a knife through a melon. Can't you give these honest lads their beer and have done with it?

[Shepherds *advance hopefully*.

Landlady

We don't sell beer.

Jewish Gentleman

You grasp the idea, lads, don't you? We don't sell beer What are you? Shepherds?

1st Shepherd

Yes, sir. We weren't wishful to be troublesome. Me and my two sons be keepin' our sheep on the hills yonder, and, it bein' a cold sort o' night, Sam and me come along to get a little drop to our supper.

Jewish Gentleman

I see. Well, I haven't got any beer, but here's wine, if that'll suit you. Sit down and have a quick one before you go.

1st *and* 2nd Shepherds

Thank you, sir. Very good of you, sir.

[*They gather about the* Jewish Gentleman—*he gives them wine*.

Jewish Gentleman

All right, hostess, that will do. (*Exit* Landlady, *working off*, *left* (*L.U.*).) Now, tell me, my good friends, how are things going with you? Do you rub along pretty well? Or do you want a rebellion against the Government, and a new Messiah and all that kind of thing? You can talk quite freely to us. We shan't give you away. My friend here is studying social conditions, aren't you, Phil?

253

GREEK GENTLEMAN

Yes; I am very much interested in your Jewish religion and politics; but they are terribly complicated. This, for instance, your Messiah as you call him—what does that word mean, Yussuf?

JEWISH GENTLEMAN

Christos in Greek, Christ, the Anointed One.

[During this long conversation, the rest of the travellers settle down to sleep. The 1st SOLDIER stands sentinel at the door, right; the other goes to sleep. The lights in the other two braziers die down, leaving only the group of the two GENTLEMEN and the SHEPHERDS clearly lit, and a beam of moonlight on the stable door. Dim down front spots and No. 3 batten gradually.

GREEK GENTLEMAN

Ah, yes. Messiah, Christ, I understand. Now, this anointed one—what is he? A king or a priest? Or is he some kind of hero or demi-god, after the fashion of our Hercules?

JEWISH GENTLEMAN

My dear man, these shepherds have never heard of Hercules.

GREEK GENTLEMAN

Never mind. I like to get the reactions of the common people to all these academic questions. What do you think of Christ, my good friends?

1st SHEPHERD

Well, sir, I don't rightly know. Some say he's to be a great prince, born of the royal house of David—him that was a king in Israel, you know, sir, long ago, wonderful rich and powerful, notwithstanding he began life as a poor shepherd, no better than us. But others say he'll be a mighty chieftain, more after the style of Judas the Maccabean, and lead a great rebellion against Rome. But I do hope and trust it won't be that way, sir—not in our time, anyway.

254

Jewish Gentleman

You don't want a rebellion, then?

1st Shepherd

That I do not, sir. Rebellions and civil wars and such never do no good to us poor folk.

2nd Shepherd

Come now, Father, I don't know. They say the Messiah will restore the kingdom and do away with oppression and taxes, and bring back the good old days, with milk and honey for everybody.

[*About this point*, Joseph *comes out of stable door* (*C.B.*). *He quietly wakes the* Maidservant, *who goes off left* (*L.U.*), *to look for* Landlady. Joseph *returns to stable*.

1st Shepherd

Why, so he may; but there'll be a sight of poor souls ruined and slaughtered first. No; life's hard enough on the poor, as it is, without no wars. We're well enough off as we are, with King Herod. You'll find, sir, it's mostly the upper classes as complains about King Herod's government. He don't bear too hard on the farmers, all things considered. Of course some of the tax-gatherers puts the screw on cruel, but, saving your presence, gentlemen, I think they mostly gets their orders from the Emperor, and him living 'way off in Rome, maybe he don't quite know the way they go on here.

2nd Shepherd

Maybe, when Messiah comes, he'll explain matters to the Emperor. You know, sirs, there's some say he won't be a king at all—but a poor, good man, the servant of the people. Something more in the nature of a prophet, like, same as Elias, or it might be Nathan, what spoke and rebuked King David when he behaved so unjust to Uriah the Hittite.

[*Enter* Landlady, *left* (*L.U.*), *with lantern. She goes briskly in at stable door* (*C.B.*).

1st Shepherd

Yes, or a holy priest, more after the fashion of Aaron or Melchisedek, as will take away sin and bring the people back to righteousness—for there's a sad deal of worldly living these days, and men don't keep the Law as they did. Some of the young people don't seem to believe in nothing but dancing and going to prize-fights and having a good time.

2nd Shepherd

That's right. And there's a young chap I know, that's employed in the theatre, as they call it, at Jerusalem, says the goings-on there is something shocking—men dressed up like women with masks on, acting heathen pieces full of smut and nastiness, and tumblers and chariot-races, and a terribl deal of betting and gambling. It ain't right, to our way thinking. I expect Messiah will put a stop to all that.

[*The* Centurion *reappears, left, and passes silently across the back of the stage, the moonlight catching his helmet as he goes past the stable. He goes out, right.*

1st Shepherd

Ay, so he will, I dare say. But he won't do it by making wars. People don't act holier in war-time, they acts more sinful. And what with soldiers stravaguing up and down, looting and pillaging and destroying the cattle and the crops, it's bad business for everyone. No, we don't want no more wars.

Greek Gentleman

Upon my word, Yussuf, your countrymen seem to be very sensible fellows. Here's to you, shepherds, and I hope, when your Messiah comes, he'll turn out to be a prince of peace. If you ask my opinion——

[Landlady *comes briskly out of stable door, with* Joseph *following.*

Landlady

There now, didn't I tell you so?

Jewish Gentleman

Hullo! what's the matter with our good hostess now?

LANDLADY

It's no good talking that way to me, Joseph ben Heli; this is
an inn, not a lying-in hospital. Of all the tiresome things!
No, indeed I can't help you—I've got far too much to do.
Perhaps there's some one among the company that can
oblige. Excuse me, ladies, is there anybody here that's a
midwife?

FATHER

Eh, what? Yes, my missus is a very good hand in that line.
Wake up, Hepzibah, you're wanted.

[MOTHER *gets up.*

MOTHER

What is it? (FATHER *whispers.*) Oh, yes, of course.

LANDLADY

ery good of you, I'm sure. I wouldn't have had this
appen for the world. It all comes of being soft-hearted and
letting people in against one's better judgment. She's in the
stable over there, in the far corner—you'll know it by the
rown ox being there. Here, take this lantern.

JOSEPH

I'll carry the lantern to light the kind midwife.

LANDLADY

Indeed, my good man, you'll do no such thing. We don't
want any husbands hanging around. This is a woman's job.
Oh, dear! oh, dear! we shall none of us get any sleep to-
night. And I don't suppose for one moment you thought to
bring any proper swaddling-clothes with you.

JOSEPH

Yes, ma'am, indeed we came provided. The midwife will
find everything needful in our saddle-bags.

[MOTHER *disappears into stable. The family group settles down
again.*

LANDLADY

Well, that's a mercy. Bless me, what an upset!

Isp

257

JEWISH GENTLEMAN

Sweet mistress, do I gather we're expecting an addition to the company?

LANDLADY

Yes, indeed, sir, and I'm sure I'm very sorry for all this disturbance. It's this man's wife been taken with her pains, sir, and I really don't wonder, riding up all the way from Nazareth, and over these bad roads. It's a wicked thing, sir, isn't it, that decent folk should be jostled about and sent travelling willy-nilly, just because the Government takes it into its head to have a census.

1ST SHEPHERD

Ah! it's a shame, that it is.

JEWISH GENTLEMAN

Very trying indeed.

LANDLADY

We had to bed them down in the stable—along with the ox and the ass—and where we're to put the child, I really don' know. There isn't a cradle in the place. I had one, but I gave it to my daughter when she married. You'll have to use the manger, that's all. I'll go and find you some old sacking to line it with.

JOSEPH

God will reward you for all your kindness.

LANDLADY

Oh, well, it's all in the day's work, I suppose.
[*Exit* LANDLADY, *left* (*L.U.*).

1ST SHEPHERD

We'd better be getting along to the sheep now. Thank you kindly for the wine, sir. Good luck to you, Master Carpenter. May your good lady have a light childbirth.

2ND SHEPHERD

Ay, truly, and bring you a bonny baby to bless you.
258

JOSEPH

I thank you both from my heart.
[*Exeunt* SHEPHERDS, *right. Gate is noisily barred after them.*

JEWISH GENTLEMAN

Take courage, good man. These things happen every day.
It's sure to be all right. Here, I'll have a wager with you.
What odds will you lay me it's a boy?

JOSEPH

It would be robbing you, young sir. I know it will be a boy.

GREEK GENTLEMAN

Hark at him! Every father is certain it will be a boy.

JEWISH GENTLEMAN

And every Jewish mother is certain it will be the Messiah.
Isn't that so, carpenter?

JOSEPH

That is so.

JEWISH GENTLEMAN

And what are you going to call your Messiah when you get
him?

JOSEPH

His name shall be called Jesus; for he was so named of an
angel before he was conceived in the womb.

GREEK GENTLEMAN

Jesus? and what does that mean?

JEWISH GENTLEMAN

Oh, it's quite a common Jewish name. It means liberator,
a deliverer, a saviour—that sort of thing.

JOSEPH

He is to be called Jesus, because he shall save his people from
their sins. The angel said so to his mother.

259

He seems to have been a very communicative and explicit angel. What else did he say to your wife?

JOSEPH

He said, "The Holy Ghost shall come upon thee and the power of the most High shall overshadow thee; therefore that holy thing that shall be born of thee shall be called the Son of God."

GREEK GENTLEMAN

The son of a god. The expression seems very familiar. Our Greek mythology is full of such tales. Personally, I am an agnostic, but I am always willing to learn. Pray tell me, carpenter, did the god manifest himself in a shower of gold, as Jupiter did to Danae?

JEWISH GENTLEMAN

Be quiet, Philip. The God of Israel is nothing like your heathen deities. He is a spirit, and works, not after the flesh, but after the spirit. Besides, your own philosophers will tell you that your Olympic myths are themselves no more than symbols of the working of the spirit upon the flesh.

GREEK GENTLEMAN

So they say, indeed. But I believe the whole thing is nothing but a pack of fairy-tales.

JEWISH GENTLEMAN

I don't know, Philip. Sometimes I have wondered whether the Son of God, when He comes, might not fulfil your prophecies as well as ours. The hearts of all men have felt obscurely that God should somehow reveal Himself—walk as a man with men—I do not know. Does not Aeschylus speak somewhere of a Zeus that should know human suffering?

GREEK GENTLEMAN

Yes; in the *Eumenides*. But I thought your God was rather an exclusive deity, and never troubled Himself about any but His chosen people.

JEWISH GENTLEMAN

I know. But we insist very loudly that He is God of the whole earth. One would expect Him to take some interest in the outlying portions of His dominions. What do you say, carpenter?

[PHARISEE *gets up and comes across, right.*

JOSEPH

I do not know at all, sir. I am a plain ignorant man. I try only to do my duty and obey the word of God without asking too many questions. But here is a Pharisee coming across to us. He is no doubt learned in the Scriptures. Perhaps he can tell us.

JEWISH GENTLEMAN

Why, if it isn't my old friend Zadok. You seem to be restless, sir. I hope our talk hasn't disturbed you.

PHARISEE (*with more concession to common humanity than he has shown up till now*)

The snoring of Aaron ben Isaac the merchant is a curse more intolerable than all the ten plagues of Egypt. The bellowing of fat bulls of Bashan is silence by comparison.

GREEK GENTLEMAN

You have come in time to settle a theological argument. My friend here says that the God of Israel is lord of the whole earth, and in consequence the Messiah will be the saviour of the Gentiles as well as of the Jews. Do you support that opinion?

PHARISEE

Certainly not. It is blasphemous and ridiculous. He will set his foot upon the necks of the nations, and the heathen will be cast into outer darkness with wailing and gnashing of teeth. I hope you are answered. This inn seems to be very noisy to-night. I am going outside to try and get a little peace and quietness. (*He goes out by door to stair, left (L.U.), passing* LANDLADY, *who goes into stable (C.B.).*)

261

GREEK GENTLEMAN

What a very dogmatic person! It must be marvellous to feel so positive about everything. I never feel certain of anything.

JEWISH GENTLEMAN

That is the malady of you Greeks—you are blown about with every wind. Ours is to shut ourselves up tight in tradition and exclude every breath of fresh air. If only we could somehow wed the purity of our religion to the intellectual vigour of your philosophy! Well, never mind. Sing to us, Philip, and take our minds off our worries.

GREEK GENTLEMAN

Will it not disturb the company?

JEWISH GENTLEMAN

If they can sleep through each other's snoring, they can sleep through anything. Sing softly.

GREEK GENTLEMAN

Very well. (*Sings.*) "Golden Apollo——" (*He breaks off; to* JOSEPH, *politely.*) You will excuse my singing about Apollo. The words are of no importance, but the tune is pretty. (*Sings.*)

> Golden Apollo,
> > lord of the burning bow,
> Thy brow with sacred fillets bound
> And deathless laurel crowned;
> Singer and seer, whose splendour lights the sun,
> Sweet, terrible one!
> Swift as the swallow
> > thy searching arrows go.
> Then smite, lord, smite the heart of desire
> With thy celestial fire.

[*The* CENTURION *comes in, right, and speaks to the* SENTRY, *who wakes his companion to go on guard in his place. The* CENTURION *picks his way slowly across the stage, lending momentary attention to the song and going to stand by entrance, left.*

262

Master of vision
                    throned on the circling wheel,
Immortal born of mortal birth
That once didst visit earth
And as a servant humbly walk with men;
Turn, turn thee again,
Mighty physician
                    Whose hand can harm and heal,
And quench, lord, quench thy heavenly dart
For it doth rive the heart.

[MERCHANT *rolls over with a loud snore and snort; they all laugh.*

JEWISH GENTLEMAN

There is the comment of the commercial mind. You may ive his ears, but never his heart. Try again.

GREEK GENTLEMAN

There is no more to that song. Take the lute yourself.

JEWISH GENTLEMAN

I will sing you an old Jewish tale. (*Sings. After verse* 1, *the other two join in the chorus.*)

Adam and Eve stood under a tree,
                    (*Four rivers in Paradise*)
A sweet and comely sight to see
For they were fair as fair could be,
Adam and Eve beneath the tree
                    (*Paradise, Paradise,
                    God is all in all*).

And on the tree the branches grew
                    (*Four rivers in Paradise*)
Adorned with leaves of tender hue,
And they were fair as fair could be
And Adam and Eve stood under the tree
                    (*Paradise, Paradise,
                    God is all in all*).

[*An ox lows.*

263

JOSEPH

Listen! What was that?

GREEK GENTLEMAN

Only an ox lowing. Sing the next verse.

JEWISH GENTLEMAN (*sings*)
And on the branch a beauteous flower
   (*Four rivers in Paradise*)
Budded and bloomed from hour to hour,
The flower that on the branches grew
Adorned with leaves of tender hue,
And it was fair as fair could be
And Adam and Eve stood under the tree
      (*Paradise, Paradise,*
      God is all in all).

[CENTURION *goes out, left.*

And in that flower a fruit of gold
   (*Four rivers in Paradise*)
Lay hid within the petals' fold,
The petals of the beauteous flower
That budded and bloomed from hour to hour,
The flower that on the branches grew
Adorned with leaves of tender hue,
And it was fair as fair could be
And Adam and Eve stood under the tree
      (*Paradise, Paradise,*
      God is all in all).

[*An ass brays.*

JOSEPH

Listen again.

GREEK GENTLEMAN

It is only the braying of an ass. Go on. Never mind the
competition.

JEWISH GENTLEMAN (*sings*)
But Eve put forth her hand anon,
   (*Four rivers in Paradise*)

264

And bit that fruit unto the stone,
The strange, forbidden fruit of gold
That hid within the petals' fold,
The petals of the beauteous flower
That budded and bloomed from hour to hour,
The flower that on the branches grew
Adorned with leaves of tender hue,
And the tree withered down to the ground so bare,
And Adam and Eve stood naked there;
   (Paradise, Paradise,
   God is all in all).

But when the stone had fallen to earth,
   (Four rivers in Paradise)
It brought another tree to birth,
That tall and stately grew anon,
The tree that sprang from that fruit stone,
The strange forbidden fruit of gold
That hid within the petals' fold,
The petals of the beauteous flower
That budded and bloomed from hour to hour,
The flower that on the branches grew
Adorned with leaves of tender hue,
And it was fair as fair could be,
And Adam and Eve stood under the tree
   (Paradise, Paradise,
   God is all in all).

Greek Gentleman

Well sung, all! There is nothing like music to pass the time
away. How goes the night?
 [Centurion *reappears, left (L.U.).*

Joseph

It is the dark hour before the dawn. Hark!
 [*The cry of the Child is heard.*

Jewish Gentleman

That sounds more like it. Congratulations, carpenter.
 [*Enter* Landlady *from stable.*

GREEK GENTLEMAN

Here comes our good hostess, grinning from ear to ear. How about it, mistress? What's the news?

LANDLADY

Come hither, Master Carpenter, and see! Your good lady is lighter of a splendid son.

JOSEPH

Praise be to God!

JEWISH GENTLEMAN

I should have lost my bet. Congratulations again. So you were lending a hand after all, hostess? You seem very much pleased about it all.

[CENTURION *works his way down on left.*

LANDLADY

Well, sir, when it comes to babies, even innkeepers has their feelings. And the dear mother is such a sweet person—it's a pleasure to do anything for her. A beautiful child, and both doing fine. Come along, father, and have a look. You'll be that proud you won't know yourself.

JOSEPH

The dayspring from on high hath visited us.

[JOSEPH *follows the* LANDLADY *into the stable. The* CENTURION *crosses briskly left to right in front of the platform.*

JEWISH GENTLEMAN

Well, well—that bit of excitement's over. Hullo, Centurion, you still on the prowl? Have you heard the glad tidings? The carpenter's wife has presented him with a son.

CENTURION

The gods be favourable to the boy!

266

Greek Gentleman

And there you are! Kingdoms rise and fall, wars are waged, politicians wrangle, trade suffers, poor men starve, philosophers exchange insults and agree in nothing except that times are very evil and mankind rapidly going to the dogs. And yet, when one more soul is born into this highly unsatisfactory world, everybody conspires to be delighted.

Jewish Gentleman

And every time his parents are persuaded that he's going to turn out something wonderful, whereas, if they only knew it, he's destined, as likely as not, to finish up between two thieves on Crucifixion Hill. It all makes me feel very old and disillusioned.

Centurion

Don't you worry, sir. You'll get younger as you get older.

Greek Gentleman

At any rate, I suppose we can now hope for a little sleep.

[*Knocking at the gate.*

Oh, Hades!

Voice (*without*)

Now then, what the devil do you want?

Voices (*without*)

Let us in! Let us in! We have news, news, news!

Centurion

News? What does that mean? (*Shouting.*) Porter! open the gates! (*Softly.*) Might be a rebellion. You never know. Look alive there! (*He moves up behind the two* Gentlemen. *The* 1st Soldier *springs to his feet and joins the* 2nd Soldier *at the entrance. The* Landlady *enters from the stable, and the* Landlord *from the left.*)

Landlord

A rebellion? God forbid! (*Shouting.*) Keep the gate shut!

267

LANDLADY

Oh, please, dear Captain, don't let them in! We shall all be murdered in our beds.

CENTURION

If there is news, we must hear it. (*Shouting.*) Open the gate.

[*Gate unbarred.* SHEPHERDS *enter noisily; the* SOLDIERS *bar their way.*

Now, then, fellows! What's all this noise about? (*He signs to the* SOLDIERS *to let them through. They stand guard again behind the* SHEPHERDS.)

SHEPHERDS

Show us the Child that is born to-night! For we have seen a miracle.

MERCHANT (*waking suddenly*)

Hey! hey! Robbers! murder! help! Keep off! Let me go! I'm only a poor traveller! I've no money on me! Help! help!

[*Everybody wakes up. Tumult.*

[*Bring* SHEPHERDS *centre and bring up arena flood slowly to full during their story.*

CENTURION

Be quiet, there!

JEWISH GENTLEMAN

It's all right, Aaron ben Isaac. Nobody's being robbed.

LANDLORD

You've had nightmare.

GREEK GENTLEMAN

It's only some shepherds, who say they've seen a miracle.

MERCHANT

Miracle, indeed! I thought I was being murdered. This inn is disgracefully run. I shall complain to the authorities.

1ST SHEPHERD

Indeed, indeed, sirs, a wonderful thing is come to pass.

268

MERCHANT

Oh, go to Gehenna! (*He rolls himself up again and resolutely closes his ears.*)

CENTURION

Quick, fellows! Your story.

1ST SHEPHERD

Sir, we were in the fields, keeping watch over our sheep this night. And as I sat, looking eastward toward Beth-Shemesh, I beheld a great light, as though the sun were rising an hour before its time. And even while I looked, my son Matthew spoke to me, and said: Father, said he, what is this? Is the sun rising in the west? Then I turned myself about, and saw as it might be a ring of fire, all about the earth, and the hills and trees glowing like copper in the furnace.

2ND SHEPHERD

Ay, and the fire burnt up and up to the very pole, putting out the stars.

3RD SHEPHERD

And out of the fire, out of the sky—I cannot tell how, but so it was—there came an angel, great and terrible and shining. And we were sore afraid.

2ND SHEPHERD

Ay, that we were. But the sheep weren't afraid, not they. And that's a strange thing too.

1ST SHEPHERD

Then the angel spoke, clear as anything. "Be not afraid," he says, "for behold I bring you glad tidings of great joy which shall be to you and all people. For to you," he says, "is born this day in the City of David"—that's here, sir, you know—"a saviour, which is the Lord Messiah."

JEWISH GENTLEMAN

You hear, Philip? The Lord Christ. Zadok the Pharisee should be listening to this. What's become of him, by the way?

Greek Gentleman

Oh, he cast himself into outer darkness some time ago.

Jewish Gentleman

"Joy to all people"—you are sure the angel said, "to *all* people"?

1st Shepherd

Certain sure, sir. And we was just thinking as how there might be a many babes born in the city, and how was we to know, when he says, "This," he says, "shall be a sign to you. Ye shall find the babe wrapped in swaddling clothes and lying in a manger." So I looks at Sam, and Sam looks at me, and then, all of a sudden we sees the heavens open and thousands, ah! millions of angels, more than a man could count and singing that beautiful—Oh, sirs, listen! listen! There it be again—going right away over the roof, as clear as clear.

Angels' Choir (*distant*)

Glory to God in the highest and in earth peace, goodwill towards men.

[*Repeat chorus, crescendo and dying away again; dim arena flood to about quarter as song passes.*
Pause.

Centurion

Look here, I don't understand a word of all this.

1st Shepherd

Couldn't you hear nothing?

Centurion

Not a word.

Greek Gentleman

Nothing whatever.

Landlady

They've had too much to drink, that's what it is. You didn't ought to have given them that wine, sir.

JEWISH GENTLEMAN

I don't know. I fancy I did hear something—but it was very faint.

CENTURION

This is all a pack of nonsense. Go home, you shepherds, and let's hear no more of this. (*He turns to the* TRAVELLERS, *who are beginning to talk.*) Quiet, everybody. Get back to bed. Show's over.

[*The* TRAVELLERS *subside.*

1ST SHEPHERD

But may we not see the Child?

CENTURION (*after a brief hesitation*)

You may see him. But for his own sake, don't let your story come to King Herod's ears.

JEWISH GENTLEMAN

Come with me, shepherds. I'll show you the way. (*He leads the* SHEPHERDS *up centre.*) Listen! That is the Mother singing to her son.

[*The* CENTURION *sits on edge of platform, a menacing black shadow between the audience and the brazier.*

The curtain before the stable-door is withdrawn to disclose the HOLY FAMILY. (*Take out spot batten.*)

The GREEK GENTLEMAN (*lost in the shadows*) *has picked up the lute and accompanies* MARY's *song.*

MARY (*sings*)

Balow-la-lee, my little king,
　　What shall we do to comfort Thee?
Canst Thou for whom the angels sing
　　Content Thee with balow-la-lee,
　　　　　　Balow-la-lee?
Balow-la-lee, my royal child,
　　There's little we can give to Thee,
A manger-bed, a mother mild,
　　The ox and the ass for company,
　　　　　　Balow-la-lee.

[1ST *and* 3RD SHEPHERDS *on the side of stable-door;* 2ND SHEPHERD *and* JEWISH GENTLEMAN *on the other.*

1ST SHEPHERD

Your pardon, mistress. May we come in and see the Baby?

MARY

Surely, good shepherds. Come in and welcome.

JOSEPH

Tread softly. Do not wake Him.

MARY

He is already awake. Look, He is smiling at you.

1ST SHEPHERD

All hail, little king! See, here is a woollen fleece to be your royal robe.

2ND SHEPHERD

All hail, little king! Here is a shepherd's crook, to be your royal sceptre.

3RD SHEPHERD

All hail, little king! Here is a twist of flowering thorn to be your royal crown.

MARY

My Son shall remember you all when He comes into His kingdom.

JEWISH GENTLEMAN

Madam, I fear I have come unprovided. I was not expecting a revelation. But if ever your Son and I should meet again, I will have a rich gift ready for him.

MARY

Sir, we shall not forget your goodwill. What is your name?

JEWISH GENTLEMAN

I am Joseph of Arimathaea.

[*The* SHEPHERDS *play a pastoral tune upon their pipes, and the Tableaux Curtains close. From behind:* Landlord! landlord! . . . Up, you lazy slaves! will you lie there till noonday? . . . Saddle the asses and bring my reckoning. . . . Oh, dear, I never got a wink of sleep all night. . . . Has anybody seen my slippers? . . . Confound you, sir, you've knocked my flask over. . . . Git over, hoss—ah! would you then? . . . You have overcharged me by five pence. . . . Landlord! landlord! (*Fading away.*)

[*If gauzes are used, drop them on* NATIVITY TABLEAU, *blackout, and let voices fade off in the dark; then bring up spot on fore-stage as* KINGS *re-enter.*

BALTHAZAR

Caspar!

CASPAR

Melchior!

MELCHIOR

Balthazar!

CASPAR

I looked for wisdom—and behold! the wisdom of the innocent.

MELCHIOR

I looked for power—and behold! the power of the helpless.

BALTHAZAR

I looked for the manhood in God—and behold! a God made man.

CASPAR

Up and to horse! Make haste! for the Star has moved on before us
And the east is pale with the dawn. We must ride by faith.

273

MELCHIOR
Following the light invisible.

BALTHAZAR
Following the Star.

CURTAIN
(*or, if there is no front curtain, the Kings go out left*)

FINIS

THE JUST VENGEANCE

DRAMATIS PERSONÆ

(in order of their appearance)

THE RECORDER, *Angel of the City.*
GEORGE FOX, *the Quaker.*
THE AIRMAN.
EVE, *Mother of Mankind.*
MARY, *Mother of our Lord.*
ADAM, *the First Man.*
CAIN ⎫
ABEL ⎭ *his sons.*
PERSONA DEI.
GABRIEL, *Angel of the Annunciation.*
CAIAPHAS (*previously an Inquisitor*).
HEROD (*previously a Rich Man*).
PILATE (*previously a Judge*).
JUDAS (*previously an Informer*).
EXECUTIONER (*previously a Roman Soldier*).
AN ANGEL.
A SOLDIER.

PERSONS OF THE CHORUS

INFORMER (*afterwards* JUDAS).
INQUISITOR (*afterwards* CAIAPHAS).
RICH MAN (*afterwards* HEROD).
JUDGE (*afterwards* PILATE).
ROMAN SOLDIER (*afterwards* EXECUTIONER).

Men	*Women*
EARLY MARTYR.	PROTESTANT MARTYR.
SAMUEL JOHNSON.	HUNCHBACK.
LUNATIC.	HARLOT.
POTTERY WORKER.	WIFE.
LABOURER.	WIDOW.
UNEMPLOYED MAN.	MOTHER.
SAILOR.	SLAVEY.
BEGGAR.	PAUPER.
CHIMNEY-SWEEP'S BOY.	CHILD.

The whole action of the play takes place in the moment of the
AIRMAN'S *death.*

The Just Vengeance was originally performed in Lichfield Cathedral on the occasion of its 750th Anniversary Festival, June 15th–26th, 1946, with the following cast.

THE RECORDER, Angel of the City	SEYMOUR GREEN
GEORGE FOX, the Quaker	FRANK NAPIER
THE AIRMAN	GORDON DAVIES
EVE, Mother of Mankind	ROWENA ROBINSON
MARY, Mother of Our Lord	DOROTHY BOND
ADAM, the First Man	PERCY CARTWRIGHT
CAIN ⎫ his sons	MICHAEL INGHAM
ABEL ⎭	PETER BAYLISS
PERSONA DEI	RAF DE LA TORRE
GABRIEL, Angel of the Annunciation	BARRY BRIGG
AN ANGEL	DONALD HARPER
A SOLDIER	FREDERICK LAWRENCE

PERSONS OF THE CHORUS

AN INFORMER (afterwards JUDAS)	DENNIS RUDDER
AN INQUISITOR (afterwards CAIAPHAS)	JOHN HARRIS
A RICH MAN (afterwards HEROD)	CHARLES ROFE
A JUDGE (afterwards PILATE)	PAUL RICE
A ROMAN SOLDIER (afterwards EXECUTIONER) ⎱	WALTER PULLEN
EARLY MARTYR	HENRY ROBINSON
PROTESTANT MARTYR	JOYCE CRESWELL
SAMUEL JOHNSON	CHAPMAN DAVIES
HUNCHBACK	KAY HUDSON
LUNATIC	LESLIE PARKES
HARLOT	MARY BLACKBURN
POTTERY WORKER	ALBERT HARRISON
WIFE	MARGARET SALT
LABOURER	GEORGE COATON
WIDOW	JESSICA BASSETT
UNEMPLOYED MAN	MALDWYN WORMAN
MOTHER	JANE CARR
SAILOR	MARCUS WHICHELOW
SLAVEY	DOREEN EDGAR
BEGGAR	ALBERT HOUGHTON
PAUPER	BARBARA PRATLEY
CHIMNEY-SWEEP'S BOY	ANDREW SALT
CHILD	MARGARET HODGKINS

Producer: FRANK NAPIER

The music specially composed by ANTONY HOPKINS

INTRODUCTION

THIS PLAY IS FOUNDED upon two passages, one from *The Divine Comedy* and the other from (I think) Thomas à Kempis, although I have unhappily mislaid the reference. They are complementary, and together form an almost complete statement of Atonement theology, and of the coinherence of Christ in His mystical body, the Church.

The first, which gives its title to the play, is in the seventh canto of the *Paradiso*, where Beatrice interprets the saying of Justinian:

> "My infallible intuition tells me that you are wondering *how the just vengeance justly was avenged*. . . . Because he would not endure, for his own good, the rein set upon his will, the man who was never born (Adam), in condemning himself, condemned all his offspring; wherefore the human race lay sick for many an age in great error, until it pleased the Word of God to descend to earth, where, by the sole act of His eternal love, He took that nature which had gone astray from its Maker, and joined it to Himself in His own person. . . .
>
> "As for the penalty, then, inflicted by the Cross, if it be measured by the nature thus put on, never did any bite so justly; and in like manner, never was any so monstrously unjust if we look to the Person who suffered it, by whom that nature was assumed."
>
> (*Para.* VII. 19. 899.)

This, with its affirmation of the true God-Manhood, presents the act of Atonement from God's side. The second, affirming the coinherence, presents the response from Man's side: "Whoso will carry the Cross, the Cross shall carry him," and should be taken in conjunction with Rom. viii. 22, "the whole creation groaneth and travaileth in pain together," and Col. i. 24: "Who now rejoice in my sufferings for you and fill up that which remaineth of the afflictions of Christ in my flesh for His body's sake, which is the church."

279

In form, the drama is a miracle-play of Man's insufficiency and God's redemptive act, set against the background of contemporary crisis. The whole action takes place in the moment of the death of an Airman shot down during the late war. In that moment, his spirit finds itself drawn into the fellowship of his native city of Lichfield; there, being shown in an image the meaning of the Atonement, he accepts the Cross, and passes, in that act of choice, from the image to the reality.

Being concerned as it is with the eternal witness of the Church to the central doctrine of the Incarnation, the play contains no "original thought about . . ." and no "new interpretation of . . ." anything whatever. "Originality" in such matters is out of place: the thought is that of the Church and the interpretation that of her doctors and confessors. Readers will recognise echoes from many other writers, ranging from the Apostles and canonised saints to Charles Williams and T. S. Eliot, and Dantists in particular will take pleasure in picking out and attributing to their rightful owner the lines and images from the *Comedy* which occur at frequent intervals throughout. It is, however, only right that I should make personal apology and acknowledgement to the greatest of Christian poets for having translated and lifted bodily the first six lines of the hymn *Vergine Madre* (*Para.* XXXIII. 1–6).

The curious story of George Fox's vision in the streets of Lichfield is narrated in his *Journal* for 1651.

I should perhaps add a reminder that the verse, as well as the whole architecture, of *The Just Vengeance*, is constructed for performance in a cathedral, rather than for reading in the study, and that the choruses assigned to the Choir were written for music. The circumstances called for a stylised presentation, moving in what may be called large blocks of action rather than in the swift to-and-fro of dialogue; the emphasising of important affirmations by repetitions; and a rhythm enabling the actor's voice to overcome those acoustical difficulties which, in a large ecclesiastical building, no arrangement of microphones can wholly eliminate.

RECORDER

You, citizens of Lichfield, here at home,
And you that out of other cities come,
Or towns, or villages both great and small,
To keep with us our glad high festival,
Be welcome to this House of God, which hears
Now the third quarter of a thousand years
Strike on the clock of history. May she stand
To tell her story in this English land
Until the fingers of slow time come round
To their last moment, and the trumpets sound!
Alas! alas! the hardest stones decay,
Man in his rage may blast the walls away
And make destruction where he once gave glory;
But neither sin nor time can kill that story—
That fact—of man's gread need, and God's great pity
Which we show here in terms of our own city,

[*Here the* CHORUS *enters.*

Playing all parts as best we may. But yet
We, who are actors, bid you not forget
That all these images on which you look
Are but as pictures painted in a book—
No more like that they bid you think upon
Than this small yellow disc is like the sun;
Though, in a picture, this might stand for that,
And the great sun take no offence thereat.
See now, the citizens, in proper order
Displayed from first to last, with me, Recorder
And Angel of the City, at their head,
Wait here to welcome one who is newly dead.
To him the ageless tale shall all be shown,
And through his eyes you'll see, as through your own.

[*Enter* GEORGE FOX, *from the back of the church, having his
shoes in his hand and a Bible under his arm.*

281

Fox

Woe to the bloody city of Lichfield! Woe to the bloody city
of Lichfield!

[*He goes about the church.*

Choir (*whispering*)

Lichfield! Lichfield!
Whisper the name of the city through the oblivion;
Let the name stir like the scurry of mice in the wainscot,
In the tapestries, under the floorboards; whisper the name
In the patter of dead leaves on the window; whisper
Among dry bones in the valley of Jehoshaphat;
Lichfield! Lichfield! whisper the name of the city.

Fox

Woe to the bloody city of Lichfield! Woe to the bloody city

Choir (*a little louder*)

The city! the city! speak the name of the city!
The articulated name in the confusion of syllables;
Speak the coherence, speak the squalors and splendours,
Speak the remembered streets, the familiar houses,
Speak the skyline and the Cathedral spires,
Speak order, speak unity, speak the name of the city.

Fox

Woe to the bloody city of Lichfield! Woe to the bloody city!

Choir (*louder*)

Call the city! call home the blood of the city!
Call the blood out of the alien shadows!
The sorrow with the kindred, the guilt with the derivation,
The flesh and the blood, the bread and the wine of the city.

Fox

Woe to the bloody city of Lichfield!
282

CHOIR (*loud*)

Lichfield! Lichfield! cry the name of the city!
Cry in the dark wood and under the iron lintel;
Cry the sweat, cry the blood, cry over the banners!
Cry across the rivers the name of the city of Lichfield!
(*Softly.*) Listen!

[*In the sudden pause the feet of the* AIRMAN *are heard running from a great distance.* FOX *sits down and begins composedly putting on his shoes.*

CHOIR (*resuming quietly*)

The feet of the young man, the feet of the fallen,
The feet of the forgetful running back to remembrance,
The feet of the future hurrying home to the past
In the sudden cessation of time, the eternity of the city.

ONE VOICE

"For I am a citizen of no mean city."

CHOIR (*loudly*)

Proclaim

Tarsus! Proclaim the citizenship of Rome,
Jerusalem, Athens, Byzantium, London, Lichfield!
Proclaim the Republic! proclaim the Empire! proclaim the
    name of the city!

[*The* AIRMAN *has run up the aisle and stumbles panting on to the steps of the stage.* FOX *helps him up.*

FOX

Friend, thou art welcome. Pray compose thyself:
Thou art within the city.

AIRMAN

In Lichfield?

FOX

Ay,

For thee it is Lichfield.

AIRMAN

                       The plane took a long time falling;
The fire was everywhere. I hope the others baled out;
I never saw them after I—lost touch.
The trees went past so quickly, catching me up
From behind, and the darkness roared so. The worst of it
Was to have no sense of direction. One comes to rely
On navigation. If one knows where one is going
It is not so bad. But those huge vegetable shapes,
And the long processions under meaningless ensigns,
And the noise without speech—it was a kind of terror
I had not experienced; though I was always terrified
On operational flights—but that was different;
One belonged to something; the thing that got me down
Was the sense of belonging nowhere. It went on for ages.
And then, you know, I heard a sound that I recognised;
Somewhere, very far off, a voice said "Lichfield"
Quite clearly; the darkness suddenly focused itself
And was going somewhere, like an enormous tunnel
With the name, like light, at the end of it. So I ran
Towards the name—there was only that to run to—
And found myself at last in my own city.

FOX

Friend, it is very well that thou hadst a concernment
For this or for that; they that are concerned for nothing
Do not come back to this city or any other.

AIRMAN

Well, I am here. What am I supposed to do?
The voice that called me seemed to threaten the city;
I thought about bombing, of course; but the lights are up
And the houses standing—only the people are strange,
As though they were ghosts and could not speak to me;
You are the only person whose voice I can hear—
Was it you that called in the forest?

FOX

                       The word of the Lord
Came to me at the entering in of the city,

Bidding me cry. So I put off my shoes,
For the word of the Lord was like a fire in me,
And I went up and down the streets, crying aloud:
"Woe to the bloody city of Lichfield!"

AIRMAN

Yes,
That is what I heard.

Fox

As it was given to me
So I cried, and I cried in the market-place
And to and fro in the several parts of it,
And no one laid hands on me. And while I cried
"Woe to the bloody city," I seemed to see
A channel of blood running along the streets,
And the market-place appeared like a pool of blood.
Was that not strange?

AIRMAN

Was it so very strange?

Fox

And all that time, not one of these people here
Stayed me, or asked what I said. They sat unmoved,
Or went about their business, no way astonished;
Was that not strange?

AIRMAN

Why should they be astonished?
They have seen and heard too much; blood in the headlines,
Blood in the bodiless voice from the loud-speaker,
Blood in the siren-song and the drone of the bombers,
In eye-witness stories and columns of statistics;
They have hardened their hearts so that they may not break,
Deafened their ears, lest thought should split the brain;
The time has gone by when you could startle people
With words like that—they have grown used to numbering
Death by the million.

Fox

Yet every man dies once,
Once, and no more. A universe is extinguished

Every time a soul goes out of it—
The same universe, in a million deaths or one.
The one is the important figure; the rest are ciphers.
The single death which each endures by himself
Is never multiplied, though it is reckoned in millions;
Nor diminished by any division, though a million men
Were summed in a single man dying once for all;
That is the final irreducible integer
Of each man's reckoning. We die into something
As we are born into something; but the act of death,
Like the act of being born, is an individual matter,
As thou hast discovered.

AIRMAN

As *I* have discovered?

FOX

Thou.

AIRMAN

I see. You mean I have had it. Well, I can take it—
(*Uncertainly*) I suppose. What next? Where do we go from
    here?
Who are you, by the way?

FOX

That which is seen to thee
Is the figure of one who one day came to Lichfield—
George Fox the Quaker.

AIRMAN

The Quaker? (*Embarrassed*) I died fighting.
You wouldn't approve of that.

FOX

We are peaceable people.
When a man smote me I turned the other cheek;
He was abashed.

286

Airman

Was he? it takes more than that
To abash some people.

Fox

We had a most precious meeting,
And many souls were turned to the Lord. I heard
Afterwards, that the fellow who smote me died
In poverty, of an ugly disease. Vengeance
Belongs to the Lord; my hands were guiltless towards him.

Airman

That pleases you? If I hated a man like that——

Fox

I did not hate him.

Airman

Have it your own way;
But if I were so pleased that something beastly had happened
To a man, because of something he did to me,
I almost think I'd rather feel guilty about it.

Chorus (*swaying and whispering*)

Guilty, guilty, whisper the guilt of the city.

Airman

I mean, if there is a God—I suppose you know
Whether there is or not——

Fox

Thou shalt know too.

Airman

Why should He do my dirty work for me?
Why should my hands be cleaner than other people's?
I can't explain what I mean, but it doesn't seem fair.
(*Defensively*) I know what you're going to tell me: it was
a judgment;
I don't care; I don't like it.

I was doing the Lord's work;
When he smote *me*, the blow fell upon Christ
As such blows do; and the judgment overtook him.

AIRMAN

Perhaps he thought he was doing the Lord's work too.
The thing's a muddle; that's what you righteous people
Never seem able to see. We try to do right
And someone is hurt—very likely the wrong person;
And if we do wrong, or even if we do nothing,
It comes to the same in the end. We drop a bomb
And condemn a thousand people to sudden death,
The guiltless along with the guilty. Or we refuse
To drop a bomb, and condemn a thousand people
To a lingering death in a concentration camp
As surely as if we had set our hands to the warrant.
Should we have waited for judgment? We did wait,
And innocent people died. *We* are the judgment.
We have no choice between killing and not killing;
We can only choose which set of people to kill—
And even at that, the choice is made for us;
I did not choose; perhaps I ought to have chosen?
I was told to go and I went. I killed; I was killed.
Did any of us deserve it? I don't know.
You can stand there and say your hands are clean;
I cannot. But you were lucky. You could be meek
And go to prison, and not take others with you.
We who are tied in this damnable cat's cradle
Where there is no choice except between bloody alternatives
Have a fraternity which you know nothing about.

CHORUS

Fraternity, fraternity, the fraternity of the city.

AIRMAN (*violently*)

Why did I have to meet *you*? Where are my brothers
Who can lay grimy hand to hand with me
Without dread of contamination? fellow victims
And fellow criminals in the exchange of blood?

Exchange, exchange, in the market-place of the city.

Fox (*mildly*)

Friend, I fear me thou art a man of blood,
And an ignorant man; there is no fraternity
And no exchange, except in the blood of Christ—
But howsoever, thou hast aroused the city.
  [Fox *retires and sits reading his Bible.*

RECORDER

Son of the city, called home by the city,
You have called up the city in the power of exchange.
Look! the city holds out its hands to you.
Whose will you take?

CHORUS (*dispersedly*)

Will you take mine? or mine?
The hand of the victim? the hand of the executioner?
The child's hand? the traitor's hand? the rich? the poor? the
    oppressor?
Scavenger? murderer? scholar? tinker? tailor?
Soldier? sailor? apothecary? plough-boy? thief?
How do you understand the bond of the city?
Child of the city, what do you know of the city?

EARLY MARTYR

You that died, did you die in our brotherhood?
I was a martyr for Christ. Diocletian
Was Emperor. There was a slaying of Christians in Lich-
    field.
Our blood ran down the streets and ways of the city,
And the market-place appeared like a pool of blood.
I know what I died for. Do you know what you died for?

ROMAN

You that killed, did you kill in our brotherhood?
I was a Roman under Diocletian;

They told me, those who would not worship the Emperor
Betrayed the city; they told me to slay and I slew.
I know what I killed for; do you know what you killed for?

Protestant Martyr

They burnt me at the stake for the blessed Gospel
And the Protestant faith——

Inquisitor

You died a heretic.

Protestant

How could I tell? I was no learned doctor—
Only a woman, who had learned to love
Our Lord quite simply in His holy Book:
They tangled me in my talk——

Inquisitor

Away with her!

Labourer

Why grumble, lady? At least you died for *something*—
I never stole the sheep they hanged me for;
D'ye call that justice?

Informer

I was an informer,
Running with the hare and hunting with the hounds—
I stole, and sold my fellow thieves; the law
Needs men like me. Are you for law and order?

Judge

There must be order: we must keep the peace—
Sometimes with dirty tools; and if sometimes
The wrong man's framed, or if a stupid jury
Brings in a senseless verdict, can the judge
Do anything but shrug, and wash his hands?

Consider the case of our Lord Jesus Christ—
Judas betrayed Him, Caiaphas accused Him,
Pilate summed up in His favour—the jury hanged Him.
If you are looking for your fellow murderers
You will find more of them in the city streets
Than on the judge's bench.

POTTER

Who murdered me?
I worked here in the potteries, and the work
Poisoned and killed me. All the choice I had
Was, work and die; or, die for lack of bread.
The city is served so.

UNEMPLOYED MAN

I had no work;
If I'd died fighting in the first world-war
A grateful city would have carved my name
Upon a monument—but for the living
The city had no use.

RICH MAN

Why blame the city?
Everything has its price; if flesh and blood
Are cheap, that is the way of things.

HARLOT

My flesh
Was bought and sold in the market of the city,
Which spat on what it purchased. They who fouled me
Scorned me for being foul, and their sleek wives
Drew back their skirts from me.

WIFE

I was a wife,
Hard-working, decent; and my husband said:
"Be still, be modest, do not paint your face.
Leave that to harlots—you're a married woman."
So I obeyed my husband, and he sneered
At his pale wife, and gave himself to harlots.

[*She falls weeping into the* HARLOT's *arms.*

WIDOW (*to* WIFE)

At least you had your husband; death took mine
And left me childless; and I saw the city
One graveyard.

MOTHER (*to* WIDOW)

Death was merciful to you;
My children lived to break their mother's heart.

CHILD

I was a child whom no one ever wanted.
I don't know what I did to offend the city
That men should send me crawling through black chimneys
While other little boys were playing ball.
Do *you* know, mister?

HUNCHBACK

Look! I was a woman,
And I was ugly. No one gave me children.
Was it my fault that they were never born,
Young man? And what have you to do with me?

PAUPER

Were you a pauper?

SAILOR

Did they feed you on weevils?

SLAVEY

Did you sleep in a basement with black beetles? Spend your
    youth
With scuttles and slop-pails?

LUNATIC

Were you a lunatic?
Afraid of the world? of yourself? Were you mad? mad? mad?

[*The* AIRMAN'S *nerves give way under this assault, and he
retreats into the arms of* DR. JOHNSON.

JOHNSON

My name was Samuel Johnson; I was learned,
Poor and industrious; and God thought it well
To visit me with a scrofulous disease
And dim my vision. Yet I loved the city,
And was a merry old dog for all my trouble,
Save that sudden ugly melancholy
Took me at times, and terror of the judgment.
And most of us are so—our learning blind,
Our industry made poor, our souls half-sick,
Our little laughter mixed with fearfulness;
The city is made of such. What did you think?
Sir, what cord was it drew you back to the city?
Fancy or fact? Was it a rope of sand
Or a steel hawser? Why do you seek the city?

AIRMAN

What can I say to you? Sir, there have been times
When there seemed to be a happy and high meaning
In the mere pattern of the city's life; women
Shopping with string-bags, while the ends of the earth
Waited upon them; boys set free from school
Under the drifted gold horse-chestnut leaves
Hunting for conkers; elderly men in pubs
Exchanging slow speech over a pint of ale;
Girls' laughter; the double ebb and flow of the tide
Daily through the factory gates; long lines of streets
Silently going somewhere, made for a purpose;
Houses, like safes, with locked-up secrets in them;
The noise of a crowd, mysteriously unanimous,
Like a band, each instrument playing its own tune
To make one music; drays and buses and cars
Moving and stopping for lights or a raised hand;
Pealing of bells; clocks ticking and striking;
Movement of feet and wheels on the surface of things,
Carried triumphant on the hidden intricacy
Of pipes, sewers, cables—the dark functioning
Of distribution. There have been times, I say,
When all this seemed like a miracle and a glory;

And then, like the switching-off of a light—nothing;
Only a crawling of maggots among carrion
In a muddle of petty squalors. If one could find,
Somehow, a way to make the glory endure!
But it only comes by moments. When my plane
Dropped, that was one of the moments. I saw the city
Shine to me. That was the last thing I saw.

RECORDER

Son, you have come to the place of the images,
As all men come, whose eyes are not shut fast
Against redemption, drawn to the moment of glory
By that god-bearing image, whatever it was,
That carried the glory for them; some, most happy,
Leaping directly to the unveiled presence
Of Him that is Himself both image and glory;
Some indirectly—this in a woman's eyes,
That in a friend's hand or a poet's voice
Knowing the eternal moment—and you, in the city.
Wherefore you must make your answer now to the city,
And to me, that am the Recorder of the city.

AIRMAN

I'm sorry—I don't quite get you.

RECORDER

                              What is your claim
To citizenship?

AIRMAN (*uncertainly*)

                    I was born here. . . . Oh, do you mean,
What have I done for the place? Not much, I'm afraid;
I was killed too soon. I meant to do lots of things—
Set up in business, marry and settle down,
And start a family; take an active interest
In education and politics; work for improvements
In the economic system; I rather thought
Of writing a book one day; but I had no time,
Except to be killed—and kill. Perhaps that counts
As service? The city should know—that seemed to be
The only thing it wanted of me or anyone.

294

What matters here is not so much what you did
As why you did it: the choice behind the action;
The deed is the letter; what you believe is the spirit.
Except a man believe rightly he cannot be saved,
Not even by suffering. Can you recite your creed?

AIRMAN (*mechanically*)

I believe in God . . .

CHORUS (*picking him up and carrying him along with it*)
. . . the Father Almighty, Maker of Heaven and earth; and
in Jesus Christ . . .

AIRMAN

No! no! no! What made me start off like that?
I reacted automatically to the word "creed"—
My personal creed is something totally different.

RECORDER

What is speaking in you is the voice of the city,
The Church and household of Christ, your people and
    country
From which you derive. Did you think you were unbegotten?
Unfranchised? With no community and no past?
Out of the darkness of your unconscious memory
The stones of the city are crying out. Go on.

AIRMAN (*loudly, and with determination*)

I believe . . .

CHORUS (*overriding him*)

. . . in Jesus Christ His only Son our Lord; who was conceived by the Holy Ghost, born of the Virgin Mary, suffered
under Pontius Pilate . . .

AIRMAN (*desperately*)

Stop it, I tell you!
That is exactly what I do *not* believe in—
I do not believe in all this suffering—
I do not see the sense of a suffering God—
Why should anyone suffer?

RECORDER (*drily*)

Why indeed?

Go on.

AIRMAN (*angrily*)

We have seen too many people crucified. . . .

CHORUS

. . . crucified, dead, and buried; He descended into Hell. The third day He rose again from the dead; He ascended into Heaven; from thence He shall come to judge the quick and the dead. . . .

AIRMAN

Judgment! wait—there is something I want to believe—
They say there is no such thing as Heaven or Hell,
Or anything after death; I do not know;
It seems I am dead, and therefore there must be something,
Somehow. That being so, I have this to say:
That if there is going to be judgment, I want justice.

RECORDER

You shall have it—more, perhaps, than you bargain for;
Always supposing, when it comes to the point,
You know justice when you see it, or are prepared
To accept it when you know it. Now go on.

AIRMAN

I believe . . .

CHORUS

. . . in the Holy Ghost, the holy Catholic Church, the communion of Saints, the forgiveness of sins, the resurrection of the body and the life everlasting.

AIRMAN

I do not understand a word of all that.

RECORDER

Leave the understanding to the Holy Ghost,
The holy Catholic Church and communion of saints,

296

So far as they are in you, and you in them.
Now that the city and Church have confessed in you
What they believe, and your memory still believes,
Tell me what it is you think you believe.

AIRMAN

I believe in man, and in the hope of the future,
The steady growth of knowledge and power over things,
The equality of all labouring for the community,
And a just world where everyone will be happy.

RECORDER

Child, that is well; but when you speak of equality,
Happiness, justice—who will be equal and happy?
Who shall have justice done them?

AIRMAN

Everybody.

RECORDER

Do you mean these?

CHORUS

Who will give justice to us?
Where is our happiness? Where is our equality
With the aristocrats of the future, borne on the backs
Of the toiling proletariat of the past?

AIRMAN

The past is dead. We must turn our backs on it,
Forget it, bury it. I denounce the past.
The past has turned the world to a living hell.
We must build for the future.

RECORDER

You are the dead and the past.
Must *you* be forgotten?

CHORUS

Must you be forgotten with us?

RECORDER

Must *you* be denounced?

CHORUS

Denounced with us and the city?

AIRMAN

No! that's not justice! I believed in the future—
I fought and died for the future.

CHORUS

Did we not die?
You were our future; did we not die for you? Speak!
What did you do with the future we fought and died for?
Was your world just? Was your world happy?

AIRMAN

No;
But what could I do? I had no time; I was killed;
It was not my fault, but the fault of the old people.

CHORUS (*generation after generation, from the most recent
to the earliest*)

It was not our fault, but the fault of the old people.

AIRMAN

You accuse one another—you try to shift the burden
Back to the beginning, as though you were not responsible,
As though there were something wrong with Man himself,
I will not believe it. The future man shall be good,
Happy and free, walking the world in justice;
Else I have died for nothing. Why was I killed?
I died for your sins—you are my murderers,
Sacrificing me as a victim without choice.
I have no part in you.

CHORUS (*going away*)

You have no part in us—
No part in the dead, no part in the living city.

AIRMAN

What have I done? I have turned them back to ghosts—
The phantom faces with the unseeing eyes;
I did not mean what I said—oh! do not leave me!
Do not send me back to the dark forest!

RECORDER

You have renounced the past—will you have the future?
Shall we call up the voice of the undead future?

AIRMAN

Call up the future? Yes; I believe in the future,
The happy and grateful future. No; I dare not!
I could not bear it if I were to hear them say:
"It was not our fault, but the fault of the old people."
(*To the* CHORUS) Forgive me, I was wrong: we are victims
     together
Or guilty together; if we have betrayed the future
We will share the blame—and if we have died for the future
Let us believe the future is worth our dying.
But I want to know why we have no choice;
I want to know why there is no justice,
And why it is that everything we do
Turns to a horror we never contemplated;
I want to know what it is all about,
And whether the thing makes sense. I have lived; I have
     died;
I have a right to know.

RECORDER
What says the city
To the son of the city?

JOHNSON
Sir, it appears to us
Th.. .his young man is fundamentally sound;
..nough sadly ignorant and confused in mind,
Nevertheless, he recognises the city,
And the city him.

By his and our goodwill;
Wherefore, that he may fully understand
Where, how and why his good will forged his choice,
Sir, we require you in the name of the city,
Show him the Images.

RECORDER

With all my heart;
Let you and you and you and you and you
(*indicating the* ROMAN, INQUISITOR, INFORMER, JUDGE *and*
     RICH MAN, *who go off*)
Go play your chosen parts in that great play
Wherein the princes of this world are judged
By Him they judge, and you who are the jury
Stand with the Prisoner in the dock and hear
Your sentence on yourselves; and we will show you
The image of man who was made in the image of God;
And God in the image of man; and the image of justice.

CHOIR

Celebrate man, exalted in the image of man,
Strongest and weakest of things! His life is a span,
A breath—death
Creeps to him through a filter. He measures the stars,
He tames the lion, humbles the unicorn, yokes
The lightning; earth shakes with his strokes.
He makes and mars; plenty is his postillion
And famine fawns at his heels; his wheels
Extend dominion; fear is his running footman.
His sculptured monuments outlast the bones
That built them, and his songs outlast their stones;
He heals what first he wounded; he wounds what he heals.
Call upon man in the time of trouble—man
Shall hear. Cry in his ear for fear.
"Save, Lord, we perish!" Cry through the hurricane,
And you shall see and hear
What help there is in the might and the image of man.

300

[The Upper Stage opens, disclosing Eve *and* Mary *with the Tree of Knowledge.* Eve *comes forward;* Mary *remains working at a piece of scarlet cloth.*

Eve

What do you want? You must not disturb Adam.
He is busy inventing something—the old task,
Trying to undo the curse. My sons are out,
Cain in the vineyard, Abel tending the sheep.
I am here alone with one of my young daughters
Whose work it is to weave the purple and scarlet
For the veil of the Temple. What can I do for you?
I am Eve, the Mother of all mankind,
And all my children are very welcome to me.

Recorder

Ancestral Eve, this latest of your sons,
Newly arrived into the Place of the Images,
Desires to look on the Image of the First Men
Who were made in the Image of God; because it seems
That no man can choose justice, but is bound
Either to suffer or to deal unjustly,
Or both at once, whatever he attempts;
And each one lays the burden of guilt and grief
On the men before him, back to the very beginning
As though Man's very nature were to blame—
And yet he says that he believes in Man.

Eve

O my poor child, you must not believe in us—
It is too true that guilt is bred in you,
Not to be bred out but by being reborn
To a new knowledge by a Heavenly Word,
As we, alas! were terribly reborn
To a new knowledge by the word of the serpent.

Airman

What knowledge, Mother? Is not knowledge good?

Eve

Knowledge of good is good; and that we had.

AIRMAN

Knowledge, they say, is power; is that not good?

EVE

Power to know good is good; and that we had.

AIRMAN

How can one know good without knowing evil?
We are not animals, but thinking men;
It is our privilege to know good and evil
And choose the good, or so it seems to me,
And so grow nearer to the image of God.

EVE

O child, O child, that was the serpent's word—
(How well he has learnt his lesson! how the poison
Runs in the blood!) "Ye shall become as gods
Knowing both good and evil." Then the trap
Shut down. We had forgotten we were creatures.
We could not know as God knows, by pure knowledge,
Only as men know, by experience.
What we desired in knowing good and evil
Was simply the experience of evil:
We chose it and we had it.

AIRMAN

All the same,
If there is evil, it is well to know it.

EVE

There was none, till we chose to know it so
What we knew then was what we had always known—
There was nothing else to know; only the world
That God had made and seen to be very good.
But after we had eaten the sad fruit
We knew it by experience differently.
We knew doing and making as labour and sorrow,
Love as possession and lust and jealousy,

302

Difference as hatred, blessed luck as envy,
The holy and glorious flesh as living carrion,
And death had a new countenance; we knew it
As—death. Hush! hush! we must not speak such words
Nakedly. When we had eaten we knew we were naked,
And made aprons for that and a good many other things.
Death—and birth; it was only after the Fall
That I conceived and brought forth Abel and Cain:
Both of them are my sons—but Cain is the first-born.

CHOIR

Lo, now, the image of the works and ways of Adam!
Knowledge growing as the tree grows in the garden—
Knowledge for Cain, and knowledge also for Abel,
Knowledge for Abel and Cain; but Cain is the first-born.

Lo, now, the riches of the knowledge of Adam!
Riches running as the river runs from the well-spring—
Riches for Cain, and riches also for Abel,
Riches for Abel and Cain; but Cain is the first-born.

Lo, now, the power of the riches of Adam!
Power that gathers as the clouds gather in the mountains—
Power for Cain, and power also for Abel,
Power for Abel and Cain; but Cain is the first-born.

[*Enter* ADAM *carrying an axe.*

ADAM

Cain! Abel! Where are those boys? Mary, my dear,
Run to the fields and fetch your elder brothers;
I have something here to show them. Where's your mother?

[*Exit* MARY *above.*

EVE

Husband!

ADAM

Oh, there you are! Well now, this time
I think you'll say I've really earned my dinner;
Give me a kiss—call me your clever Adam,

Who toils all day to do away with toil
And now and then makes progress. . . . What? What's that?
Company? Why, the more the merrier!
Children, applaud your father's new invention,
Which will go far to circumvent the curse
And usher in the new progressive age
Of leisure and prosperity.

[*Re-enter* MARY *with* CAIN *and* ABEL, *and sits down on the steps with her work.*

Ah, Cain!
Come here, my boy. Here, Abel—look at this;
Is that, or is it not, a useful tool?

[*He hands the axe to* CAIN.

CAIN (*appreciatively*)
Nice, very nice.

[*He hands it to* ABEL.

EVE
What do you call it, Adam?

ADAM (*irritably*)
What can it matter what the thing is *called*?
How like a woman!

ABEL
Cheer up, Mother dear—
Just call it marvellous.

ADAM (*with offended dignity*)
It is called an axe.

EVE
Why axe?

ADAM
Because I choose to call it so.
Of course, you do not ask me what it *does*,
Which is what really matters.

EVE (*meekly*)
> What does it do?

ADAM

Increase the power of a man's arm tenfold.
[*He settles down to deliver a lecture.*
You see, the curse laid on the human race
Is labour—without hard, back-breaking labour,
And sweat and toil that leave no time for pleasure
We make no progress. Progress, as you know,
When one gets down to it, is just the task
Of shifting things about from place to place
Quicker and quicker, so as to get more
Of everything at once. (*To* CAIN) If you could reap
And bind and thrash and stack a field of corn
All in one day, instead of many days,
That would be progress. (*To* ABEL) Or if you could go
By some swift engine to your furthest field
And shear your sheep and bring the fleece back here
Within an hour or two, you'd call that progress.
[*Applause.*
The day will come for men to do such things,
By multiplying power in such a way
That one man's hand may do the work of many.
This axe, then, is an instrument of power:
It works upon the principle of the lever.

EVE

What's that?

ADAM

> My dear, I'm talking to the boys;
Women don't need to know these things.

EVE

> Of course not.

ADAM

If you'd not been in such great haste to *know*
There in the garden, we should all be now
Much better off.

Eve

Indeed, that's very true—
My sin was of the intellect.

Adam

It was.

Eve

So now I must not use my intellect?

Adam

No; we've been through this argument before;
Women must have no further opportunity—
They can't be trusted. You should have sent for me,
I would have sent the snake about his business,
My sole mistake was listening to *you*.

Eve

Your sin was of the heart. Dear, chivalrous Adam!
You were so noble—never shall I forget.
"If God sends death," you said, "we'll die together;
You are my Eve—my woman, right or wrong."
Kind Adam, I'd not rob you of your heart
Although it made you sin; I hold it here,
And I can twist it round my little finger,
Can't I?

Adam

You can, my womanly sweet Eve.
Kiss me.

Eve

You won't be angry any more?

Adam

No, no.

Eve

You'll tell me all about the axe?

Adam

Yes, if you like.

306

(*to* CAIN)

You would not have, because they were so dry
No crops would grow there. In a rocky cleft
I found—guess what!—a quite new spring of water
Which certainly was not there yesterday.
Isn't that wonderful? It gushed and ran
Among the stones, and some of it was lost—
But if we made a conduit——

CAIN

What do you say?
You found a water-spring upon your land?

ABEL

Yes. God is good. Perhaps He likes the lamb
I sacrificed. I chose it carefully.
Or else it was sheer bounty.

CAIN

Sacrifice!
Did I not sacrifice as well as you?
Why should He like your offering more than mine?

ABEL (*gaily*)
I don't know, brother; it was just my luck.

ADAM
Call it God's providence.

CAIN
It isn't fair!
Why should my brother have more luck than I?
I am the first-born.

ABEL
That was *your* luck, brother,
The water-spring is mine.

309

CAIN

> This is not justice—
> I sacrificed, I prayed; if God were just
> He would reward me too. I am the first-born—
> Why should I toil and moil at carrying water
> While you, the younger, laze beside your stream
> Singing psalms in the sunshine?

EVE

> Cain!

ADAM

> My son,
> Control your tongue!

ABEL

> Why are you so unkind?
> Indeed you are very welcome to the water.
> We'll make a conduit from my fields to yours.

CAIN

> I won't have charity, I'll have my rights.
> Don't talk of luck or providence to me!
> Must I have your permission to draw water?
> Must I be grateful? Must I kiss your hand,
> That am your equal and your elder? No!
> To-day we usher in the great new age
> That makes one man's hand as the hand of ten—
> I tell you, we'll have no more blundering luck,
> But only opportunity and power!
> Out of my way!

EVE

> Abel!

ADAM

> Cain, for God's sake!

CAIN

> I'll teach God to make favourites.
>   [*He strikes* ABEL *down.*

ABEL

Brother!

CAIN

So.

EVE

Abel! . . . He's killed him. . . . Murderer!

ADAM

Justice of God!

Mary, go in—this is no place for girls—
You that are men——

[MARY *runs in, dropping her work.*

EVE

Why are you standing there?
Do you not see that he has killed my son?
Seize him! . . . O Abel!

[*The* CHORUS *make a half-hearted rush at* CAIN, *who keeps them off with the axe.*

CAIN

Back, you fools! I am armed.

[*They drop back.* ADAM *goes up to him.*

What do you want, good man?

ADAM

I am your father;
I charge you by my holy authority,
Put down that weapon.

CAIN

Weapon? Now we have come
To the exhortations and the moral sanctions.
I am your son, your first-born; and this weapon—
Is it, or is it not a useful tool?
Useful perhaps for more things than you thought of.
You bid me put it down—by your authority!
By *what* authority, my clever father,
You that put power into the hand of Cain?

CHOIR

Where is salvation? who shall deliver Adam?
Power and knowledge and wealth are only a man's work,
Mighty for good and mighty also for evil;
All men are Abel and Cain; but Cain is the first-born.
    [EVE *covers the body of* ABEL *with the scarlet cloth.*

FOX

And the Lord said unto Cain: "Where is Abel thy brother?"

CAIN

And he said: "I know not: Am I my brother's keeper?"

FOX

And He said: "What hast thou done? Thy brother's blood
crieth unto Me from the ground. And now thou art cursed
of the earth and it shall not yield thee her fruit; a fugitive
and a vagabond shalt thou be in the earth."

CAIN

My punishment is greater than I can bear—
Cursed and driven away and dispossessed;
I shall be a fugitive and a vagabond,
And every one that findeth me shall slay me.

FOX

And the Lord said unto him: "Therefore whosoever slayeth
Cain, vengeance shall be taken on him sevenfold." Thus
saith the Lord.

CAIN

Thus saith the Lord—and lets the wolf go free;
I am a marked man; keep your hands off me.

EVE

Alas! alas! must I lose both my sons,
One by injustice and the other by judgment?
O Cain, my first-born, will you not say you are sorry?

312

Ask pardon? Plead with your dead brother's blood
To speak for you, as the dead lamb's blood speaks
On the altar of sacrifice? What will you do, poor child,
Alone in the desert with the barren earth,
Outlawed by God and man?

CAIN

                    Don't trouble, Mother;
Your heart's too soft—I shall live long enough
To breed a race of Cains; and you shall see
The sevenfold vengeance—seven-and-seventyfold—
Before we have finished. Let the earth be barren!
We will build cities, and work in iron and brass,
And you shall bring your corn and oil and wine
And your fat cattle, and your souls, and sell them
To buy that produce. You can keep your axe;
We will make axes for all of you. Let me pass.

[*He goes in under the stage. The curtains of the Upper Stage are
closed.*

CHOIR

God is not served with engines
                    He takes no pleasure in horse-power,
Neither delighteth
                    in the speed of any man's going;
What though your two hands
                    span the dawn and the sunset
When one is the hand of Abel
                    and one is the hand of Cain?

RECORDER

So shall the seed of Cain take vengeance on Cain;
Though you slay innocence and outlaw guilt
You cannot undo the brotherhood of the blood.
Every man and every woman of you
Is the whole seed of Adam, not divided
But fearfully joined in the darkness of the double self.
Do you not know it? do you not feel it, all of you,
In the bone's marrow, in the labyrinth of the brain,

In the ambiguity of dreams—the twofold will
Purposing life and death? Do not you all
Suffer with Abel and destroy with Cain,
Each one at once the victim and the avenger
Till Cain is Abel, being condemned for Abel,
And Abel Cain, in the condemning of Cain?

CHORUS

A: Shall we not have our blessing? We are Abel.
B: Shall we not have our birthright? We are Cain.
C: We all are men, and shall we not have justice?
A: Our name is Abel; you have murdered us—
    Are you not Cain and shall we not have justice?
B: Our name is Abel if you take revenge,
    And you are Cain, and shall we not have justice?
A: Cain shall go free, for we will not be Cain;
    We will be innocent though we do no justice.
C: Alas! your innocence has let loose Cain,
    You too are Cain, and shall we not have justice?
A: If you take vengeance on us, we are Abel
    And you are Cain, and shall we not have justice?
B: Brother, what is your name?
C: My name is Cain
    And Abel.
A: Brother, what is your name?
B: My name
    Is Cain and Abel.
C: Brother, what is your name?
A: My name is Cain and Abel.
All: God send justice!
    The blood of Abel cries out from the ground.

Fox

Vengeance is mine, saith God; I will repay.

EVE

O no, no, no! that is a fearful saying!
God shall take vengeance? God Himself repay?

Still in man's retribution some small shame,
Remembering the contributory guilt
Which wronged the wronger and excused the wrong—
Some prudent terror of the back-recoil
Of that great clumsy engine men call justice—
Must stay the judge's hand and wring out mercy,
Though grudgingly, and less for mercy's sake
Than policy. But what sort of dreadful thing
Can be the vengeance of the innocent,
Who, being all wronged, need not subtract the score
Of his own debt from the appalling total?
You that cry out so loud for right and justice,
Do you mean *justice*? deed and word and thought
Judges in yourselves by one eternal measure
Of absolute and incorruptible right?
I do not think so. When you call for justice
You would make God your bailiff, to collect
Your legal dues; but not your almoner,
Still less your judge. Alas! you cannot bend
God to your service; yet He may hear prayers—
Sometimes His vengeance is a granted prayer,
When a corrupt heart gains its whole desire
And finds itself in Hell. Children, take heed,
And do not pray for justice; you might get it.

Adam

Wife, I think you have spoken the hardest word
That ever man gave ear to. *Not ask justice!*
That word of yours would overthrow the temples
And bring the state down headlong. Man's first cry
Is still for justice. Children utter it,
Accepting both reward and punishment
So long as they are dealt out equally
To all alike.

Eve

But must we be so childish?
It's in my mind that there is something else—
A kind of mercy that is not unjust,

A not unmerciful justice—if we could see it;
Something that, once seen, would commend itself,
Not to be argued with. The serpent argued,
And all his words were true: but that truth lied.
But God's word was that we should find a Man,
The image of His argument bodily,
Whose heel of flesh should bruise the serpent's brain
Visibly. Will you not pray God send that sight?
For our sad eyes see nothing now but death.

ADAM

Children of men, kneel down and pray with us,
The parents of your Abel and your Cain,
The derivation of your life and death,
Adam and Eve. O God, over our dead
And banished blood we cry. Roll back our sins
That like the leaves of the accursed tree
Shut out the face of Heaven.

[*During the following litany the curtains of the Upper Stage open slowly and disclose the Gates of Heaven.*

CHORUS
Roll back our sins.

ADAM

From the blind skill that has no understanding,
The knowledge that has no wisdom, the glib speech
That has no vision, from the heartless brain
And the brainless heart.

CHORUS
Deliver us, good Lord.

ADAM

From the black chaos that blasphemes creation,
From the disordered will that spews out judgment,
From the dark greed that binds us in subjection
To our desires,

316

ADAM

From the proud virtues that are our undoing,
From the harsh righteousness whose name is murder,
From the liberality whose name is treason,
From the weak and the strong, from our right and our
    wrong,
Our worst and best,

CHORUS

Deliver us, good Lord.

ADAM

From all the gods made in the image of man,
From all the worship of man in man's own image,
From the corrupt alike and from the barren
Imagination,

CHORUS

Deliver us, good Lord.

CHOIR

Open the gate! that we have sinned we know—
The sole admission
Brings no remission
Of our despair; life cannot be lived so
In division without vision,
Frustrate, disconsolate,
Knowing so little, destroyed by what we know.
No, no,
Better in a sharp derision
Break, burn, scatter us at a blow,
Blow us away in the blast of the world's fission
Disject, disintegrate—
But yet You hold us to our hard condition
And You will not let go.
Open the gate, O Lord, and legislate
Late though it be, for us who wait,

Weighted by our contrition,
Mocked of ambition,
Yet stubborn to believe that You will show,
Though how, we do not know,
Some order in the State.
State terms, state conclusion, state decision,
Speak the name of the City. Open the gate,
Throw open the gate, throw
Open the gate, show
The image of truth in the place of the images, show,
Show!

[*The Gates of Heaven open, disclosing the* PERSONA DEI, *with* GABRIEL *and another* ANGEL.

PERSONA

I the image of the Unim ginable
In the place where the Image and the Unimaged are one,
The Act of the Will, the Word of the Thought, the Son
In whom the Father's selfhood is known to Himself,
I being God and with God from the beginning
Speak to Man in the place of the Images.
You that We made for Ourself in Our own image,
Free like Us to experience good by choice,
Not of necessity, laying your will in Ours
For love's sake creaturely, to enjoy your peace,
What did you do? What did you do for Us
By what you did for yourselves in the moment of choice?
O Eve My daughter, and O My dear son Adam,
Whose flesh was fashioned to be My tabernacle,
Try to understand that when you chose your will
Rather than Mine, and when you chose to know evil
In your way and not in Mine, you chose for Me.
It is My will you should know Me as I am—
But how? For you chose to know your good as evil,
Therefore the face of God is evil to you,
And you know My love as terror, My mercy as judgment,
My innocence as a sword; My naked life
Would slay you. How can you ever know Me then?
318

Yet know you must, since you were made for that;
Thus either way you perish. Nay, but the hands
That made you, hold you still; and since you would not
Submit to God, God shall submit to you,
Not of necessity, but free to choose
For your love's sake what you refused to Mine.
God shall be man; that which man chose for man
God shall endure, and what man chose to know
God shall know too—the experience of evil
In the flesh of man; and certainly He shall feel
Terror and judgment and the point of the sword;
And God shall see God's face set like a flint
Against Him; and man shall see the Image of God
In the image of man; and man shall show no mercy.
Truly I will bear your sin and carry your sorrow,
And, if you will, bring you to the tree of life,
Where you may eat, and know your evil as good,
Redeeming that first knowledge. But all this
Still at your choice, and only as you choose,
Save as you choose to let Me choose in you.
Who then will choose to be the chosen of God,
And will to bear Me that I may bear you?

EVE

O my dear Lord, in me the promise stood—
Worst, weakest, yet in me. What must I do?

PERSONA

Woman, that bore the blame from the beginning,
Now in the end bring forth the remedy;
Go, call your daughter Mary, whose unsinning
Heart I have chosen that it may bear Me.

EVE

Mary!

CHORUS

O Mary maiden! Mary of pity!
Speak for us, Mary! Speak for a world in fear!

Mary, mother and maid, send help to the city!
Speak for us, choose for us, Mary!

[*Enter* MARY, *above*.

MARY

You called? I am here.

CHORUS

All that is true in us, all we were meant to be,
The lost opportunity and the broken unity,
The dead innocence, the rejected obedience,
The forfeited chastity and the frozen charity,
The caged generosity, and the forbidden pity,
Speak in the mouth of Mary, in the name of the city!

PERSONA

In the speed of the Holy Ghost run, Gabriel;
Bear Our message to Mary, daughter of Eve,
That she may lay her will under Our will
Freely, and as she freely gives, receive.

[GABRIEL *comes down*.

CHORUS

Alpha and Omega, beginning and end,
Laid on a single head in the moment of choice!
Pray God now, pray that a woman lend
Her ear to God's, as once to the serpent's voice.

Paradise all to gain and all to lose
In the second race re-run from the old start;
What will the city do now, if a girl refuse
The weight of the glory, the seven swords in the heart?

GABRIEL

Hail, thou that art highly favoured! The Lord is with thee;
Blessed art thou among women.

MARY

What may this be?

Gabriel

Thou shalt conceive in the power of the Holy Ghost
The most high Child, the Prince of the heavenly host;
This is the word that I am charged to say:
Wilt thou receive that Guest without dismay?

Mary

Behold in me the handmaid of the Lord;
Be it unto me according to thy word.

Persona

Now I put off My crown and majesty
To take the vesture of humility.

[*The* Persona Dei *takes off His imperial vesture and remains in
His alb*.

Gabriel

Rejoice, O daughter of Jerusalem,
Thy King shall come to thee in Bethlehem.

Mary (*sings*)

My heart is exalting the Lord
   and my spirit is glad of my Saviour,
Who stoops from the height of His heaven
   to look on me, maiden-in-meekness,
And all generations shall bless me
   in the sound of the great salutation,
For He that is highly exalted
   exalts me, and holy is He.

Choir

Who being the Father's Image,
   the expression and form of the Selfhood,
Thought the equal and infinite glory
   was nowise a thing to be clung to,
But came to the selfhood of Man,
   in the image and form of a servant,
Made lower and less than His angels,
   the Lord of them; holy is He.

[*The* Persona Dei *comes down*.

RECORDER

O widowed city, wake! beneath thy stones
A whispering wind goes stirring the dead bones.

GABRIEL

Rise up, dear city of God, rise up; receive
The second Adam from the second Eve.

RECORDER

Come, thou North wind, and come, thou South wind; blow
On our parched garden; bid the spices flow.

GABRIEL

Replant lost Eden in Gethsemane,
For Love's new fruit hangs from the second Tree.

RECORDER

New age, begin! bring in the golden reign!

GABRIEL

Mercy and truth, long-parted, meet again,
And righteousness and peace kiss one another.

PERSONA

Woman, behold thy Son.

MARY

Behold Thy mother.

CHOIR

O Virgin Mother, daughter of thy Son,
Lowliest and loftiest of created stature,
Fixed goal to which the eternal counsels run;
Thou art that she by whom our human nature
Was so ennobled that it might become
The Creator to create Himself His creature.

[*During the singing of this hymn,* GABRIEL *returns into Heaven,
and the gates are shut.*

PERSONA

Naked I came out of My mother's womb,
Naked God in a world of armed men.

ADAM

When we had tasted knowledge we knew we were naked.

EVE

We were afraid and hid ourselves, being naked.

FOX

Sheol is naked before Him, and Abaddon hath no covering.

CHORUS

Who shall look on Abaddon unveiled and go down naked
    to Sheol.

PERSONA

Mother and daughter, bear Me forth to the world;
Show to them who were made in the image of God
The image of the Image of the Unimaginable
From the place where the Image and the Unimaged are one.

MARY

Good Christian people, you see, this is my Son;
Be tender to Him. It was a very long journey;
The ass was footsore before we came to Bethlehem,
And there was no room in the inn. He was born in a stable,
And I wrapped Him in linen and laid Him in the manger
Between the ox and the ass. The angels sang
And the simple shepherds worshipped; the wise kings
Brought incense and myrrh and gold. Then Herod was
    angry,
And sent his soldiers to kill the little children—
They died because Herod was afraid of a little child—
But we took the ass and fled away into Egypt,
And presently, when things seemed a little more safe,
Came home to the carpenter's shop at Nazareth,

Where He lived thirty years in silence and obedience.
Consider now the work and word of the Son
Before the ass carries Him up to Jerusalem.

Persona

The Kingdom of God is come among you. I,
Being the Father's Word and one with Him,
Am here with you in the power of the Holy Ghost.
Thus saith Isaiah: "He hath anointed Me
To speak good tidings to the humble, heal
The broken-hearted, open the blind eyes,
Unloose the captives whom your sins have bound,
And to proclaim God's year of jubilee."
To-day you see all prophecy fulfilled.

Recorder

The World, the State, the Church shall see it, too.

[*Enter* Herod, Pilate *and* Caiaphas *and sit upon the Upper Stage attended by two* Soldiers.

Persona

Lo! I am come to make all these things new.

[*Enter* Judas *and stands watching.*

Recorder

And some will see and hear and then betray.

Persona

Whoso sells Me sells his own soul away.

Recorder

Behold, against the princes of this world
The banners of the King of kings unfurled!

Chorus (*dispersedly*)

Is it He that should come? or do we look for another?
Can he do what he says? These things are hard to believe.

324

I am sad. I am sick—his touch would heal me, perhaps.
He may be a quack. One does not want to look foolish
Or get into trouble. We thought we saw visions of angels.
But visions are dreams, and the thought is betrayed by the
    wish.

HARLOT

Why do you hesitate? I, who have nothing to lose,
Being so utterly bad, will fall at His feet.
Pity me, sir.

PERSONA

I will. You are forgiven.
Be glad, and sin no more. Sin-burdened souls
Come unto Me, and I will give you rest.

[*The* CHORUS *draws close to Him.*

CAIAPHAS

What is the meaning of this blasphemous folly?
No man can cleanse from sin but God alone.

PERSONA

Truly. Go now and say what you have heard
And seen.

[*He lays His hands on* JOHNSON.

Look up, dim eyes, behold the sun!

[JOHNSON *falls at His feet. He lays His hand on the* HUNCH-
BACK.

Stand upright, crooked limbs, and walk with God.

[*The* HUNCHBACK *is healed.*

You that are haunted with a spirit of fear——

[*He lays hands on the* LUNATIC.

LUNATIC (*shrieking*)

No, no! Let go! Take off your terrible hands,
Strong Son of God—let go!

325

PERSONA

Come out of him!

[The LUNATIC *is healed.*

CHORUS

Hosanna, Lord! O Lord, have mercy on us!

JUDAS

It looks as though there might be something in this.

[He comes down.

Hosanna!

CHORUS

Hail! Hosanna!

EVE

Alas! alas!
Turn pitying eyes this way, O Son of Man!

PERSONA

Woman, why do you weep?

EVE

See here, see here,

This was my son!

PERSONA

Mother, unloose your arms—
Wake, murdered innocence! Rise up from the dead!

[He raises ABEL.

CHORUS

Hosanna!

HEROD

What's all that noise?

SOLDIER

A prophet, sir.

HEROD

Prophet? Oh, well! He might start some new craze
To make a dull world seem less wearisome.
Hey, you there! Is there anything I can do
To save me from the boredom of myself?

PERSONA

Sell all you have, and give it to the poor,
And come and follow Me.

HEROD

Follow you where?

PERSONA

To the gallows, if need be.

HEROD

Preposterous!

[*He takes no further interest.*

PERSONA (*sitting with the* CHORUS *about Him*)

Listen, My children. In the olden time
The law was made for sin: an eye for an eye,
A life for a life; requital, not revenge.
But I say this: the Law indeed must stand,
But do not seek the Law. Give, and forgive,
And make no claim; for what the Law concedes
Is your bare merit, grudgingly allowed,
Grudgingly taken; but the gifts of love
Are gifts, beyond desert, beyond desire—
And the meek heart inherits all the earth.

PILATE

You can't do things like that. It is not justice.

PERSONA

Oh, no! there is no justice in the Gospel,
There's only love, which does not seek its own,
But finds its whole delight in giving joy
Unasked.

PILATE

Dreams, dreams. Men are not governed so.

PERSONA

Oh, if you want the Law, you shall have law,
Your own harsh measure, pressed down, running over,
Returned into your bosom. What you choose
You choose, and it is yours for ever—*that*
Is the great Law, of which no jot or tittle
Changes. But if you choose Me, you choose Love.

CAIAPHAS

And who are you, to set yourself above
The Law? You know who gave the Law to Moses?
Speak! was it not the God of Abraham?

PERSONA

Your father Abraham longed to see My day—
He saw it and was glad.

CAIAPHAS

What do you mean?
Whom would you make yourself?

PERSONA

Ere Abraham was
I am.

[*The* CHORUS *hide their faces.*

CAIAPHAS

O monstrous!

JUDAS (*hastening across to* CAIAPHAS)
How much will you give me
If I betray him?

CAIAPHAS

Thirty pieces of silver.

[JUDAS *signifies agreement and returns.*

328

AIRMAN

Sir, that your law is good we well believe;
But how to keep it? Will the seed of Cain
Forgive, or seek forgiveness, or be meek?
Was it worth while—forgive my bluntness, sir—
That God should be made man, only to say
To man, "Be perfect," when it can't be done?
A rough-and-ready rule that can be kept
Is something; but impossible demands
Will only serve to make us desperate.

PERSONA

Only Myself can keep My law in you;
Merely to hear My words and nod approval
Is nothing—'tis a house that's built on sand.
I must be closer to you than your marrow,
The sight of your eyes, the thought within your brain.
I say, unless you eat My flesh and blood
And make My substance and My self your own,
You cannot live. I am your bread, your wine;
I give My body to be broken for you
That I, in you, may break and give yourselves
For all the world. No man has greater love
Than he who lays his life down for his friends.

AIRMAN

Is any man worth such a price?

[JUDAS *goes to* CAIAPHAS.

PERSONA

My child,
That is a question which love must not ask,
Though some will dip their hands deep in the dish
And sell the love that fed them, Love must bear it.

AIRMAN

Is there no other way?

329

RECORDER

Sir, I am sent

To call You.

PERSONA (*rising*)

Angel, is there no other way?

RECORDER

No other way, my Lord.

PERSONA (*to* AIRMAN)

You see, there's none.
It is hard for the flesh to say, "Thy will be done."

[*He goes aside with the* RECORDER.

JUDAS (*returning with* SOLDIERS)

When I embrace him, seize him.

PERSONA

Father, alas!
If this cup must be drunk and may not pass,
I am content.

JUDAS

Hail, Master!

PERSONA

What is this?
Judas, will you betray love with a kiss?

[*The* PERSONA DEI *is taken before* CAIAPHAS, *the* CHORUS
following.

FOX

And they sought for witness against Him to put Him to
death, and found none. For many bare false witness against
Him, but their witness agreed not together.

CAIAPHAS

Why do we waste our time? Our holy court
Is not concerned with what the prisoner did,

Whether good or bad, but only with his claim:
Now, by the living God, answer to me—
Are you the Christ, the Son of God?

PERSONA
                                   I am.
CAIAPHAS
What man of woman born may dare to say so?

PERSONA
I say that you shall see the Son of man
Throned in high Heaven at the right hand of power.

CAIAPHAS
What need of witness? You have heard his blasphemy—

[*The* CITY *groans.*

He is guilty of death.

[*The* CITY *groans again.*

                    Take him away to Pilate.

PILATE
What is your accusation against this man?

CAIAPHAS
He has blasphemed; religion has condemned him.

PILATE
In that case, let religion punish him.

CAIAPHAS
The priesthood sheds no blood. We hand him over
To the secular arm. Creeds become policies—
He says he is a king.
                    PILATE
                    Are you a king?

PERSONA

Yes, but My kingdom is not of this world.

PILATE

Speak plainly, man; what is your kingdom?

PERSONA

                                    Truth;
All true men are My people.

PILATE

                    What is truth?
This is some harmless mad philosopher—
The State cannot concern itself with truth;
Thought must be free; religious toleration
Is Caesar's motto—we don't care, provided
People will keep the peace and pay their taxes.

CAIAPHAS

This man has stirred rebellion up in Galilee——

PILATE

Galilee?—Not within my jurisdiction.
You should have said he was a Galilean;
Why waste my time? Take him away to Herod—
Passed to you, please, for information and action.

HEROD (*yawning*)

What is all this? Something about religion?
The trouble is, it's all so out of touch
With daily life. Can't you put ginger in it?
A thrill is what we need, but in these days
There's so much competition. What's your line?
The scientific witness? Exploitation
Of fresh techniques? The new psychology?
Old truths in modern dress? Or politics—
God's contribution to the perfect state?
I hope not merely brighter services

And congregational singing. Speak up, man!
Aren't you the prophet born in Bethlehem?
They tell me you work miracles—well, begin!
Show us what you can do. You won't? No thrills—
No sales-talk. Pilate, what's this man accused of?

PILATE

Of stirring up the people.

HEROD

Stirring up? . . .

[*He dissolves into laughter.*

Stirring? . . . don't make me laugh . . . stirring the people . . .
Here, take him back—he comes from Bethlehem—
Your bit of boredom and not mine, thank goodness.

PILATE (*waving them off*)

I will chastise him then, and let him go.
Here, fellow, take the prisoner out and flog him,
And that may teach him not to call himself
A king in future.

1ST SOLDIER

Step this way, your majesty.
We'll make a king of you—and crown you too.

[*He takes the* PERSONA DEI *out of sight.*

CAIAPHAS

Pilate, this will not do; the man has theories,
That's always dangerous.

PILATE

Doesn't that depend
On what the theories are?

CAIAPHAS

No, not at all;
You said yourself that truth was not important—
Opinion is.

PILATE

I find no fault in him.

CAIAPHAS

Possibly not; but think what violent factions,
What tyrannous rule, how many bloody wars
Have risen out of words and theories
That seemed quite harmless—even virtuous—
While they were only theories and words.
You would let loose a sword upon the earth
Might sweep your Cæsar from his throne, and split
The Empire.

PILATE

How can any empire stand
Whose laws betray the innocent?

CAIAPHAS

He is guilty;
But were he not, better that he should suffer
Than bring down ruin on the innocent people.

PILATE

The people? . . . Soldier, go to the gaol and fetch
That murdering robber out—for you remind me:
This is the day when we release a prisoner
To please the people. Let the people choose. . . .
Where is the man who calles himself a king?

[*Re-enter* IST SOLDIER *with* PERSONA, *wearing scarlet robe and crown of thorns.*

IST SOLDIER

Here, sir.

PILATE

And where's the robber?

2ND SOLDIER

Here he is.

[CAIN *brought from under the stage, in the guise of* BARABBAS.

334

PILATE (*to the* CHORUS)

Look on the prisoner. (*To* CAIN) What's your name?

CAIN

Barabbas,

"Son of the father" in the Hebrew tongue;
I come, sir, of a very ancient family;
My father has many sons, but I am the first-born

PILATE

And you—what is your name?

PERSONA

Jesus called Christ.

Son of the Father and the sole-begotten.

PILATE

You know that I am placed here in authority
To set you free or send you to the Cross?

PERSONA

You could have no authority over Me
Except as God appoints you for a judge
To men; therefore the greater sin is his
By whom I was delivered to your judgment.
Yet, as men must accept, I do accept
The verdict of your court.

PILATE

Behold the man!

Consider now, you people of the city,
Which of the twain shall I release to you,
Barabbas here? or Jesus called the Christ?

CHORUS

Barabbas! we're accustomed to Barabbas—
Let us have back our old familiar sin!
Give us Barabbas! we will have Barabbas!

PILATE

What shall I do with Jesus called the Christ?

CHORUS

Crucify him!

PILATE

What crime has he committed?

CHORUS

Crucify!

PILATE

Shall I crucify your king?

CHORUS

His kingship makes too great demands on us—
He would be king of body and soul and all,
There would be nothing left of us. Away!
Crucify him!

CAIAPHAS

If you let this man go
You are not Cæsar's friend; there is no room
In one allegiance for both Christ and Cæsar.

CHORUS

Crucify! crucify!

PILATE

This is not justice.

CHORUS

Crucify him!

PILATE

I take you all to witness,
I wash my hands of this. On your head be it.

CHORUS

His blood be upon us and upon our children.

336

ADAM

O sons and daughters, consider what you have done—
How you have pulled the judgment of Cain upon you:
You are all the children of one father—you,
Judas and Caiaphas, Herod, Pilate and Cain—
The sons of Adam who was the son of God.

EVE

See how you have pulled the death of Abel upon you!
Are not all of you born of the same womb?
Now you are all involved in the same disaster,
In the intimate bond of the blood—all you, and Cain,
And Abel and Christ, the sons of Eve and Mary.

CHORUS

Crucify! crucify! let him be crucified!

[*The voices of the* IMAGES *stop abruptly and leave the* AIRMAN *shouting all by himself.*

AIRMAN

Crucify! crucify!

[*He becomes aware of the silence round him.*

           What on earth am I doing?
That is not in the least what I meant to say;
I can't think what came over me.

RECORDER

                The voice of the City.
Speaking in one of its less inspired moments—
Or in one of its moments of greatest inspiration;
For the priesthood of the City is a true priesthood;
And the prophetic heritage still inalienable
By any corruption; the City never speaks truth
So surely as when it does not know what it's saying.

PILATE

The voice of the people has condemned the prisoner;
The voice of the people is the voice of God,

The Empire truckles to the divine voice.
And minor officials do wisely to know their place
And truckle accordingly. Take him to the Cross.

Herod

Take him by all means, so far as I am concerned,
He did not come up to what I expected of him.

Caiaphas

This is a very satisfactory ending.
God is avenged, the Laws of the City are safe;
Everybody's weakness has been successfully exploited
In the best interests of society: it is wonderful
To see how all things work together for good.

Judas

I have sinned; I have betrayed the innocent blood.

Caiaphas

What is that to us?

Judas
                    Nothing at all,
Brother, although you are art and part with me.
There is no exchange in sin; when guilt is shared,
It is only as two men share the same disease
But cannot divide it; each has the whole disease,
And cannot give it away, although he gives it.
In death, you see, none can deliver his brother,
And the brotherhood of Cain is of that kind.
This guilt is yours and mine—altogether yours,
Altogether mine; it cannot be called "ours"—
Sin cannot say that word.

Persona
                    But I can say it,
Because our brotherhood is not in the sin
But in the blood—the fatherhood of God

And the motherhood of the first and the second Eve.
The yours and the mine can belong to both and either
By division or exchange, if you choose to make it so.
Say that the guilt is Mine; give it to Me
And I will take it away to be crucified.
It is all so very much simpler than you think:
Give Me the greedy heart and the little creeping treasons,
Give Me the proud heart and the blind, obstinate eyes (*to*
    CAIAPHAS);
Give Me the shallow heart, and the vain lust, and the folly
    (*to* HEROD);
Give Me the coward heart and the spiritless refusals (*to*
    PILATE);
Give Me the confused self that you can do nothing with;
I can do something.

JUDAS

You? What can you do?
No one can help me; I do not want to be helped.
Though I cast back guilt and price to the place they came
    from,
I shall find them again when I go to my own place.

[*He throws the money back to* CAIAPHAS.

CAIN

There is a place in the desert for them that refuse hope,
Where one may lie for ever and hug the thing that one
    hates,
And fear becomes desire in the final fixation of choice.

PILATE

I do not think there is any way out of these problems;
One is always at the mercy of events and the world-
    situation;
One takes the thing as one finds it and makes the best of it:
I do not believe there are any ultimate standards.

There is a place in the desert for them that refuse faith,
Where one may fall for ever in a pit that has no bottom,
Endlessly adapted to a fixed monotonous change.

CAIAPHAS (*to* JUDAS)

You will suffer for this insolence (*to* PERSONA) and you, too;
I am not a sinner; I have nothing to reproach myself with;
I have kept the Law and been perfectly right throughout.
Fools and criminals get what is coming to them,
Or how could the City stand? It is quite grotesque
To say that we, who administer the laws of the City,
Are guilty of blood; it is they, not we, who are guilty.

CAIN

There is a place in the desert for them who refuse charity,
Where the iron heart is bound in the bond of its own iron,
Enduring justice, since that is what it thought it inflicted,
Having no humility to see the injustice of justice.

HEROD

I do not see what all this fuss is about:
We are in the world for what we can get out of it.
Plenty of comfort, and entertainment for leisure
Are all I ask for; I ordered no crucifixions;
You earnest people are always crucifying somebody.
I don't interfere—no doubt you do it on principle—
I do not pretend to be intellectual.

CAIN

No;
But there is a place for your sort. There is a place
In the desert for those that have lost the good of the intellect;
Fathomless circles of perfectly meaningless nonsense—
Crucifixions, too, of an unredeeming sort,
In the everlasting exile. This way, brothers;
Here we receive exactly what we have chosen
And can practise on one another to all eternity.

[*Exeunt* CAIN, HEROD, PILATE, JUDAS *and* CAIAPHAS *under the stage.*

RECORDER

Guilt cannot carry guilt; can neither absorb it
Nor yet give it away; there is no subtraction
And no division in the mathematics of sin—
It can only add and multiply guilt with guilt,
Answering cruel injustice with no less cruel
Justice; yet without justice, where is the City?
Only the innocent can ever carry the guilt,
Only the soul that has never consented to sin
And is not concerned to justify itself
Can accept the whole guilt—the open injustice
And the hidden iniquity in the heart of equity—
Carry them away, purge them and sterilise them,
Taking them into itself and making conclusion.
What will you do, citizens, what will you do?
Since you cannot put down injustice without the Law,
And the Law is of sin, and turns to sin in your hands,
Because each one of you is at once Abel and Cain?

FOX

And Aaron shall confess over the scapegoat all the iniquities
of the children of Israel, and all their transgressions in all
their sins. And the goat shall bear upon him all their
iniquities into a land not inhabited, and he shall let go the
goat in the wilderness.

PERSONA

Now am I twice condemned; in the blood of Abel
Unjustly, and justly in the blood of Cain;
All men are so, and God, being made man,
Must walk the road that man chose for himself,
Carrying man's sin and innocence to the cross;
Thus it becomes Us to fulfil all righteousness.

CHORUS

Bind on the back of God the sins of the City;
Bind Him for Judas, bind Him for Herod, bind Him
For Caiaphas, Pilate and Cain; bind the wrong,
Bind the wrath and the tyranny, bind the treason,

Bind the fear and the folly, the greed and the grudging,
The disease and the death, the lies told in the market,
The familiar fireside slander, the traffic in blood,
The lazing, the lust, the cruel insatiate wheels,
The needs and neglects, the callousness of the possessors,
The envy of dispossession; bind the City,
The plundered earth, the dull disconsolate streets,
The splitting wood and the sweating stone, the smoke
And the reek, the glare and the glitter, the filth of the
    kennels,
The slums and the stews, the soil and shame of the City.

Bind on the back of God the laws of the City;
Bind Him for the priest; bind Him for the assessor,
For the upright judge and the incorruptible jury;
Bind Him in fetters, bind Him in just retribution,
Bind Him in discipline; bind the surgeon's knife,
The physic, the fasting; bind the holy war,
The weapons of defence, the armies of occupation;
Bind Him in power and in penalty; bind the rod,
The rule and the righteous judgment; bind the City,
The school, the asylum, the spires of the Cathedral,
The Courts of Justice, the police, the prison, the dock,
The gallows, the stern and salutary institutions,
The state and the standards, the shambles and sewers of the
    City.

[*The Cross is laid upon the back of the* PERSONA DEI, *and He is
led away about the church by the* SOLDIERS, ADAM, EVE, ABEL
and MARY *following, with four* SINGERS.

SINGERS

What is this you have done to Me, O My people?
Was ever such unjust vengeance? Am I not God?

CHOIR

God of the substance of the Father, begotten before the
    worlds;
God altogether; from everlasting to everlasting.

342

How shall I answer to Thee, O God my God?
Was ever so just a vengeance? Am I not Man?

CHOIR

Man of the substance of His Mother, born in the world;
Man altogether, in body and mind subsisting.

SINGERS

Is not this well done, that the Godhead should stoop to the
    Manhood,
Lifting it back to God, being God and Man?

CHOIR

Who, although He be God and Man,
Yet He is not two, but one Christ.

  [*The* PERSONA DEI *falls.*

MARY

You that are men, made in the image of God,
Will you see all the burden laid upon one Man's shoulder?
For the flesh faints and falls with the heavy weight of the
    glory,
But the power of the Godhead is enough for all mankind.

RECORDER

Who will carry the cross and share the burden of God
Now, in the moment of choice when the act and the image
    are one?
When the angels of Heaven, who are ignorant of sorrow,
Are helpless to do for God what only man can do?

  [*The* CHORUS *run down to carry the Cross.*

MARTYR

I am ready to carry the burden of the oppressor.

HARLOT

I will carry the shame.

LABOURER
I'll give a hand with the toil.

JOHNSON
I'll make a shift to carry my dear Lord's pain.

LUNATIC
And I will carry the fear that shatters the heart and brain.

WIFE
I will carry the bitterness of betrayal.

UNEMPLOYED
I'll take the poverty.
WIDOW
And I the grief.

MOTHER
I will bear man's ingratitude.

CHILD
And I
The ignorance, that suffers and knows not why.

SINGERS
Lift up your hearts. Hosanna!

CHOIR
We lift them up unto the Lord. Hosanna!

SINGERS
Whoso will carry the Cross, the Cross shall carry him.

CHOIR
For the whole creation groaneth and travaileth together,
Making up that which is lacking of the sufferings of Christ.

344

Lift the Cross! Lift the banners! Bring the King to the City!

CHOIR

Meek, riding on an ass, bring Christ into Jerusalem!

AIRMAN (*at the foot of the steps*)

Sir, I understand now what I ought to do.
Am I too late to bring to the wood of Your Cross
Whatever in me is guilty and ought to be crucified?
Whatever, being innocent, is privileged to die in Your
    Death?

PERSONA

The moment when you meet Me is never too late,
Though the moment of death and moment of choice were
    one.
Take up the Cross and come and follow Me,
For you shall carry the burden of bewilderment:
We shall find one another in the darkest hour of all.

  [*They go up to the place of crucifixion, the* CHORUS *remaining
upon the steps.*

EXECUTIONER

It is thought proper, sir, for the executioner
To ask the criminal's pardon; ours, you see,
Is a nasty job whichever way you look at it.
The city needs us, as she needs shambles and sewers;
It is our duty to carry out the sentence,
Not try the case; we cannot pretend to know
Whether you are guilty or innocent; either way
The job is nasty; therefore we ask your pardon,
Since, howsoever, our intention is to the City.

  [*Here the* SOLDIERS *crucify the* PERSONA DEI *upon the Upper
Stage,* MARY *and the* AIRMAN *standing at the foot of the Cross.*

PERSONA

Father, forgive them; they know not what they do.

AIRMAN

Sir, You are privileged to forgive them so;
But we know what we are doing; we, Christ's Church,
Who sin and suffer with the whole creation,
Not without understanding, self-condemned
For our misdeeds, assenting to the judgment
Which we must still endure, assent or no;
Yet somehow trusting that our free assent
Will "turn necessity to glorious gain"
And make our penalty count as sacrifice.
Look now! we are but thieves of righteousness,
Pocketing up Your merits as our own
And from Your treasure paying back to You
The debt we owe You. Lord, will You remember,
When You return to rule us in Your Kingdom,
How ragged, poor, and beggarly we were
Till we laid hands on You, and so accept
What is not ours to give You?

PERSONA

Verily
This day shall you be with Me in Paradise.

AIRMAN

Blessed indeed, thrice blessed are the dead
Who die in Christ. But what will You bequeath
To those who live, still prisoners of the hope
That like a tiny child seems every day
Ready to die, it is so frail, which yet
Will not let go its hold on life and us?
Is there some strong and natural tenderness
That can feed hope, and which that hope, grown strong,
Can in its turn sustain until You come
To be reborn in us and in the world?

PERSONA

Woman, behold thy son; behold thy mother.

[*The* AIRMAN *brings* MARY *down to the* CHORUS.

AIRMAN

O Mary of the seven swords of sorrow,
Come home with us, come home; the time is near
When the great night shall cover us all over,
Closer than death and darker, the thick blind
Pressure and stifling darkness of the womb.

[*Here the curtains of the Upper Stage are shut.*

O it is hard, this dying into life,
Helpless and hid, without communication
And with no contact left but through the blood.
Now we are nothing at all—only a pulse
Ticking out time; I am dying, Egypt, dying,
Dying into nothing, dying into nothing, nothing. . . .

PERSONA (*from behind the curtains*)

Eloi, eloi, lama sabachthani!

AIRMAN

I did not know—there is a worse deep still
Under the dark and the silence. Iron teeth
Closing down like a cramp. What is the name
Of the wringing horror? If I knew its name
There is a word of power that might command it,
Here in the bottom of the forgotten world
Where God's face never comes, but only man
Suffers and bleeds in the darkness. You, then, You—
You that are Man here in the dark with me,
Tell me the name, that we may break its jaws
And both go free. . . . Oh, no, I have remembered;
Its name is justice; it cannot be commanded,
Only endured. Why then, we will endure it,
Helping each other as we may.

PERSONA

I thirst.

AIRMAN

Once, long ago, You gave us bread and wine
But all my wine has turned to vinegar.

If it will serve, then all I have is Yours—
If there is anything left in me at all
That was not always Yours.

PERSONA

        It is accomplished.
Father, into Thy hands I commend My spirit.

AIRMAN

This is it. This is what we have always feared—
The moment of surrender, the helpless moment
When there is nothing to do but to let go. . . .
"Into Thy hands"—into another's hand
No matter whose; the enemy's hand, death's hand,
God's. . . . The one moment not to be evaded
Which says, "You must," the moment not of choice
When we must choose to do the thing we must
And will to let our own will go. Let go.
It is no use now clinging to the controls,
Let some one else take over. Take, then, take . . .
There, that is done . . . into Thy hand, O God.

MARY (*sings*)

See now, you shepherds and mages wise,
How helpless laid in other hands
The very Lord of glory lies
Wrapped head to foot in swathing bands.

CHOIR

In swaddling-bands and strong grave-bands.

MARY

Noël, noël, Emmanuel
Is sleeping sound and doth not stir,
Then go your way, before Him lay
Your gold and frankincense and myrrh.

348

Your funeral spices mixed with myrrh.

FOX (*over music*)

So on the third day, very early in the morning, the women came to the sepulchre, bringing the spices that they had prepared. And they found the stone rolled away from the sepulchre.

ANGEL

Whom seek you in the sepulchre, O citizens of Christ?

WOMEN

Jesus Christ of Nazareth, O citizens of Heaven.

ANGEL

He is not here; He is risen as He said; behold the place where they laid Him.

[*The curtains are opened, to disclose the* PERSONA DEI *standing before the Cross of glory.*

CHOIR

Speak, speak, speak the name of the city,
The new name, the true name, where the King and the City
    are one;
Call us by name, who came
Out of the blind places, to the blinding of the white sun.
Answer to our surprise,
Seeing with our eyes,
The obscure demanding
Of bowels and bones and heart, each feeling part
Made suddenly plain in the brain and understanding.
Deal gently with us, because we are so much astonished
To find ourselves thus replenished. Lord, have pity
On our bewilderment; speak! speak peace O, Lord, to the
    City.

PERSONA

I the Image of the Godhead bodily
In whom the Godhead and the Manhood are one,

349

Born into time, begotten from everlasting
Of the Father's love, by the gift of the Holy Ghost,
In whom all Heaven subsists; who, being in Heaven,
And being made Man, descending out of Heaven,
Bore for man's sake to set My feet in Hell:
I the end, and I the beginning of all things,
Call My Christendom out of the waste places,
Call the dry bones back from Jehoshaphat,
Call My multitudes in the valley of decision,
Call you home to Myself, in whom your selves
Find their true selfhood and their whole desire.
What has astonished you? Shall not I keep faith
Now with My chosen, and give you all you chose
When you laid your will in Mine in the moment of choice
And bade Me choose for you? When you chose Me
You were made Mine; and I am yours for ever.
That which you gave, you have. All you who choose
To bear with Me the bitter burden of things
In patience, or, being burdened without choice,
Choose only to be patient, whether you give
Your bodies to be burned, your hearts to be broken,
Or only stand and wait in the market-place
For work or bread in a long tediousness,
Think, it is I that stand and suffer with you,
Adding My innocence to redeem your guilt,
And yours with Mine, to ransom all mankind.
This is My courtesy, to make you partners
With God in your own rescue, nor do anything
But by your love and by your will consenting.
Come then, and take again your own sweet will
That once was buried in the spicy grave
With Me, and now is risen with Me, more sweet
Than myrrh and cassia; come, receive again
All your desires, but better than your dreams,
All your lost loves, but lovelier than you knew,
All your fond hopes, but higher than your hearts
Could dare to frame them; all your City of God
Built by your faith, but nobler than you planned.
Instead of your justice, you shall have charity;

Instead of your happiness you shall have joy;
Instead of your peace the emulous exchange
Of love; and I will give you the morning star.
Rise up, My mother Mary and come away,
Rise up, My daughter Eve and My sweet son Adam,
Rise up, My city, rise up, My church, My bride!
For the time of your singing is come, and My bright angels
Unwinter hosanna in the perpetual spring;
So enter My Father's house, and there take seizure of the
    crown laid up and the incorruptible treasure,
Where the endless Now is one with the moment's measure,
The truth with the image, the City one with the King.

CHOIR (*with trumpet-echo*)

God is gone up. . . . God is gone up. . . . God is gone up
    with a merry noise, with a merry noise . . . and our
    Lord with the sound of the trumpet.

[*Here the* PERSONA DEI *goes up into Heaven, with the people
going up lovingly together after Him; and the* ANGELS *give to each
of them a new robe and a palm of gold.*

CHOIR

Well done, good and faithful servants,
Enter now into the joy of your Lord.

The earth is yours, and the voice of sounding metal,
The gold and the iron and the brass, the clarions of con-
    quest.
You shall command the eagles, you shall laugh at leviathan;
The striped tiger shall sit with velvet feet
At the hearth; you shall be made glad with the grape and
    the wheat;
Nothing at all shall offend you, no snare shall enmesh—
You shall praise God with the glorious and holy flesh.

The sea is yours and the waters, with the voice
Of the dropping rain; O lute and harp, awake!
Rivers shall not drown love, nor the floods o'erwhelm it;
You shall be poured out with the cataract, ride the tide,

351

Run with the stream; beauty shall mould and hold you;
You shall fill up the cup of all delight; your art
Shall praise God with the moving and sensitive heart.

The air is yours, the wind that bends the cedars
And breathes in the reeds, the bodiless mighty voice
That comes and goes unseen; you shall be keen
To pierce and pass between a thought and a thought;
Nothing shall stay you or stain; by south and north,
East, west, you shall go forth and turn again—
You shall praise God with the searching and subtle brain.

The fire is yours; the fire mounts up to God
Beyond the angels of the spheres, whose strings
Are tuned too deep and high for mortal ears;
You shall possess that music; you shall go
Secure among the mysteries; the sun
Shall harm you not by day nor the moon by night—
Your soul shall praise God, and your spirit shall fathom the
    depth and the height.

MARY (*sings*)

Behold our City, how wide it spreads its gyres,
How great the company of the robes of light!

CHOIR

The City is yours; proclaim the name of the city!
She is set on a rock; she cannot be moved; her foundations
Are everlasting adamant; she stands
Foursquare; her walls are order; her streets meet
In the market-place of exchange; there is joy in her houses;
Her King has called her Zion; she was built without hands.
Proclaim the city!—Hosanna! God is her light.
Proclaim the city!—Hosanna! God is her strength.
Proclaim the city!—Hosanna! God is her confidence.
Proclaim the City! Proclaim Salvation! Proclaim Christ!